FORGOTTEN HERO
OF BUNKER VALENTIN

D0533246

MICHÈLE CALLAN lives in County Dublin and is Harry Callan's daughter-in-law and carer. Together they attend Second World War commemoration ceremonies in Ireland and Germany. They annually visit the German graves of the five Irishmen who died while constructing Bunker Valentin.

www.forgottenheroofbunkervalentin.com

This book is dedicated to the thirty-two
Irish-born British Merchant seamen and all
the other slave labourers who worked on
Bunker Valentin and to the memory
of all those who died there.

FORGOTTEN HERO
OF BUNKER VALENTIN

MICHÈLE CALLAN

The Collins Press

First published in 2017 by
The Collins Press
West Link Park
Doughcloyne
Wilton
Cork
T12 N5EF
Ireland

A CIP record for this book is available from the British Library.

Paperback ISBN: 978-1-84889-301-6
PDF eBook ISBN: 978-1-84889-605-5
EPUB eBook ISBN: 978-1-84889-606-2
Kindle ISBN: 978-1-84889-607-9

Typesetting by Carrigboy Typesetting Services
Typeset in Garamond
Printed in Poland by Drukarnia Skleniarz

CONTENTS

AUTHOR'S NOTE

I FIRST MET HARRY IN 1979 when my then boyfriend, Michael, introduced me to his father. Harry was working for the B&I shipping line at the time. I learnt that he had been a deep-sea sailor before that and was eventually told that he had been a prisoner of war in Germany. I also learnt that conversations about this time were a 'no go' area and that Harry never talked about this period of his life.

Twenty-two years later, Harry, who was now my father-in-law, began to tell me a little about his early days at sea and his war years. When, eventually, in 2012, I asked Harry if I could write his story, I had no idea what to expect nor that I would travel with him to Germany to where he had been a prisoner.

Forgotten Hero of Bunker Valentin: The Harry Callan Story is written in the first person so that the reader can hear Harry's voice, just as he spoke to me.

Michèle Callan

An official photograph showing prisoners working on the construction of Bunker Valentin during the Second World War.

FOREWORD

It's dark – very dark. They're jammed up against me – on all sides. Clickety-clack, clickety-clack – I'm on a train. But it can't be a train – no seats – no windows. Stop crushing me! Packed together like animals. NO! I'm not an animal! What's that smell? Fear – I'm afraid. GET OUT! Got to get out. Crying – who's crying? LET ME OUT! I have to get away.

It's cold – I'm so cold. I'm hungry – starving. My clothes are wet. Why? I'm wearing an army uniform? I'm not Army – I'm Merchant Navy. Where's my ship? Have to get to my ship – have to get home. RUN! I'm running but I'm not moving.

GESTAPO! No, no, God, NO! Don't hit him – please don't hit him. I'm crying. I can't let them see me cry. Clomp! Clomp! They're coming for me? Down, rolling, tumbling down into a hole. Dirt is falling on me. They're jammed up against me – on all sides. Bodies. Dead bodies. Packed together – crushing me. Glassy eyes staring at me. GOT TO GET OUT OF HERE!

I'M ALIVE! I'm shouting, screaming. Why can't they hear me? I scramble over them – the bodies –

clawing my way out. Got to get out of here! From the darkness a hand reaches out to shake me. 'No, no, please! I'M ALIVE!'

'Harry, Harry. It's all right, Harry, you're safe. I'm here.'

I recognise my wife's voice. Suddenly, I am awake, my face wet with tears. Will these nightmares ever stop? I have woken the children again and Anne goes to comfort them. When she returns I turn out the light and we lie there together in the darkness. I do not talk about my night terrors. Soon her breathing changes. I am glad but, like most nights, I am afraid to go back to sleep. It is safer to be alert. Stay awake!

1

EARLY DAYS IN DERRY

I WAS BORN IN Derry on 19 November 1923, to Matthew and Nellie (née Keenan) Callan. We lived in 7 Derryview Terrace, Waterside, and I was the sixth of nine children. There were George, John, Matthew Edgar (whom we called Edgar – not to confuse him with Father), Baby Robert (who died at birth), Nan, me, Gerry, Eileen and then Baby Willie, who died at six months. George was six when I was born and I was four when Baby Willie died.

Derryview Terrace, just off the Strabane Old Road, was a mile from Derry city. It was a small estate of seven two-up two-down houses, with four Catholic and three Protestant families. We were Catholics. As a child, my boundary was the tarmac surface of Craigavon Bridge: I was not allowed to cross the bridge or walk into the city alone and I never broke that rule. Some small boys were fascinated by the trains at the Great Northern Railway Station, on the far side of the river, but the real fascination for me were the street lights on the bridge itself. The only light in the Waterside was at the crossroads known as 'top of the hill', but at night, from our house, we could see the twinkling lights of Craigavon Bridge.

Relatives of the Callan family outside the family home in
Waterside, Derry, in the 1940s.

Ireland was still recovering from a bitter civil war when I
was born. In 1922 the Treaty had been signed between Great
Britain and Ireland. Of the thirty-two counties, twenty-six

became the Irish Free State or *Éire*, later the Republic of Ireland; six, with a predominantly Protestant population, became Northern Ireland under British rule and part of the United Kingdom. I was not taught any of this history at school.

Granny and Granddad Keenan lived across the Border in a small thatched cottage in Ballyshannon, Donegal, 58 miles from Derry city. Like many small landholders and farm labourers, my grandparents hired themselves out as 'tattie hokers', that is, each year they travelled to Scotland for the potato picking. They worked eighteen hours a day from June to November, in all weathers, and hoped to earn enough to live on for the rest of the year. Their staple diet in Scotland was potatoes, bread, jam and tea, and while there, they slept in a barn, called a bothy, where the beds were made of piled-up potato crates with straw mattresses and a blanket on top. There was no form of heating. One year, on the ferry home from Scotland, Granny Keenan went into early labour and my mother, Nellie, was born.

My paternal grandfather, George Callan, was the railway station agent at the local Waterside Station. When he died, my father took over this position and remained there until he retired. Grandfather's brother, James, owned a general grocery shop on Strabane Old Road. Along with foodstuffs, he also sold paraffin and coal. I knew nothing about my paternal grandmother, whose name was Anne Edgar. Her sister Ellen was a Protestant, but as my father's family were all Catholic, it is possible that my grandmother converted to Catholicism when she got married.

My parents married on 25 November 1915. I have very few memories of my mother, but I remember the sound of her long skirts swishing across the floor as she walked

View from the Callan family home looking out over the River
Foyle and Derry city, *c.* 1946.

up and down the kitchen, her hugs and feeling safe in her
arms. I remember her getting cross with me once, just
before my fourth birthday. The bigger boys in the estate
lit a fire in the lane beside our house and I went out to see
it. A piece of paper blew out of the flames, hit my shin
and burnt me. I rubbed it, which made it worse, and ran
crying to my mother. She gave me such a scolding while she
bandaged my leg. I sobbed, feeling sorry for myself. Then
she gathered me into her arms and hugged me. After my
brother Willie was born, Father's Aunt Ellen came to live
with us because Mother was very sick, in bed. She died in
1927; I was only four years old.

Aunt Ellen, whose surname was Edgar, was a spinster
and a great baker. Every day she baked an India-meal loaf
and a big soda bread. All the cooking was done on the range
and in winter, it heated the house and dried the clothes. We

were very lucky as we always had coal to burn. After Mother died, Aunt Ellen, Nan and Eileen slept in the double bed in the back room. In the front room, Father, Gerry and I slept in one double bed, while John, George and Edgar slept in the other.

There was no running water in the house; we shared a spring-fed well with our next-door neighbour. Everyone had to have a bath on Saturday. Aunt Ellen boiled water in the stew pot many times, to fill the galvanised bath. She and the girls had theirs earlier in the day, while later in the evening, Father washed first, followed by each one of us boys. Enclosed in a small shed in the yard was a dry toilet, so called because there was no flushing water. It consisted of a raised seat over a pipe, which ran to a large pit, called the 'midden'. The 'pit man' came once a month to empty the midden. Occasionally the pipe became blocked with effluent and then one of us got the job to clear the blockage with a shovel. I really hated this job but there was no escaping when it was my turn.

The Waterside Boys' School was a two-roomed, two-teacher school and a ten-minute walk away. Teacher had a blackboard, which stood on wooden legs and could be turned over, so that she could use both sides of it. We wrote on slates with chalk. I was five when I started school. Nan went to the Waterside Girls' School, farther up the road, and I had to wait for her and Edgar to bring me home for dinner in the middle of the day. Father also came home for his midday meal, which consisted of vegetable soup and a pot of steaming potatoes. We finished school at three o'clock and played until teatime, after which we did our homework. No matter what age we were, bedtime was nine o'clock for all the children. A lot of Catholic families in those days knelt down together in the evening to say the Rosary. We did not because Aunt Ellen was a Protestant, but she always reminded us as we got into bed: 'Don't forget to say your prayers.'

We had a hot meal every day and so were better off than many living in the Waterside. Father often took bread to some of the poorer families, while on his way to work. For most of my Catholic friends, Friday was the day they got the best dinner of the week – they had salt herrings.

When I was six, my father's sister and her husband, John Jarvis, came to live in our house. We were told that Aunt Mary Jane had 'married out', that she was no longer a Catholic but a Protestant, like her husband John. Not everybody accepted mixed marriages, but because Father was also from a mixed marriage, he agreed to sublet the parlour to them and it became their home. They cooked, ate and took their weekly bath in that room. Aunt Mary Jane worked in one of the local laundries, in Derry city. Her husband, like many men in mixed marriages, found it very difficult to get a job at that time. He drank a lot. Father did not approve of John Jarvis' drinking.

In summer 1930, Father got passes for the Donegal Line train and Aunt Mary Jane took Nan, Eileen, Edgar and me to the seaside village of Bundoran, 66 miles away. Derry people would say, 'We're just going over to Bundoran for the day.'

Although they were crossing the Border into the Irish Free State, there were no border checks, so it meant nothing to them. I wanted to go to the beach but Nan said,

'Come on, we are going to see Granny.'

'Granny who?'

'Granny Keenan. Our granny. Come on!'

Harry, aged seven, on his First Holy Communion Day.

Nan told Aunt Mary Jane that we wanted to visit Granny, and we all headed off to walk the 5 miles to Ballyshannon.

It was dark inside the thatched cottage. Granny Keenan sat hunched over the fire and poked it angrily. She was very cranky and I was afraid of her. We children were sent outside to play. In our excitement, we chased each other into the cottage. Granny was not pleased and, taking a hazel switch from beside her chair, she swung out with it and did not care who she hit. My sisters and brother felt the sting of it across their legs and they cried out. I escaped the switch but I never visited Granny Keenan again. I preferred to stay with Aunt Ellen and help her with the weekly wash and changing the bed linen.

Each morning, Father left for work at six o'clock, without his breakfast. We children all took our turn to light the range. From the age of seven, I took my turn, too. Once the range was lit, Aunt Ellen came downstairs and made breakfast for us. We always had a bowl of porridge, bread, butter and tea. We all took turns, on our way to school, to bring a breakfast to Father. And on Saturdays, we had to wash the floors in our house for Aunt Ellen. Once that job was finished it was bath time.

On Sunday mornings, Aunt Ellen made sure we were all ready to go to Mass with Father. I do not remember her going to church on Sundays. As Catholics, we had to fast from midnight on Saturday until after Mass on Sunday. That was not a hardship for us. We never had anything to eat after midnight any day! When we got home, Aunt Ellen had shop bread – which we called cake – butter, jam and a big pot of tea ready. Some of the local men visited the pub after Mass for a pint, but Father never drank or smoked; instead, he sat down to read his newspaper. After dinner, we children walked for miles in the countryside. I'm sure Aunt Ellen was glad of the peace and quiet.

In 1930, gas lighting came to the house. The landlord installed one lamp in the front room, one in the kitchen and one in the hall; now we did not need the oil lamp any more but we still used candles going to bed.

I had a happy childhood: we made our own cricket bats and our own little four-wheel trollies to race each other down the hill. In autumn we went 'progging' (the local term for stealing!) apples from the orchard and in winter we made sleds.

Christmas was always wonderful in our house. Father carried home a Christmas tree, which we decorated with little white candles. Before we went to bed on Christmas Eve, our stockings were hung on the back of the bedroom door. I can remember putting my hand in and taking out an orange, an apple and two shiny pennies, which we spent on sweets. After first Mass, we ran home to the wonderful cooking smells. We had turkey or goose with potatoes and lots of vegetables followed by Aunt Ellen's plum pudding and cake. Aunt Mary Jane and John Jarvis joined us for our Christmas feast.

One of our neighbours, Leslie Moore, had a fruit shop on the Strabane Old Road, near Callan's shop. He imported pears, oranges and bananas and also sold apples. Sometimes on a Saturday, he took me to the shop to help him. If he had overripe bananas, he gave them to me as payment for my work. He always said, 'There you go, Harry; they're very good for you that way.' I brought home my 'wages' and shared them with my family.

Although I liked school and never missed a single day of it, only students with high marks could apply for scholarship exams and go to Senior School, or college. So at fourteen and a half I left school and went looking for work.

During his spare time, my eldest brother, George, built a beautiful radio set and wooden windmill, which acted as a generator for its huge battery. The radio was given its own shelf in the kitchen, as it was considered to be a piece of furniture with a case of inlaid fretwork, which George had carved. He and Father liked to listen to it in the evenings. When George married Molly Dobbins in 1942 and went to live in Burnfoot, Donegal, he dismantled it, piece by piece, to take it over the Border on his bicycle and rebuilt it in his new home. But he still had to cross the Border twice a day as he worked in the Midland Railway Station in Derry.

My brother John was a great dancer at jigs, reels and waltzes, but there were no dance halls in the Waterside. Neighbours sent out word that they were going to have a 'do', which meant furniture was removed temporarily and a space cleared for the musicians and dancers. Once, when I was about fourteen years old, John bought new dancing shoes and told me that I could break them in for him, by wearing them in the house. Oh, they were lovely shoes – black leather, shiny with laces – I loved the feel of them on my feet; they were a big change from my laced boots. John showed me a few dance steps, which he said I would need to know if I ever went to a dance.

In 1938, when my other brother Edgar was sixteen, he joined the Royal Navy and I took his job as messenger boy in my granduncle's grocery shop. Granduncle James got his money's worth out of me! For 2 shillings and 6 pence (a half-crown, or 30 pennies) plus the bacon ends, I worked from eight o'clock in the morning until eleven or twelve o'clock at night. I took grocery orders in the shop, loaded the cart and delivered them. I cleaned out the stables, swept the yard, watered and fed the horse. Sometimes, I brought the midden cart into the field and spread the waste there. I used the sickle to cut vegetables like cabbages, kale and turnips for the shop and I used the scythe to cut the high grass along the ditches surrounding his land. On Saturdays, I hauled twenty 10-stone bags of coal onto the cart and delivered them to customers. In summer, when the grain boats came into Derry, I loaded twenty sacks of grain into the cart; each sack weighed 2 hundredweight. It was exhausting work. One day towards the end of that summer, I went home after a day unloading grain. Father, who was sitting in his chair beside the fire, turned to me and said, 'I don't want you going back there to work again. Tell him you're finishing up Saturday.'

'All right, Father.'

When I went into work and told my granduncle, he asked why.

'Father doesn't want me working here any more.'

So Granduncle said to me, 'I'll give you a raise of another half-crown, if you stay on.'

I did not go home to discuss it. 'No, Father says he doesn't want me working here any more. So, that's that!'

I wonder how different would my life have been, if I had taken the raise and stayed on in the shop. But I did what Father told me to do.

It was September 1939 and I was at home with no job and nothing to do. I went to see Paddy Coyle, the manager in the Broo (as we called the Labour Exchange) and a near neighbour from Strabane Old Road. He looked up and smiled at me when I came into his office.

'So, young Callan, what are you here for?'

'Father told me to come to see you.'

'Are you looking for a job?'

'Yes.'

'All right, give me your particulars.'

So I gave him my name, address, date of birth, where I went to school, that I could read, write and do arithmetic. About a week later, a letter arrived from the Health Authorities. I said to Aunt Ellen,

'God, this must be a good job I'm getting.'

'Why?'

'I have to go for a medical examination, to Belfast, tomorrow.' I just wanted a job and never thought to ask what it was. I found out when I started training.

There was a return train ticket in the envelope. Father gave me thruppence and told John to match it, so that I could buy my dinner in Woolworths. Woolworths sold everything from pots and pans to clothing, groceries, wool, confectionery, ice cream and toys. And it had its own dining room. They advertised that nothing in their store cost more than 6 pennies and I had sixpence in my pocket! The next morning, I went with Father to the Waterside Station, where I got the train for the two-and-a-half hour trip. I did not pay any attention to the scenery outside, or to the towns I passed through, even though it was my first adventure on my own.

The Medical Centre was only ten minutes away from Belfast Station, York Street. I seemed to be the only one there, so it was not long before I heard my name called. As I was never sick, this was the first time I could remember visiting a doctor and I was a bit nervous. The doctor gave me a good examination: eyes, ears, throat and even an X-ray of my lungs. I did not know that tuberculosis was rife at that time and employers did not want to employ anyone with TB.

'You'll have to get your tonsils out,' the doctor said. 'An appointment will be set up for you at the City and County Infirmary in Derry.'

When my medical examination was over, I went to Woolworths and got a plate of stew, potatoes and a pot of tea – all for thruppence. I bought myself some hard sucky sweets and then walked back to the station where I caught the early afternoon train to Derry. I still had money in my pocket. Two days later, in the first week of October, the letter with my appointment for the City and County Infirmary – known locally as the Waterside County Hospital – arrived. Off I went, by myself, to have my tonsils removed the next day. I was there for a week and was the only young person in the ward. The nurses did not want me to be idle, so they asked me to roll bandages for them. By the end of the week I was well enough to go home.

On 13 October 1939, a letter arrived from the Ministry. Enclosed with it was a train ticket to Belfast, a boat ticket to Holyhead, a second train ticket to the Gloucester Docks, a third one to the Sharpness Station, and instructions to report to the training school on the Sharpness Canal. I found out that Gloucester was in southwest England, close to the Welsh border, but nothing about the Sharpness Canal. My new job would give me board, lodgings and a pay packet. It did not take me long to pack. I wrapped my two cotton shirts in a paper parcel and some sliced bread and butter, which Aunt Ellen gave me for the journey, in another parcel; I had no other possessions. At the Waterside Station I met Father.

'Good luck now, son, and take care.'

'I will so, Father. Thanks.'

'Away you go now, don't miss the train.'

There were no hugs, but I did not expect any. I took the seven o'clock train to Belfast and from there, boarded the overnight boat to Holyhead; it was a calm sailing. There was nothing to see through the darkness, so I walked up and

The Gravesend Sea School *Vindicatrix* at her canal berth, Sharpness, in 1953.

down on the deck all night. At eight o'clock we docked in Holyhead. The station agent in Holyhead told me to show my letter and ticket to the other station agents and they would direct me to the correct platform for each stage of my journey. It was about six o'clock that evening when I eventually reached Sharpness Station. I was tired, hungry and cold. No one else got off the train. I was on my own on the short walk from the station to the training school. I could not believe my eyes when I got there; in front of me was an old ship called *Vindicatrix*.

2

TRAINING FOR MY NEW JOB

EVERYONE ELSE HAD arrived already: I was the last of the group of trainees for 1939. One of the lads met me and escorted me on board. He told me to report to the purser and showed me where to go. I knocked on the door.

'Enter!'

I stepped into a storeroom. A uniformed man sat behind a desk; he was the purser.

'I'm Harry Callan, I was told to report here for training, for my job. Here's my letter.'

'Welcome, Harry! We'll get you kitted out and down to the mess room for your tea. The lads will show you where to go. Classes in the morning but you'll be called on time.'

'Thank you, Sir.'

He handed me all my working gear: underwear, socks, trousers, a jacket that fastened at the waist, and something called a hammock. I had no a clue what a hammock was. I found out later. The purser called one of the lads, who brought me to the noisy, crowded mess room. We had bread, jam and pots of tea, and afterwards, we sat around chatting. I found out that I was one of fifty trainees on board; I was the only one from Ireland.

Eventually, we all headed down the stairway to the sleeping deck below. The other lads showed me how to set up my hammock. One end had a loop on it, which I hooked onto a post, and the other end had a cord, which had to be tied to another post. It took practice to get the level right. Getting into it was a laugh! I wobbled all over the place and landed on the floor. I tried climbing into it front-ways; I put my right knee up, then my left, but that did not work. I watched the other lads. They got in back-ways, sitting into it, bringing one leg up, then swinging in the other leg. I copied them, and eventually managed to climb in and not fall out.

Wearing underwear for the first time in my life felt strange; sleeping in it felt stranger still (I had only ever slept in my shirt). The fabric of the hammock was canvas and it tucked in around me like a cocoon. I pulled the blanket over me and was surprised to find that it was comfortable and cosy; I didn't miss the body heat of my brothers, or my father. Fortunately, the hammock was really snug, as there was no other heat on the sleeping deck, which was in the bottom of the ship.

I heard nothing, until the following morning,

'5.30 a.m. lads! We'd better get moving!'

I took down my hammock and hung it, with the others, on what the lads called the bulkhead. The deck was then free for us to use as an exercise area. I followed the others to the washroom on the top deck, and the toilet out on the dock.

It took me a while to learn my way around the ship. I found out that a stairway led up to the mess deck, which was divided into the mess room, where we ate our meals and had our lessons; the saloon for the captain and officers, who were our teachers; and the galley, where the meals were cooked and dishes washed. There was another stairway, up to the top deck, which held the washroom, the lifeboats and the captain's quarters.

At 6 a.m., those on galley duty headed to the galley to prepare our breakfast and the rest of us grabbed buckets and mops to scrub the decks. At 8 a.m., we stopped what we were doing and went to the mess room where we tucked into porridge with watered-down Lyle's Golden Syrup on it, a slice of bread and a cup of tea with no sugar. Rationing had started and sugar was a luxury item. We were told there would be none at sea, either. Like everyone else in Great Britain at this time, we got used to rationing.

After breakfast, an officer gave us our tasks; cleaning the mess room, washing dishes, cleaning the galley and scrubbing down the stairways and floors. When we were finished, we sat in the mess room until another officer arrived and then we started classes. He began to teach us about navigation and how to sail a boat. He asked us if we had any questions, so I put up my hand.

'What are we training for?'

'Don't you know?'

'No, Sir.'

'You're training to go to sea. Do you want to go?'

'Oh, I'll go, all right, I just didn't know what the training was for. No one told me that I was going to sea, I was just told to come here for training.'

'That's all right, so.'

And I began my training.

The officer took us up on deck, where he showed us the lifeboats and the different parts of the ship. I was on the *Vindicatrix* for three months. The main thing I remember, during that time, was the cold, especially at the end of November and the month of December. Apart from the ovens in the galley, there was no form of heating on board. The only time I was warm was when I was in my hammock.

The Merchant Navy was very strict about cleanliness; our very first lesson was about personal hygiene; our second lesson was about keeping the outside and inside of the ship clean, at all times. There would be no slovenliness on board a British Merchant Navy ship. These lessons were well learnt, and were to save some of our lives, later, during the war.

We had to learn about ropes; splicing and making knots; boat handling, which was getting the lifeboats into the water and back onto the ship again; rowing; lifeboat drills; signalling; knowledge and use of the compass; cleaning brass; scrubbing decks; preparing food and serving meals in the mess and saloon – basically all the skills a seaman needed. At midday, we stopped for an hour for dinner. We got meat with every dinner. For some of us, it was like having a feast every day.

We had more classes in the afternoon, which ended at 4 p.m. Those of us not on galley duty had free time until 5 p.m. when we went back to the mess room for bread, usually with raspberry jam, and a cup of tea. The only day I remember getting supper was Sunday, when we got a slice of batch loaf, dripping and a mug of cocoa, made on water. After tea, we had more free time, which we spent either in the mess room, or below deck in our sleeping quarters. We chatted, played cards, read mystery novels or cowboy books. At 10 p.m. we climbed into our hammocks. We were plunged into darkness when one of the officers called, 'Lights out!'

On board, we had the skipper, whom we also addressed as 'Captain', or quietly among ourselves, the 'Old Man'. The captain's cabin was on the top deck, above the saloon, and the washrooms were at the other end of this deck, above the galley. The captain slept on board, as he was in charge of the whole ship. We had a second skipper, who was a working skipper, called Captain Angel. He was responsible for the upkeep of the ship and its supplies. We also had on board the purser, who looked after us, and the chief steward, who was in charge of the galley and our galley training. There were other officers who came on board, every morning, to train us for ship life.

Originally, our Merchant Navy School was on land, at Gravesend in Kent, just south-east of London, but when Great Britain entered the war, the British authorities were concerned about the safety of the school in the event of a Luftwaffe attack. It was decided to move the students to the *Vindicatrix,* on the Sharpness Canal in Gloucester. The accommodation for the training officers was on shore, in a few prefabricated, corrugated-steel Nissen huts that belonged to the school. For the recruits of 1941 and after, there was a library, music room, games room, a small shop and post office installed in newer buildings, but for us there was none of these luxuries.

After breakfast on Sunday mornings we all went up to the top deck, which was open to the elements, and Captain called out, 'C. of E., step forward!'

Thirty lads were Church of England; they stepped forward and were taken off the ship to go to church, where afterwards they got tea and biscuits. Twenty of us stayed on board and had no church service. Although there was a Catholic church near Sharpness, the priest never came down to the ship; there were more Catholics on board than just me. While the 'C. of E.' lads were at church, we were free to sit around, go for a walk along the canal, or up to the village. The only other time we went ashore was to use the toilet block on the quayside, and when we had to take our turn on night-watch duty.

There were two night-watch shifts, 10 p.m. to 2 a.m. and 2 a.m. to 5 a.m. We were paired off and given one gun between us; we would argue over whose turn it was to carry it. We had to walk up and down the quayside in darkness, which was not so bad for me, because I was used to having no streetlights, but some of the city lads didn't like it. It was very quiet, or so I thought at first, but after a short while I could hear the canal water lapping against the bank, or the plop of a fish as it jumped.

We thought we were great doing 'sentry duty', as we called it. We were keeping the enemy at bay; it was an adventure. We practised saying, 'Who goes there?'

We hoped that no one would answer. If someone did, what were we supposed to do? If it was the enemy, we were finished: we'd had no firearms training and there were no bullets in the gun! On cold nights we could see our breath in front of us, and were glad if it was not our turn to hold the gun; that way we could put our hands in our pockets. After a four-hour shift it was great to climb into my hammock to get warm. I liked the second shift, because it ended at 5 a.m., which meant we called the others to get up, then climbed into our hammocks and snuggled into our blankets until dinnertime: we were let off other duties and classes for the morning.

We had to wear our lifejackets for lifeboat drill. These were blocks of cork, covered with material sewn together in a band, which we strapped around our chests and over our shoulders. We hated wearing them. There were stories of people jumping off the *Titanic,* into the water, and forgetting to hold down their lifejackets. When they hit the water, the lifejacket was forced upwards and the hard cork broke their necks. Even though I could not swim, I hated wearing that jacket; it was bulky and awkward, tying the cords was difficult and I was afraid of getting my neck broken.

It was great fun learning how to row the lifeboats. The officer in charge let us enjoy it at first but after a while we were called to order and shown how to use the oars correctly. We eventually got the hang of it. We were trained, too, in the duties of a cabin boy and how to look after the captain's cabin. The duties were to bring tea to the captain in the morning, clean his cabin and make his bunk.

Then there was my training in the saloon, which I enjoyed. I had to learn how to set a table correctly, with linen and cutlery, how to serve the meals in the saloon, to the captain, the second skipper, training officers and any guests the captain might have. After their meal, I learned how to serve tea, or a little demitasse cup of coffee. I could not believe it when I saw that there was sugar in the saloon for the captain and officers' use.

Captain Angel was very strict. He expected us to be well behaved and to pay attention in class. He tolerated no larking about or joking while he was on duty; in particular, there was to be no whistling, as this could give away our position to the enemy. When we heard that, every time Captain Angel walked past us, a group of lads started whistling. Of course, once Captain Angel turned around, we were diligently setting about our duties.

'Were you whistling, boy?'

'Whistling, Sir?'

'Not I, Sir. Did you hear someone whistling?'

'Get about your duties.'

'Yes, Sir.'

It became a game with us, and I do not think Captain Angel minded too much.

In December, some of the lads who had been on board the *Vindicatrix* before I arrived finished their training. They were now known as the 'Vindi Boys' and went to work on British Merchant Navy ships. New trainees started to arrive, and those of us who were still on board were considered the 'old hands' now. In 1939, I didn't have to pay for my training but from 1941 onwards, a training fee was charged to new recruits. I spent Christmas on board the *Vindicatrix*. Christmas morning came and when we went up on deck, the captain called out, 'C. of E., step forward!'

The Church of England lads went on shore while the rest of us stayed on board. When the lads got back to the *Vindicatrix,* they returned to the wonderful aroma of cooking coming from the galley. We were treated to a turkey dinner, with vegetables and potatoes, and afterwards we had plum pudding and custard. We lounged around in the mess room for the rest of the day; we could not move we were so full. There was no contact with home as we were still in training, and had to get used to the fact that we were going to sea and would not be in touch with our families for long periods of time. I didn't mind really: apart from the fabulous dinner, it was just another day for me.

My training finished on 17 January 1940. Now I, too, was a 'Vindi Boy'. There was no graduation ceremony, just a visit to one of the Nissen huts where I was given my kit bag.

In it were the following: 2 pairs of shoes, 2 pairs of dungaree trousers, 1 pair of blue trousers and a jacket, 3 striped jumpers, 3 white suits, uniform buttons, white shoes, 1 peaked cap, vests and underpants, 3 shirts, 3 pairs of socks, 2 towels, 2 pairs of pyjamas, a toothbrush and comb, a notebook and a training school badge.

That kit bag was great: it held everything and I just threw it over my shoulder – better than a case any day! The purser gave me a train ticket to London and my instructions:

'You're to report to the Royal Mail Line Office, beside the docks. They're expecting you. You're to join one of their ships, the *Highland Monarch.*'

'Yes, Sir. Thank you, Sir.'

On the same day, I made the four-hour journey from Sharpness to London. Unfortunately, I arrived to find she had already sailed. The agent in the Royal Mail Line Office sent me to the Seaman's Mission and told me to wait there until I heard from him.

It was the first time I'd had a room to myself and it felt strange sleeping there. It was very quiet. I stayed for two days until I was told that the Royal Mail Line Office was looking for me.

They sent me to a Royal Mail Line boat, the *Culebra,* and I signed on as cabin boy. She was running between Britain and the West Indies, i.e. sailing on a regular route, and had docked in London for a week while being unloaded. I 'worked by' and stayed on board her at night. 'Working by' meant that while the ship was docked, a seaman could get board, lodgings and pay, while working on board. I could go ashore, once my work was done and could stay ashore all night if I wanted to, but I had to be back on board in time for my morning duties. I shared a cabin with an assistant steward, and a second steward by the name of Richard Knight, called Dick, who took me under his wing. He seemed old to me but was probably about thirty at the time.

When I first went on the *Culebra*, I got excited when I saw the hand basin with hot and cold taps but was quickly brought back to earth when Dick said I had to get my water from the galley.

Then I asked Dick, 'If we want a bath, or shower, where do we go to have one?'

'Your bucket, out on deck – there.' He pointed to an area outside the galley.

I filled my bucket from the galley with hot water, went out on deck, stripped to my underwear, soaped down, poured the water over myself, towelled and dressed very quickly. That was my bath. There was no toilet on the *Culebra*, just the heads, where I learned to hang my backside over the ship's rail; that was some experience! There was a frame, with a screen around it, for a bit of privacy, which just covered the lower regions. It was possible to be seen from the waist up and it was better than nothing, but if it was rough at sea, the screen was taken down. I didn't like that, but I had to get used to it: it was the same for all of us. If we were in port, a large barrel was hung over the side and we used that. It was then either emptied when we moved out from port or taken out by some of the crew in one of the lifeboats, and emptied where the tide could take it. Eventually, the Port Authorities banned this practice and built toilets on the docks, but truthfully, they were worse than the barrel over the side.

Dick invited me to go with him to visit his mother who lived in Kent. We would have to stay overnight as it was a two-hour train journey. Mrs Knight had a quiet and genteel voice and was delighted to see Dick. She lived in a cosy, two-up two-down house, with wallpaper in all the rooms and carpets on the floor. I had never seen this before.

Mrs Knight could only give us tea and bread in the morning because of rationing. She apologised but I understood and thanked her for her hospitality. Dick said his goodbyes to his mother and we were on board the *Culebra* by 8 a.m. and signed on for a sailing to the West Indies; it was 19 January 1940 and I was sixteen.

3

MY LIFE AT SEA

FOUR DAYS LATER, on 23 January 1940, we cast off from Southend Pier, London. I was seasick for the first few days; all I wanted to do was to lie down and die. But I was a seaman now. There could be no lying on in my bunk, feeling sorry for myself. I was the pantry boy and my duties included washing the dishes. I would drop the dishes in the sink, run out on deck to vomit over the side, then go back to washing dishes. In and out, in and out, all day long; I could not eat anything. When I finally got to my bunk, I thought I would be grand there, but no: I was sick all night and had to keep a bucket beside me.

On my second day at sea, although I still had to go out on deck once or twice, I began feeling a bit better. It was while I was out on deck, dry retching, that a bosun's mate came up behind me and suddenly I felt a hand on my backside. I jumped away from the rail, in shock; I didn't know what was going on, but Dick Knight was coming out on deck, and he saw the incident.

'Go back inside, Harry. Are you okay, son?'

'Yes, Dick.'

As I went back to my duties in the pantry, I heard Dick warning the crew member to keep away from me in the future. That evening he said to me, 'Harry, you're at sea now, son. Don't let anyone ever, ever touch you like that again. If anyone on this ship ever does, you report him to me, immediately. Do you hear me, now?'

'Yes, Dick. Thanks, I will.'

Then Dick told me about some of the things that can happen at sea to young lads. I'd had no idea that such things went on and made sure to keep out of everyone's way after that talk.

When the chief steward gave me an apple, four or five days later, and I was able to eat it, I knew that I had got my sea legs. It was the tastiest apple I can ever remember!

When the Second World War was declared, Britain adopted a convoy system. I knew nothing about this and was surprised to see so many ships together. That evening, I asked Dick about them. He explained that the Germans were in our waters and that our Navy would give us protection until we got past Ireland and into the safer waters of the Atlantic. Each convoy consisted of between thirty and seventy, mostly unarmed, merchant ships. Our convoy was OG-16F, which meant 'outward going sixteen fast ships'. Once the Navy left us, we would be on our own.

The full meaning of what Dick was saying did not strike me at the time. I was still on an adventure. I loved the sea and was enjoying my work. I had not seen anything of war yet.

My day started at 5.30 a.m. At 6 a.m. I brought tea to the bridge, then set to scrubbing the two companionways, one leading from the pantry to the saloon and the other, from there to the captain and officers' quarters. The bell system was used aboard the ship to regulate the duty-watches and my meals revolved around the 'seven-bell' ring, so at 7.20 a.m., when the seven-bell breakfast started for the two-man watch going on the 8 a.m. shift, I had bread, butter and a cup of tea in the galley, after which I washed dishes. At 8 a.m., the captain and officers were served their breakfast. The crew, on the other hand, had to queue on the open deck to collect all their meals from the galley, and carry them down to the mess deck below. At 9 a.m., I cleaned the captain's quarters and made up his bunk. At 11 a.m., I had twenty minutes to eat my dinner, in the galley, just before 'seven-bell dinner' for the change of watch. At 1 p.m., I tidied up the pantry and then I got a break for a couple of hours.

At 3 p.m., cups of tea were served, in the saloon, on the bridge and to the men on watch. At 3.30 p.m. 'seven-bell tea' was served to the watch going on duty at 4 p.m. I ate a quick tea in the galley before laying the table for the evening meal. At 5 p.m., tea was served to the captain and officers. Afterwards, the crew had theirs. When everything was washed and ready for the next morning, I cleaned the pantry and finished for the day, usually around 6 p.m.

In my cabin I liked to chat to Dick and the assistant steward, and enjoyed their stories of life at sea. I also read books. My favourites were cowboy or detective stories. I had to get used to all the new sounds: the engines and the different noises they made, the sea lapping on the side of the ship and the crew walking around in the mess room above. I realised that I had got used to them when I could fall asleep without hearing them any more. But any change in the engine, if it stopped, or slowed down, would jolt me awake.

I would have hated to work in the engine room. I felt sorry for the trimmers, firemen and greasers. The

SS *Culebra* – Harry's first ship.

Culebra was a coal burner. The three trimmers shovelled coal through the small hatch to the engine room; the six firemen maintained the fires, and kept the boilers going; they also loaded the coal on board, and ensured that the bunkers were balanced, so that the ship did not list. The three greasers continuously greased all the nuts and bolts, so that the engines ran smoothly. I do not know how they stuck the constant noise, the intense heat and the dreadful coal dust. Because the engines never stopped, they had three shifts, and had to wash after each one, on deck, in front of the galley; they needed buckets of hot water. We were not allowed to sit to meals, in the mess room, unless we were clean. The captain was very strict about that.

The *Culebra* carried grain to the West Indies and returned with spices, teas and other dry goods. It took nearly a month at sea to get there and another month to get back. There was no fridge on the *Culebra* to preserve our food, and no other port of call. Instead, situated on the port side, opposite the galley, she had an icebox, which was a large wooden structure like a walk-in cupboard. Before we left port, two men with claw hooks lifted a couple of very large blocks of ice into the icebox, where large quantities of mutton, beef and dairy products were stored. As the ice melted, the amount of spiced and pickled food on the menu increased. When we arrived at our destination port, fresh ice blocks and victuals were loaded on board for the next stage of our journey.

On our second week out, we hit rough weather. The storm washed waves up over the ship as she lurched. In the pantry, seawater poured under the door. In order to stay on my feet, I had to brace myself against the sink, holding tightly to the edge of it with one hand, while washing dishes with the other. The wind screamed. I never heard anything like it before, and although orders were being shouted out, I could not hear what anyone was saying to me. During storms, it was the bosun's job to ensure that security ropes were put in place around the decks. Battling with wind and water, the crew clung to those ropes in order to carry on with their duties.

My shift ended and I tried to go down to my cabin. With great difficulty, I left the pantry and staggered into another world. I was immediately soaked by the sea and the rain. I grabbed the rope as the wind tried to pull me away. But I was not scared. I did not want to go overboard, that's for sure, but the screaming wind made it exciting – it was another adventure. As I made my way along the gangway, crossing one hand over the other, following the ropes, I recited a rhyme in my head, 'one hand for the company and one hand for me'. A couple of times, I lost my footing but finally managed to get down the companionway. I was glad to close the door behind me, strip off my wet clothes and get into my bunk. I don't know how long that storm lasted because I fell asleep.

The next morning, on my way back to the pantry, some of the crew met me and said, 'Well, for a first tripper, you did all right. You've come through your first hurricane, son!'

A hurricane! I hadn't ever heard of hurricanes and had thought this was just a very bad storm. At first I thought the *Culebra* had come through it in one piece, but I noticed that the steel hatch covers were missing. Most of the ships at that time were installing steel hatch covers to stop bombs dropping through into the holds and setting fire to them. In port, it took a crane to lift them off, but that hurricane had lifted those steel hatches off like pieces of paper, and thrown them overboard during the night. The hurricane had also blown us off course. The meat supplies were gone and the ice had completely melted, too. We had tinned corned beef in the ship's stores for backup, and so we had that for dinner.

For me, everything was new and every day was an adventure. I saw the ocean in a completely different way. At home in Derry, I was able to see the Atlantic, but I had never seen waves like these. I could not believe the size of them and the way they came crashing over the *Culebra*. One day there was great excitement. Some of the crew called me.

'Harry, come out here, quick! You've got to see this.'

I came out of the pantry and joined the others at the rail. I saw dolphins for the first time but did not know what they were. There must have been at least fifty of them jumping out of the water and playing in our wash. It looked like they were having fun with us, then they went out in front, as if they were pointing us in the right direction, and they swam away, jumping out of the water and diving back down; they were so fast we could not keep up with them. Too soon, the show was over and we all went back to our duties.

We arrived at Bermuda, our first port of call, in the West Indies on 16 February 1940. We docked, unloaded some grain and took on other cargo, victuals and ice. While we were docked, we were allowed to go ashore. Dick explained to me that I could get a 'sub' on my wages, which were £2 a month; a 'sub' for me was 5 shillings. The captain would not allow any crew member to have all his money going on shore. It was a strange sensation when I once more stood on firm ground. I realised that I was rolling from one foot to the other, my body expecting the ground to shift under me; it felt weird.

Bermuda was beautiful. There were carriages, bicycles and horse-drawn traps everywhere. It was warm, and everyone dressed in brightly coloured clothes, even the men. Such a change from home. The ladies wore wide-brimmed hats. There were palm trees and bushes with huge blooms on them and flowers that I had never seen before. I still had to work on board, but during my off-duty times, I could go on shore leave and each time I was stunned by the beauty of the place.

On 20 February 1940, we left Bermuda to sail to Kingston, Jamaica. We were one crew member short as the assistant cook, a Jamaican, had not come back on board. I never knew what happened to him, but I was promoted to the position and, as well as my pantry duties, I now worked in the galley. There was a crew of thirty-eight on board the *Culebra*. My new job included making the bread to feed us all, so Cook showed me how to make batch loaf. Baking bread on a ship was not easy: yeast was frozen and had to be thawed; it took 5 stone of flour and sugar (which Cook kept under lock and key) to make enough loaves each day. The basin was as big as our tin bath at home; it took hours of kneading before Cook could bake the loaves in the oven and in between I had to attend to my pantry duties.

'If only Aunt Ellen could see me now!' I thought.

I could not get another sub, so I chose not to go ashore in Jamaica. We left Kingston on 9 March and two days later arrived in Port-au-Prince, Haiti, where I went on shore leave, but I had been spoilt by the beauty of Bermuda, and soon returned to my ship. We left on 16 March and arrived at Hampton Roads in south-eastern Virginia six days later. That same day, we left for Halifax, Nova Scotia, arriving on 26 March, where we took on ice and victuals, before leaving there on 29 March. We rendezvoused with our convoy, HX31 (the name indicated a convoy of thirty-one ships out of Halifax), and headed back across a calmer Atlantic, reaching Liverpool on 13 April 1940. The following day we sailed around the coast of England into London Docks, arriving safely in the afternoon with a cargo of grains, spices and other dry goods. In London, I signed off and was given my Discharge Book.

The Discharge Book was a seaman's passport. It contained his personal details, next-of-kin name and address, shipping route record, standard of work and character reference. It was signed by the captain and the port office, who gave it to the seaman when he signed off his ship. When he signed onto his next ship, he handed it in at the port office. The captain studied this book, when deciding to take a new seaman on board. I have four Discharge Books covering my life at sea and each record has 'impeccable behaviour' noted. I am proud of that.

I collected my wages, went to the Seaman's Mission and got a room. Some of the men staying there told me about a pub they frequented and I went along with them. The landlady of the pub, who was very friendly, knew her customers. She ran a clean house, tolerated no fighting or gambling, and watched everything. Men played fiddles and tin whistles and every so often, a name was called out, followed by, 'Come on, give us a song!' Someone would start to sing and after a few lines most of the pub joined in.

The men with me were drinkers but I did not drink alcohol. They told me that they were buying rounds. When it came to my turn, I went up to the bar, to call the order. The landlady came over to me.

'What's your name, son?'

'Harry, Mam: Harry Callan.'

'Are you off?'

'Yes Mam, I'm taking some time off.'

She saw the row of pints and shorts I had ordered, and spotted that I was not drinking myself.

'Have you money on you?'

'Yes, Mam, my wages.'

'Give them here to me and I'll mind them for you. Those lads will have them off you in no time. Come in here to me every evening, and I'll give you some for the next day.'

I handed her my money. I trusted her.

There were two Irish girls working in the pub and they agreed to show me around. I enjoyed listening to their chatter, it reminded me of Nan and her friends, and they treated me like their big brother. Every day I called for the girls and we walked around the town or the parks; sometimes we went to the pictures. Each evening, I went back to the pub and helped out and at the end of each night the landlady gave me some of my money for the next day. Then one day, around 17 May, the landlady said to me,

'Harry, you don't have much money left. Have you decided what you're going to do? Are you going to go back to sea?'

'I will, yes, Mam. Thanks for watching out for me. I had a good time here.'

I collected the last of my money, said my goodbyes and headed back to the Seaman's Mission. The *Afric Star* was in port and they were looking for crew. I made my way down to the ship and met the chief steward. He checked my Discharge Book and told me he needed a galley boy. On 20 May 1940, I signed on the *Afric Star.*

4

SS AFRIC STAR

THE *Afric Star* was a refrigerated cargo ship. On the outward journey, to South America, she travelled with empty holds, returning with fresh beef and mutton. She also had cabins for 180 first-class passengers. The cabin I shared with a cabin boy was big enough to have a chest of drawers, a wardrobe, a shower room and a hand basin with hot and cold water in it. There were toilets on board for all the crew, too. I did two trips as galley boy.

Our first trip took us from Southend via Liverpool across the Atlantic to Argentina, calling at the Cape Verde Islands, Buenos Aires, Rio Grande, Santos and São Paulo in Brazil, Freetown in Sierra Leone, and then back home to Liverpool. We left Southend on 22 May 1940, and joined Convoy OG 31F, a fast convoy, which meant that all the ships had similar engine speeds and could travel faster than 9 knots. A slow convoy could be at least five days more at sea. The Navy escorted us until we got past the west coast of Ireland; then we travelled in convoy for a while with no further protection before we split up to go to our destination ports. It was always strange travelling in convoy, close to so many other ships; usually, there was only the ocean and the sky.

SS *Afric Star* c. 1926.

Sailors on the 4 a.m. watch were our alarm clocks. Because the galley was not locked at night, the sailors on night watch were glad to warm themselves at the stove and appreciated that Cook let them make tea. In return, they made sure that the fires kept burning low all night. Although it was not part of their duties, some even took the ashes out and threw them overboard. At 7 a.m., I called the cook with a cup of tea and cleaned his cabin when he headed to the galley. There was a crew of seventy-two on board the *Afric Star*. The galley staff consisted of the chief cook, second cook, baker, vegetable cook, assistant cook and butcher, galley boy and pantry boy. She also carried a few passengers. One of my jobs was to peel potatoes – I got sick of peeling potatoes!

In the Merchant Navy, seamen were those who had formal training, while sailors were men with experience of the sea. During wartime, many seamen joined the Royal Navy, so the Merchant Navy took on sailors to fill the gap. One of the sailors, a friendly chap by the name of Billy English, came from Arklow, County Wicklow. He used to stop by for a chat and sometimes helped me to peel potatoes; we compared growing up on the same island.

We reached the Cape Verde Islands on 2 June 1940, docked and refuelled before sailing to Buenos Aires, arriving there on 14 June. Buenos Aires was a huge, busy port and a lot of the crew went on shore leave to visit bars and enjoy themselves. I stayed on board and sunbathed up on the boat deck when not working. It took ten days to fill the hold with beef; then we sailed to Rio Grande and docked on 26 June. The next day, we sailed to Santos, Brazil, and arrived there on 30 June. There was no shore leave as the captain was waiting for our convoy rendezvous instructions. Once he received them, we left for Freetown, Sierra Leone, but Convoy SL-40F had left four days previously; we caught up and rendezvoused with them on 20 July 1940. When we arrived back in Liverpool on 5 August, I signed off.

The *Afric Star* stayed in Liverpool for three weeks and Cook asked me if I wanted to work-by on her. I agreed, because it meant that I would be paid, and have free board and lodgings, and time off, too. It also meant that the mate would recommend me to the captain for the next trip.

I noticed that the other lads dressed smartly when they went ashore. I wanted to be like them so I asked Billy where I could buy a suit. He directed me to Lewis's in the city centre. I thought Woolworths in Belfast was big, but Lewis's was even bigger! In the Men's Department, I told the sales assistant that I wanted a smart suit and everything else to go with it. He looked me up and down and then produced a measuring tape. He measured my legs, arms, chest and said, 'What kind of suit did Sir have in mind?'

Sir! He called me Sir! I had to stop myself from looking around to see who else was there.

'Well, I want to be smart, not a suit like my father would wear.'

'No problem, Sir, if you would kindly step this way, and I will bring you a selection.'

I was still only sixteen, and the sales assistant was treating me like a man – it felt good. I left Lewis's with new underpants, two pairs of socks, two new white cotton shirts, a striped tie, a pair of grey flannel trousers, a grey double-breasted sports jacket, a three-quarter length, grey woollen greatcoat and new black leather shoes. All of this cost me £5. I only had a couple of pounds left. I went on shore leave in my new clothes, taking walks in the park and the city. I glanced at my reflection in shop windows and saw a smartly-dressed working man.

I signed on the *Afric Star* again as galley boy and we left Liverpool on 29 August in an OB-205 convoy. This was an outward-bound convoy of thirty-three ships. I knew now that due to a lack of Royal Navy escort ships, we would only be give one day's escort from Donegal. Then the majority of OB convoys would disperse at a given point and sail independently to their next port of call. It was 31 August 1940 and we were about 100 miles north of the Donegal coast when our convoy was attacked. At around midnight, the German U-boat 60 fired two torpedoes and hit the Dutch passenger ship *Volendam*. There were a total of 879 people on board: 273 crew, 320 children and their chaperones who were being evacuated to Canada, and 286 other passengers. Miraculously, only one person died; everyone else was rescued. We found out later that when the *Volendam* was towed to the Merseyside Docks, the repair crew found an unexploded torpedo in her hull.

At about 2 a.m., German U-boat 59 sank a British ship, the *Bibury*. She had a crew of thirty-eight and one gunner on board. There were no survivors. At about 6 a.m., German U-boat 38 sank another British ship, *Har-Zion*. She had a crew of thirty-four. Only one survived. We heard the explosions and saw the smoke. This was my first real experience of war at sea. Cook explained what was happening. Until then, I had felt safe on my ship, especially when we were in convoy; I realised then that we were not safe at all and was frightened. I heard some of the crew muttering prayers, for those 'poor souls' and we all returned to our duties. There was nothing else we could do: we had to get to our destination. I went back to my job in the galley, and hoped to God that none of the German U-boats would find us.

Three of the ships were later torpedoed by U-boats and sunk, one just after dispersing from our convoy; the other two were slower ships and so were easy targets.

We arrived at the Cape Verde Islands on 10 September 1940 and refuelled. On 22 September we reached Buenos Aires, where we took on our cargo of beef, mutton and butter. We also docked at Santos, São Paulo and Rio de Janeiro, to fill our holds for the homeward journey. This time, I went on shore leave with other crew members in each of the ports. We went for walks and visited little restaurants or cafes. Although I enjoyed putting my feet on solid ground again, I was always happy to go back on board. The *Afric Star* was my home, at least that's the way it felt. We left Rio de Janeiro on 7 October and sailed for Freetown. On the way, we rendezvoused with other ships and met our convoy, SL-52F. As we arrived in Liverpool, the captain received instructions not to dock but to sail to Belfast Lough. We arrived there on 8 November.

By this time, the Germans were using magnetic mines and the *Afric Star* had to be fitted with degaussing gear. I was fascinated to know how it worked. Metal rods, attached to the sides of the ship, jutted out over the sea and carried electrical cable around her outer edges. As the ship's steel hull sailed through the water, the magnetic field built up. The mines could detect this and attach themselves to the ship; the degaussing gear was supposed to reduce the magnetic field, so that the mines could not find us. When I learned this I thought to myself, 'Well, that's good news anyway. We don't have to worry about mines, just U-boats, Raiders and planes. They might get us, but the mines won't!' I had heard about the Raiders *Graf Spree, Lutzow* and *Admiral Scheer,* German battleships that attacked merchant ships, sinking them with their cargo. I hoped that they would never find us.

We had no shore leave in Belfast Lough, so I made no contact with my family. It was just as well, as they would have made the trip from Derry to Belfast only to find out that I could not go ashore.

We left Belfast Lough on 14 November but we could not go back to London as it was being heavily bombed at the time, so we were diverted to Avonmouth Docks in Bristol. We arrived there on 16 November, unloaded our cargo and refuelled. I signed off, received my Discharge Book and then worked-by. There was always work to be done on the ship: even in dock, the crew had to be fed and the ship kept clean. On 24 November, five days after my seventeenth birthday, I had just finished my meal in a restaurant when bombs started falling. It was mayhem. Buildings were collapsing all around us, so I started to run for my ship. In my head I was saying, 'Got to get to my ship. Got to get home. Safe there. Safe. Run!'

I ran as fast as I could, dodging falling debris. Suddenly, a hand shot out and grabbed me.

'Where do you think you're going, son?'

It was a policeman.

'Have to get to my ship, Sir. It's there, at the dock.'

'Not tonight, you don't. Get into the air-raid shelter, NOW.'

'But my ship …'

'I said NOW.'

He pushed me into the air-raid shelter.

'And STAY THERE!'

There were a lot of people in the shelter but I did not talk to anyone. I just sat down on the floor, like everyone else, and waited. What else could I do? It was awful listening to the noise outside and knowing that everything had changed, that everything was being blown to bits. It was not my home, but I felt very sorry for the people there with me. I still had my ship. At least, I hoped to God I did and that she had not left Avonmouth without me.

The all-clear siren sounded and we began to climb out of the shelter. Whole terraces of houses were gone, and in some places, only the two end houses were left standing. I could see parts of rooms, open to the elements, wallpapered walls, wardrobes hanging askew, and clothes in rags flapping on the few trees that survived. People's homes and lives were wrecked. It was really dreadful. In all, 207 people were killed in the air raid and 187 were seriously injured. Over 10,000 homes were damaged and 1,400 people were left homeless. The *Afric Star* was still there. I was thankful to go aboard again.

Britain retaliated: the RAF began to bomb the U-boat bases in France. The Royal Navy converted cargo merchant ships into catapult aircraft ships, aircraft carriers and they armed merchant cruisers. To protect the cargo merchant fleets, they built more corvettes, frigates and escort carriers. Britain's survival relied on the merchant fleets being protected at sea, so they improved the anti-submarine weapons on the Navy ships, one of which was called the hedgehog. This was an array of mortars that would be fired ahead or to the sides of a warship so that the shells fell in a large pattern over the suspected location of a submarine. Each shell carried a charge of about 60 lb of high explosive, enough to buckle a submarine hull on contact. The hedgehog shells only exploded if they scored a hit.

In order for escort vessels to track U-boats, the Royal Navy used long-range aircraft, improved the radar and radio direction finding, and improved the sonar. Vessels were allocated to convoys according to their speeds, so that faster ships were less exposed. The Royal Navy also approved larger convoys, and allowed more escorts per convoy to defend those that faced an above-average risk of attack. Finally, Britain managed to break the Kriegsmarine or German Navy's cipher.

The *Afric Star* was ready to sail and I signed on for the third time, now as assistant cook and butcher. Due to the large loss of ships and crew, more and more seamen were joining the Navy to fight the enemy and there was a shortage of skilled galley crew. When the captain read in my Discharge Book that I had held the position of assistant cook on the *Culebra,* he considered me for the job, even though I was only seventeen. Once I told him how I had got the job and after he questioned me, he was satisfied that I knew what I was doing and he took me on. I knew nothing about butchering, however, and had to learn it as I went along. Cook helped me.

On 8 December 1940, we left Avonmouth and sailed, with no escort, for the Cape Verde Islands. It was a nerve-wracking trip because I now knew that we could be attacked from below, from the air or from another ship. Luck was with us. We arrived safely on 21 December and refuelled. We sailed to Buenos Aires on 2 January 1941, where we filled our cargo holds, up to the brim, with beef. Before the war, ships were only allowed to carry a certain tonnage, according to the Lloyds Registration. The Plimsoll line, a white line painted around the ship, had to be visible. If it went below the surface of the water, it meant that the ship was overloaded and was no longer insured. When the ships were painted grey during the Second World War to camouflage them, this mark was covered over and ships were able to take on extra cargo.

We took on two British passengers in Buenos Aires, Frank Evans and his wife, Joan. He was a civil engineer, who had gone to Argentina in 1931 and was returning to Britain, where he hoped to help in the war effort. Their ship had sailed a couple of days earlier than scheduled, so they sailed on the *Afric Star* instead. We headed for Montevideo, Uruguay, where we arrived on 18 January and picked up a third passenger, a young Argentinian lady called Sheila Jagoe. The talk among the crew was that she had been working in Britain and had fallen in love with a British lad. She travelled home to visit her family, to tell them that she was getting married and to purchase her wedding dress. I do not know how true this was, but it made a good story and the crew liked to say, 'Hasn't she the good sense? British lads are the best!'

The passenger accommodation was across from the galley, so I would see Frank and Joan standing together on the companionway, holding hands, or leaning into one another, looking out to sea and talking quietly together. I was only a young lad, but I do not think I had ever before seen two people so in love; they had eyes only for each other.

5

TAKEN PRISONER

WE LEFT Montevideo on 18 January and sailed for the Cape
Verde Islands to refuel and then onwards for Freetown,
Sierra Leone, to rendezvous with our convoy. Ten days
into our journey, we were near the Cape Verde Islands. The
weather was beautiful, warm and balmy and there was not
a ripple on the sea; it was like a millpond. We had not seen
any other ships and there had been no sign of any U-boats
either. Like all the other merchant ships, we now had a
Navy gunner on board, who trained some of us to use the
newly installed 4-inch gun on the poop deck, the shells for
which had to be loaded by hand. These were stored in the
bosun's small hatch, also called the lazarette, at the aft of the
ship, a small area under the deck where his ropes and other
equipment were stored. Because I was one of the youngest
on board, I was trained to go down the hatch to hand-feed
the shells to the gunner up top. I enjoyed this training but
hoped I would never have to use it.

The day of 29 January 1941 started out like any other day.
The crew had been fed at 11.30 a.m. and then, at midday, we
served dinner to the officers and the three passengers in the

saloon. The galley boy was cleaning up and the cabin boy was washing dishes. I served them their dinner and joined them. The three of us were eating our meal when one of the crew stuck his head around the door and said, 'There's another ship out there. We must be near our convoy.'

The Bridge had announced that we would be at the Cape Verde Islands that day, which meant we would meet ships heading for our convoy rendezvous; it was always exciting when this happened. Some of the crew moved out on deck to see if they could recognise the ship in the distance and we left the galley to join them. I enjoyed listening to the banter as they tried to guess her identity. I still could not recognise ships but the older seamen knew them by their funnel markings and even by their size and shape. This always impressed me.

'Definitely a Hamburg Amerika Line ship, lads.'

'Yeah, definitely.'

'Which one?'

'Reckon it's the *Steiermark*.'

'Reckon you're right there. Definitely the *Steiermark*.'

'Must be short on fuel, she's not moving very fast.'

'Maybe she's got engine trouble.'

And so the speculation continued. We all drifted back to our duties, the initial interest and curiosity now satisfied.

Unknown to us, the *Steiermark* had been bought by the Germans following the outbreak of war, converted into a merchant Raider and renamed *Kormoran* (HSK-8). She had a speed of 16 knots – faster than our 15 knots. The *Kormoran* was armed: she had guns on the decks, five anti-aircraft guns and torpedo tubes (both above-water launchers and below-water tubes), moored mines, ground mines and two Arado 196 seaplanes. We could not see the four guns mounted in the bow and stern, which were hidden from view by camouflage plates (pieces of metal that could be swung back by use of a counterweight, allowing the gun behind to be trained on its target). The two guns housed in the hatches were protected from view by the use of specially made coamings, which were lowered using a hydraulic system. We also had no way of knowing that the *Kormoran* was responsible for the destruction of ten merchant vessels and the capture of an eleventh during her year-long career in the Atlantic and Indian Oceans.

Both ships were heading in the same direction but instead of keeping her distance, the *Steiermark* was slowly moving closer to us. She drifted around our stern and was now on our port side.

The crew were back out on deck.

'She must be in trouble, she's drifting a bit close to us.'

'What flag is she flying, lads? Can anyone see the flag?'

'Yes, it's a Russian flag.'

'Wonder what's wrong with her?'

'Well, we'll know soon enough, reckon the Bridge is talking to them.'

We were only a few hours from the Cape Verde Islands when the disguise was dropped – the Russian flag was replaced by the German swastika. There were two loud bangs. The windows of the radio room shattered and glass flew everywhere. Our radio was knocked out. We threw ourselves down on the decks and lay there. Our engines stopped – there was silence. Not all of the crew was on deck: those below grabbed their belongings from their cabins but I did not move. I was too afraid. My lifejacket was in my cabin. If I went down to get it and something happened, would I be able to get to the lifeboat? I could not swim. If

The German Raider *Kormoran*, in the Atlantic *c.* 1940.

I moved, would they shoot me? No, I was staying where I was.

Then the order came from the captain: 'Take to the lifeboats!'

There were three port and three starboard lifeboats on board, big wooden boats with four or six oars. There were no lifejackets on them and only the few crew who had gone to their cabins were wearing theirs. On each lifeboat there was a locker up forward under the seat, which stored tanks of drinking water, tins of condensed milk, tinned corned beef and biscuits that were so hard it took a hammer to break them. Every twelve months in port they were replaced with fresh items.

We each had a job to do on our respective lifeboats – mine was to put in the plug. The adrenalin was flowing now and as I jumped into my boat, looking for the plug, I could not see it and started to panic.

'Oh God! Where is it? Where's the plug?'

Up to then, my worst nightmare had been that I would lose it. So, one day, I climbed into my lifeboat and tied it with a piece of string to the seat, up forward, directly over the hole. It was then that I realised I was already holding it. My hand was shaking. I jammed the plug into the hole and hammered it down with my fist to make sure that it was well and truly in place. My heart was thumping.

While I was busy, the other eleven were attending to their jobs. They began to lower the lifeboat. Suddenly, the Raider fired at us. We jumped out of the boat and I landed on the deck below – about 8 feet down. Someone else landed beside me but I did not look to see who it was. I lay there with my hands over my head, my face pressed to the deck. I was so scared. The firing stopped, but no one moved. In my head I was praying, 'Hail Mary, full of grace, the Lord is with thee … Please don't let me die. I don't want to die. Holy Mary, Mother of God, pray for us sinners now and at the hour of our death …'

Scared as I was, I did not dare say anything – I had to be a man. I knew if the gunner called me, I would have to go down into the hatch and feed the shells up to him as I had been trained to do. Now I prayed, 'Please God, please don't let him call me to go down into the hatch.'

The rapid firing began again. Splinters of timber, metal and glass fell like rain around me. A loud explosion close by was deafening. As quickly as it started, it all stopped. There was a terrible silence. I do not know how long I lay on the deck, waiting for an order from the captain. It seemed like an age.

'Abandon ship! Take to the boats!'

I jumped up and ran as fast as I could, up the companion-way with the others, to the boat deck above. God, what a shock! The galley was gone – completely gone. The bridge and the radio were destroyed. The lifeboats on the port side were wrecked and could not be used, so we lowered the three lifeboats on the starboard side and all seventy-five of us got into them. I could not understand what was happening – I was in shock. If I had said I was scared, I would have got a clip on the ear from one of the older men, so I said nothing.

The boats had been riddled with shrapnel and we started to take water and began to bail. Then someone said, 'There's no sign of them coming to get us. If he doesn't have us the sharks will, for sure.'

I thought to myself, 'Cripes. There are sharks and I can't swim. I'm a goner!'

Although I had not been to Mass since I left home, I was now apologising to God for not going to Mass and begging Him to save us. I did not hear anyone else, but they may have been, like me, praying in their heads. Then, I realised to my horror, that I had wet myself. I was so embarrassed; after all, I had a man's job. I glanced around at the others. No one was looking at me, but I noticed that I was not the only one who had wet themselves.

There were worse things to worry me now. We were up to our knees in water. The bailing pans were like small woks, but no matter how quickly we bailed, we were sinking. Then someone said, 'He's moving!'

The German ship drifted slowly towards us and stopped.

'God, lads, it is the *Steiermark*! Her name has been removed, look you can see the outline of it on the bow.'

I was not looking at anything except the rope ladders, which had been dropped over the side of the ship. All I wanted to do was to reach those ladders and climb up out of the water. The Germans took all seventy-five of us on board and the lifeboats sank shortly afterwards. We were lucky, I suppose: only two of our crew were injured. The captain was hit by shrapnel on his face and the lamp trimmer in his leg. They were taken to the hospital bay and were, in fact, looked after very well. Joan Evans and Sheila Jagoe were separated from us and were taken to a room beside the hospital bay. Frank Evans was put with us and he only saw his wife a couple of times after that, when we were allowed a few minutes on deck.

The front of a merchant ship, called the forecastle head, is normally divided into at least two sections for the storage of paint, deck equipment, ropes and anything that is needed to keep the ship in good order. We were marched up to the forecastle head, which was now just a wide, open space, and the doors were locked behind us. We never saw the *Afric Star* again. We were the only prisoners in that section and the light was left on, as there were no portholes. There were hammocks hanging up on the bulkhead, which, I guessed, were for us. It was very warm, so our clothes dried quickly. I noticed a big tube going up through the forecastle head from the decks below, but I didn't know why. That night I learned.

At about 6 p.m., when it was dark, the door opened and a German marine, a Kriegsmarine, gave us pots of coffee and some bread, which was black and heavy, like a brick. They gave us a table knife and we eventually managed to cut it. Then we hung the hammocks and settled in for the night. At about midnight, the Germans attacked another ship and we discovered that the big tube was a magazine lift for the guns above us. We saw nothing, but we could hear the noise of the metal shaft pushing up the ammunition in the tube, the sound of the crew outside running to their duties, the shouts of the gunners over our heads, the rattle of the guns and the torpedoes; it was dreadful. It brought back the terror of our capture. I started to tremble in my hammock, unable to hide my fear from the others. My first thought was, 'Thank God! The captain must have got a message out, it's one of ours and we'll be rescued.'

My second thought was, 'We're locked in and can't get out. What if no message got out and it *is* one of ours, but they don't know we're here? They'll blow this ship out of the water. I don't want to die on this ship!'

Eventually, the firing stopped. I had no idea what was happening. There was no more sleep for me that night. We got up in the morning, took the hammocks, hung them up on the bulkhead and were allowed go up on deck for air. It was then I realised that there were other prisoners on board. There were twenty-eight officers and one passenger from the *Antonis,* which had been captured on 16 January. There were forty-two crew members from the *Eurylochus,* which was the ship that had been attacked during the night. Thirty-six of their crew were missing. We learnt that the German Raider had been designed with various prison quarters. Altogether, there were 174 prisoners on board.

6

PRISONER AT SEA

Korvettenkapitän Theodor Detmers on the Raider *Kormoran* had a crew of 400. He treated us well, under the circumstances. We were allowed out on deck twice a day; we had our own toilet and wash facilities, hammocks to sleep in, tables and bench seats. We got pots of coffee in the morning with loaves of black bread, soup in the middle of the day, and more coffee and black bread in the evening.

There were two officers on board from the German Propaganda Department sending back footage of battles at sea and captured Allied vessels to be shown to the German people. One of them was a newsreel cameraman, Leutnant Hrich, and the other, an information officer, Leutnant List. Leutnant List spoke good English and visited us each morning to talk. The older crewmen warned us not to give him any information about our ships or training. So we made up stories about our lives before the war – all lies. He told us that he had been on the German ship *Bismarck*. He did not tell us how long he was on her nor did he tell us why he was transferred to the *Kormoran*. He asked us if there was anything he could get for us, but there was nothing. He could not get us a radio, he could not get our ship back and he could not put us ashore, so really, it was a pointless question. I think he was trying to be friendly, so that we would let our guard down and give him some useful information.

The gunners on the *Kormoran* practised every Tuesday and Thursday. They had a special gun stowed under the main deck that they used for training. Their performance was timed and they had competitions among themselves to see who was the fastest at loading and firing. They loaded the shell, trained the gun and fired, all within sixty seconds. We were allowed to watch these training sessions. The gunners enjoyed showing off to us. It was like they were saying, 'Look what we have, and what we can do. You don't stand a chance against us.'

We stopped watching them after the first week.

I found I could not keep track of time, as days rolled into weeks. The weather got colder and I no longer wanted to go out on deck in my T-shirt. The older men agreed that we were heading around Cape Horn and sailing for the Pacific. It was the beginning of February when we crossed the International Date Line. Kapitän Detmers invited us to watch the Neptune ceremony. I asked why we had never had this ceremony on the *Afric Star* and was told that it was usually a ceremony carried out by the Navy, and not the Merchant Navy, for sailors crossing the equator – or, in this case, the International Date Line, for the first time. Originally it was to honour the sea god but then became a rite of passage for new recruits and entertainment for the older hands. It would break the boredom so I was looking forward to seeing it. Bench seats were placed on the foredeck, from which we watched the ceremony. The Kriegsmarines filled a big container with water, and one of them dressed up as Neptune. The crew wore costumes, and the new recruits ended up getting dunked in the tub. It was good fun and for a moment, we were all seamen together. That was a strange feeling. Then Leutnant List came over to me and jovially said, 'Hitler will be in Buckingham Palace on 8 August 1941.'

I replied, 'I don't think he'll get that far.'

But he had put a damper on my good mood; we were enemies again. We were sent back to our prison quarters after the ceremony.

A few weeks later the captain told us that he hoped to make his rendezvous with another ship, to refuel and restock supplies, within the next four days. If this did not happen, he would put us off at the nearest land and notify the German authorities of our whereabouts. God, if he put us ashore somewhere, we stood a chance of getting away! He made his rendezvous with the tanker *Nordmark*.

The *Nordmark* was constructed, under Hitler's orders, as a cargo ship. However, she actually functioned as a fast fleet tanker, armament supply store and victualling ship. She supplied bunker oil (the oil used as fuel) and lubricating oil to the German Raiders and battleships at sea. The cargo provision rooms contained enough food for 5,000 men for thirty days. We tied up alongside her and each prisoner went over the side. In my turn, I climbed down the rope ladder, reached over to grab hold of the rope on the other side and climbed up onto the *Nordmark*. Fortunately, the sea was calm. Once on board, we were counted and then put down in the forward tank, where there were already other prisoners. The forward tank was about seven decks below and had been left empty to facilitate the holding of captured seamen.

The German supply ship and prison ship *Nordmark*.

Conditions were not as good as on the *Kormoran*. There were no hammocks, so we had to lie on the deck floor, and there were no tables or bench seats. There were no washing facilities, or toilets. We used buckets, which had to be emptied regularly. The forward tank was partly divided into cattle pens and Thomas Cooney, a prisoner captured from the *Port Wellington*, lay down on some straw in one of these. He was a man in his fifties and seemed an old man to me. He was a big, heavy fella and was not fit for all the climbing. It was very hard on him. We were allowed up on deck, twice a day, which we needed; the smells and stale air in the forward tank were really terrible. I do not remember Cooney ever coming up on deck. We had been treated pretty well on the *Kormoran* and, I suppose, I expected the same kind of treatment on the new ship. But now I was

The German battleship *Scharnhorst*.

The German battleship *Gneisenau*.

The Allied refrigerated ship SS *Duquesa*.

The German prison ship MV *Portland*.

shocked and scared again. I kept asking myself, 'Why are they treating us this way? What's going to happen to us now?'

I hated being locked in the crowded forward tank. In my head I heard Father's voice, 'Mind your manners and keep out of trouble.'

I rolled myself up tightly, kept as near as I could to my *Afric Star* crewmates, and stopped talking.

While on deck I saw three other ships at the rendezvous. When the Allied refrigerated ship SS *Duquesa* was captured, she became a supply and stores ship for the German Navy, as she was carrying 900 tonnes of frozen meat and 15 million eggs! When the *Nordmark* reached the rendezvous, she tied up to the SS *Duquesa*, on which food was cooked, for the crews of both ships and for prisoners. We were fed well while we were prisoners on the *Nordmark*, which is the only good thing I can say about her.

The other two ships were huge Kriegsmarine battle cruisers, the KMS *Scharnhorst* and the KMS *Gneisenau*. Both ships were heavily armed with three triple gun turrets apiece, fifty-eight anti-aircraft guns and six torpedo tubes. Each carried two floatplane aircraft. We wouldn't have stood a chance if we'd met them at sea. I had felt safe and secure on the *Afric Star* with our 4-inch gun on the poop deck, what I now called our 'pea shooter', because it was so small, but she would never have been a match for these ships. Afterwards, I wondered if they stayed at the rendezvous to show off their naval power to intimidate us, to tell us that the British Navy was finished. If that was their aim, it certainly worked.

The SS *Duquesa*'s original crew were among the prisoners on the *Nordmark* and they told us that the Kriegsmarine had planned to take her back to Germany with her cargo, but she was running low on coal for her burners. It was possible for coal-burning ships to refuel at sea, if a coal ship could be found. The next day, I saw that the KMS *Scharnhorst* and KMS *Gneisenau* had left and wondered if they had gone in search of one. The Germans scuttled the SS *Duquesa* and she sank with the rest of her meat cargo. They made sure that the Allies would not get their hands on those provisions.

The *Nordmark* stayed at the rendezvous point for a couple of weeks, until the MV *Portland* arrived. Before the war, she had been a cruise liner operating between Chile and Bordeaux. She still sailed the same route, but was now German owned and operated as a prison ship. The MV *Portland* collected prisoners from Raiders and other battleships, and brought them to Bordeaux, which was now in German-occupied France. While she refuelled from the *Nordmark*, all the prisoners were ordered up on deck. Once more, rope ladders were thrown over the side and we were transferred to her. We were met by armed Kommandos. When all the prisoners were lined up on deck, we were counted; there were over 300 of us. It was 18 February 1941.

The *Portland* was a hell ship. The two forward hatches were linked by a narrow tunnel and were located underneath the forecastle; we climbed down into them. We had no blankets, hammocks, toilets or wash facilities; we slept on the deck floor. The heat and smell were overpowering. Once again, we had to use buckets as toilets. Once a day, the hatch cover was opened and a small bucket of water was lowered down – one bucket for over 150 of us! Only the first few got to use it. I didn't wash on board at all and hated feeling dirty all the time. I do not remember getting coffee or bread on the *Portland*, but I do remember getting soup and I'm sure they must have given us bread because, although we were hungry, we weren't starving. The Kriegsmarines left open a small corner of the hatch cover in each of the forward hatches, but it didn't let in enough air for us; they also left the big cargo light switched on.

Some British seamen, in Forward Hatch Two, were plotting to start a small fire, with the intention that when the guards came down to investigate, they would overpower them and take over the ship. The prisoners whispered to each other about this. The older men sent back word that they were to do nothing, that the risks were too great. I heard the whispers too, and all I could think was, 'God, if they start a fire, how do we get out of here? They'll obey the older men. They have to.'

They ignored the orders from the older men and on 14 March lit a fire in Forward Hatch Two. We were unaware that anything was going on; we could detect no smoke, but the German crew must have seen it rising through the gap in the hatch cover. Suddenly, our hatch cover was lifted and the marines came dashing down the ladder, through the tunnel and into Forward Hatch Two. It was a very small fire and they easily put it out. They came back into our hatch, climbed back up the ladder and closed the hatch cover.

Before anyone could catch their breath, our hatch cover was lifted a second time. This time Kommandos climbed down, armed with batons and guns. They moved speedily from Hatch One into Hatch Two and indiscriminately lashed out, hitting anyone within their reach. They singled out the chief officer from the *Afric Star*, Mr Russell, who was tall, thin, wiry and a very nice gentleman. I could not see what was going on, but I heard the noise of the beating and I was very frightened.

We backed away as the Kommandos came through the tunnel; there was not a sound as they climbed up the ladder and closed the cover. Some of the *Afric Star* crew in Hatch One went to attend to Mr Russell, and things quietened down. Some of us sat down, under the hatch cover. I noticed Frank Evans was sitting beside me, on my right. Suddenly, the cover was thrown back again and the Kommandos started down the ladder. The first one down had a gun.

'Oh God, not again. Please, not again!'

I could not move. They walked through both hatches, checking that there was going to be no more trouble and as the last gunner went up the ladder, the hatch light went out. It was controlled by the Germans up on deck – not by us; I guess the gunner was not taking any chances. He pulled the trigger and swept that gun around in a semicircle; the noise was deafening. Frank Evans fell backwards. I was too petrified to move. I stayed sitting, even when the gun stopped and the hatch cover was closed again. As quickly as it had gone out, the light was switched back on. I heard someone say,

'He's dead.'

It was then that I realised they were talking about Frank Evans. He had been sitting beside me and now he was dead.

'Thank you, God. Thank you for not letting it be me,' I prayed, and then felt guilty that I hadn't prayed for the poor man. I didn't know what Frank Evans' religion was, but I knew that if he was a Catholic, someone should say the Act of Contrition and Prayer for the Dead. I tried to pray out loud, but could not speak, so I prayed for him in my head.

Another man from the *Afric Star*, Able Seaman Arthur
Freeman, was also injured. While some of the men attended
to Freeman, the hatch cover opened and some marines came
back down the ladder. Immediately there was silence. They
took Arthur Freeman up to the ship hospital, and they took
Frank Evans' body away, too. There were no other incidents
after that.

A few days later, all the prisoners were taken up on deck;
the older men told us we were heading towards Gibraltar.
We saw two Allied cruisers patrolling up and down the
coast – if we could see them, then they must have been
able to see us. The prisoners speculated whether or not the
cruisers would come nearer, or whether they would open
fire. They could not know that there were 300 prisoners on
board, so I hoped that they would ignore us. We were sent
back below deck; the *Portland* sailed on to her destination.

Joan Evans and Sheila Jagoe were held in a cabin up
midship. As far as I knew, Joan had not seen her husband
since we were transferred from the *Nordmark* and she was
not told he was dead until we landed in Bordeaux. She
never saw his body. Arthur Freeman also died. He and
Frank Evans are buried beside each other, in Bordeaux. I
never saw Joan Evans or Sheila Jagoe again.

The *Portland* pulled into Bordeaux on 15 March 1941.
We were ordered up on deck and then marched, in single
file, down a gangplank onto the docks, while the German
guards trained their guns on us. We lined up on the dockside
in fives to be counted. Some of the men still had their kit
bags with them, some had musical instruments, and neither
their bags nor their instruments were taken from them. I
only had what I stood up in, my now very tatty, dirty T-shirt
and trousers. I did not speak or look at the guards as I didn't

want to draw any attention to myself. When they gave the order, I just marched with everyone else. The guards did not care whether we were old or sick; they just marched us along at a smart pace and we all pushed ourselves to keep up. I did not know what would happen if I fell behind, but I was not going to find out.

About 12 km later, we reached Holding Camp 221, also called *Frontstalag* 221. We were given nothing to eat or drink along the way. The guards herded us into a barbed-wire enclosure with no actual gateway, just a gap in the wire, which was replaced when the last man went through. There were no barracks in the holding camp: we just sat on the ground and were left there. It was good to feel the air and sunshine on my face; I do not think I could have gone into a barracks, had there been one. I had had enough of crowds, dirt, bad smells and being locked up. I physically could not talk. The older men, who had been on the *Portland* with me, watched out for me and made sure I was with them at all times. They tried talking to me, but although I heard them, I could not respond.

The local French threw baguettes over the fence to us and branches of mint, which we used to make tea. I do not remember getting anything else to eat. The older men told me that we were going to be in this camp for about two weeks, but I made no sign that I understood. Later, they told me that there was a gunpowder factory close by. They wanted to shock me into a response, but I was still silent. The weather was very mild and dry for the two weeks we were there.

Eventually, thirty-two days after we arrived in Bordeaux, on the morning of 19 April we were rounded up and marched to a nearby railway station, Gare St Jean, where we were lined up in fives. A guard gave each of us a quarter of a baguette and a small tin of jellied meat, about 4 oz in weight. There was more jelly than meat in it and I could not tell what the meat was supposed to be. There were no carriages on the train, just boxcars. I had seen these at home: they were used to transport livestock to market. Now, we were being pushed forward and told to get into the boxcars; they shoved about fifty of us into each one. The voice in my head was screaming, 'Why are they doing this? We're not animals. We're humans!'

But I was helpless. All I could do was to stay with the men who were watching out for me.

We travelled for five days and five nights. There were no windows, just a few small slits under the roof for air. In one corner, some of the men pulled away a few planks with their hands, to make a hole for a toilet. It was not long, though, before the smell was awful. A seaman was lucky if he got a spot with his back to the wall and could sit down; most of us had to stand. If he moved from his spot, someone else moved into it, especially if it was furthest away from the toilet. We stopped a few times, but the doors didn't open. The taller men, who could see through the slits, were able to tell us that troop trains were passing.

On the first day of our journey we ate our tin of meat and bread. The older men had penknives and one of them opened my tin for me. We were thirsty. When the train stopped, to let the troop trains pass, we banged the sides of the boxcar and called out for water but didn't get any.

Three days went by before we stopped at a station. The doors opened; it took a while for our eyes to adjust to the light. There were German Gestapo standing in the station with their guns trained on us. We were not allowed to get out of the boxcar. We were given a ladle of soup in a small bowl, which was handed in to us by a station worker. When we were finished, we handed the bowl back. We asked for water but were given none. The door was shut again and locked.

The following evening, we stopped at another station, but again, all we got was a ladle of soup. I do not remember getting any water at all. My overriding feeling was not hunger but fear: fear of the unknown, fear of the Gestapo I saw each time the doors opened, fear that left me speechless. Eventually, on the fifth night, we arrived at a station in Bremervörde, Lower Saxony, Germany. It was just getting dark, and we were all hungry, exhausted, thirsty, bewildered and filthy. Bremervörde was a small village surrounded by farmland; farmers were still in their fields. The Gestapo, when they saw some of the people trying to give us bread and water, shouted a warning at them and roughly pushed them back. The villagers were terrified. We were lined up and marched out of the village. Along the way, people threw stones at us. They marched us about 10 km and a few of the older men, who had managed to keep some kit, just could not carry their bags any longer and dropped them along the way. Eventually, we reached our destination: Stalag XB, Sandbostel, Lower Saxony.

7

PRISONER ON LAND

WE WERE MARCHED into the camp, through the main gate, under the sign Stalag XB overlooked by German guards in a watchtower. We were led through a single gate, on the right, and into a fenced-off area that had a dirt track and row upon row of wooden barracks. Our guards left us there, locking the gate behind them. I recognised some of the older men and followed them into one of the barracks down a corridor with rooms on either side. The one we entered had bunk beds, each with a mattress, two blankets and a pillow. I crawled into one of the bunks, rolled up into a ball and fell asleep.

There was no formal regime. Prisoners could stay in bed as long as they wanted to; but always an early riser, I got up and went outside to look around. We were surrounded by a wire fence attached to 10-foot-high cement posts, which were curved at the top and strung with barbed wire. Everywhere I looked there were rows of barracks; at the furthest end, I could see through the fence into another part of the camp, where there were other British, French and Polish prisoners. There were thousands of them; they

Restored barracks in Stalag XB, Sandbostel, photographed in 2005.

were in bad condition, their clothes were in rags and they looked starved. I kept away from that end of the camp. I did not want to end up like them. I had got separated from the *Afric Star* crew during the march to Stalag XB, but the older men were good to me. I was in a daze and still could not talk. It was really frightening. I wondered if I would ever talk again.

I do not know which was worse, the wet or dry weather. Stalag XB was built on marshy ground. In wet weather, the ground became a quagmire that sucked at our feet. We got soaked going back and forth to the latrines, and if we had no wood to burn in the barracks stove, our wet clothes dried on us. In dry weather, it became very sandy. As there was always a wind blowing, it was impossible to get away from it: sand blew under the doors, through the windows, into the food, our eyes, and into every crack and crease in our bodies. There may have been calm days, but I do not remember them.

Our fenced area was close to the brick-built administration building and kitchen. The German guards picked prisoners to carry the big containers of food from the camp kitchen and leave them outside each barracks. The fish soup had not much fish in it, but was mostly bones and very salty. The sauerkraut, pickled cabbage, was hard to eat but I was hungry so I forced myself. Some of the prisoners took their sauerkraut to the latrines, where they tried to wash the salt out of it; it did not help. After a few days, the men gave up and forced themselves to eat it; there was nothing else.

In the washroom, there were six hand basins and one shower. That first morning, I showered in cold water; it felt great to be clean, or at least as clean as I could be with no soap. In the toilet block, there were two lines of twelve toilet bowls with no seats, no cubicles and no privacy. Prisoners from the other compound worked in shifts to keep our toilets clean. It cannot have been an easy job, as a lot of people had dysentery.

We had about 300 Merchant Navy prisoners in three barracks in our compound. The British Navy prisoners, in the other compound, told us through the fence that most of the barracks on their side had no bunks; just big shelves around the walls. Originally, the camp was set up as a concentration camp but the Red Cross had visited Stalag XB and insisted that barracks used for prisoners of war had to have bunks. Some changes had been made before we arrived, but only in our compound; we were lucky to get bunks!

I overheard some of the men say that they had seen and spoken to Joan Evans on the other side of the fence, near the administration barracks. She told them that she knew her husband was dead and that she was expecting a baby. I felt really guilty. I should have died; after all, he was a married man and soon to be a father. The poor woman. Now she was here by herself and pregnant. What would happen to her? I ran to the fence to see if she was still there. I wanted to tell her how sorry I was, but I did not know how I would get the words out. I wanted to turn back the clock and change where we had been sitting, but she was not there. The women had been moved to another camp.

Inside the barracks there was one small room on the right with a bunk bed in it; whoever had this room was in charge of keeping the barracks clean and keeping order among the men. There were four further rooms on the right of the corridor and five rooms on the left. There were twelve bunks in each room. In the centre of the corridor there was a 40-gallon drum which was used as the 'after dark' toilet. The double window, in each room, opened outwards. It could be opened in the morning but had to be shut at night; there was no lock on it. The double door into the barracks also had to be shut at night. No one was allowed outside after dark – anyone caught outside would be shot. Moonlight was the only light we had. Every morning, the 40-gallon drum had to be emptied; the guards assigned men from each barracks to do this. I always slipped out the window so that I didn't get picked.

By this stage our clothes were in shreds. The German guards told the French prisoners, who were in charge of the clothing store, to pass clothes over the fence to us. They threw us some pantaloons.

'Thank God!' I thought to myself.

Then one of our men said, 'Don't touch them, lads. They're full of lice!'

The guards at our side of the compound were First World War veterans, and they understood why we refused to take the pantaloons. The following day, they produced British Army uniforms for us to wear. We got trousers, jackets, overcoats and boots. Later I learned that when a prisoner died, the Gestapo stripped them of everything. All clothes were stored for reuse in the camps. I did not want to think about it too much. When I compare our treatment by our First World War veteran guards to the treatment we got later, I realise that we were very lucky at Stalag XB; the guards there had a bit of compassion.

In our first week, the guards lined us up in front of our barracks, handed each of us a board with a number on it and told us to hold it, chest high, while they took individual photographs of us. These were our prisoner-of-war numbers which were stamped onto a metal disc and attached to a piece of twine, which we had to wear around our necks at all times. My number was 90882. Shortly after we were given our prisoner-of-war numbers, the Red Cross parcels started to come. We got one every second week. In the first parcel there was a bar of soap: I could not wait to go to the shower to scrub myself. The parcel also contained a packet of tea, a tin of stew, a tin of condensed milk, a tin of fifty cigarettes and a real treat: a bar of chocolate. I was very popular because I did not smoke and shared out my cigarettes.

In my six months in Stalag XB, I saw only two prisoners punished. Each of them had to hold up a large boulder and stand under the guards' watchtower all day long. If they started to lower it, the guards would shout at them to straighten up. I moved away pretty quickly.

There were two boxers in the camp: Joe Walcott from Jamaica, an American heavyweight boxer, and Tom Keane, a British middleweight with the Royal Navy during the First World War. Most of the younger prisoners, lads of twenty and younger, spent their days aimlessly wandering around the compound. I sat and listened to them talk. Joe and Tom organised training sessions for us. Every day we did skipping, running and push-ups; then they trained us to box. I looked forward to those sessions and, one day, I realised that I had started to talk again. It was good to be able to talk.

In July 1941, three priests joined us in Stalag XB. They were missionaries who were on their way to Africa with seven religious brothers when their Egyptian ship was captured. As far as I know, they were all French Canadians from Quebec. There was Fr Piquet, Fr DeWitt and Fr Juno. Fr Piquet was in charge and Fr Juno was newly ordained. German officers must have assisted them because they arrived in Stalag XB with their trunks, which contained their vestments and chalices. The guards set aside a room in one of the barracks for the priests to say daily Mass; some of the prisoners attended. I had not been to Mass since I left Derry, but God had been good to me and I felt I owed Him my thanks. One day, when I was on my way to Mass, I met Fr Juno, a man of average height with red hair (he later grew a bushy red beard). I wanted to ask if he would like me to serve Mass for him. In school, all the boys had learnt the Latin responses to the prayers and although I had never served as altar boy, I knew what to do and when to do it. To get his attention, I put out my hand and touched his arm. I did not expect his reaction. He jumped back, turned to me, and in English said forcefully, 'You never, ever, put your hand on God's Holy Anointed.'

I could not believe it. I started stuttering an apology, but he swept past me and I never got to ask him my question.

Through the fence, some of our group were told by Navy prisoners that they were being moved to Westertimke to build a new prisoner-of-war camp, specifically for Navy and Merchant Navy men. We noticed that Navy prisoners were being marched out of Stalag XB in large numbers. Towards the end of July, when fifty from our compound were moved out, our First World War guards told us that they were joining the others in Westertimke. By the end of August nearly half of our compound had been moved out, including the priests and brothers. It was the end of September when the rest of us were moved the 30 km to the new camp. The last fifty to leave Stalag XB had to clean the barracks and the washroom. The guards came for us, marched us through the gate under the watchtower and into the waiting army lorries; the canvas cover was closed down. I began to feel sick with fear: after all, no one had sent us a message from the new camp.

8

PRISONER-OF-WAR CAMP

WE HELD ONTO THE FRAME of the lorry as we bounced along on the forty-minute journey. Was the story true, or were worse things going to happen to us? Each man was lost in his own thoughts until, eventually, we stopped. I heard the guards slamming the doors of the front cab and their footsteps coming to the back of the lorry. The canvas was thrown back and daylight streamed in. They shouted at us and we scrambled down. We were in a large square surrounded by rows of barracks on all sides; we assumed we were in Westertimke but we had no way of knowing. The guards drove off while another German guard came towards us and in English said, 'Go, find yourselves your barracks.'

The barracks looked the same as those in Stalag XB but they had seven more rooms with double or three-tier bunks: each room could hold fourteen to eighteen men. The other difference was that there was no sand.

Men called out from the barracks indicating empty places.

'Over here, lads. We have room for three here.'

'There's room in here, lads. Come and look.'

New faces brought new stories and maybe some news. I found myself a bed in a barracks among strangers. I kept to myself for a while and just listened to the older men. I soon found out a lot about the camp.

There was a high fence around the camp with barbed wire on the top. Inside that, there were rolls of barbed wire and then a clear piece of ground. After that there was a straight piece of wire about knee-high, stretched around the whole camp, overlooked by a watchtower just inside the gate. There were some rules, but not too many. Rule Number 1: never put a foot over the knee-high wire. Rule Number 2: never go outside after dark. The guards were ordered to shoot anyone who breached either of these rules.

I learned that there were actually two camps, each with its own administration and other buildings. Marlag was the Royal Navy camp and had 3,000 prisoners. The majority of them were British but there was also a small number of other Allied Nationals, mainly American and Canadian. Our camp, Milag, was about 300 metres east of Marlag and was built for British Merchant Navy seamen. Like Marlag, we too had American and Canadian prisoners. Milag was divided into two compounds, one for the officers and one for the seamen; we had thirty-six barracks for 5,000 Merchant Navy seamen. In addition to the accommodation barracks there were the post office, storehouses, prison block, fuel bunker, kitchens and eating areas. There was also a small hospital. The administration buildings and guards' barracks were outside the main gate.

There was plenty of cold water in the one large shower block, which had to cater for all of us. The toilet block was bigger than the one in Stalag XB. There were two lines of twenty-four bowls, back to back with no cubicles. There

Prisoner-of-war postcard, Milag und Marlag, 1941. (*First left, middle row*) Harry Callan; (*first left, back row*) Val Harris.

Reverse of prisoner-of-war postcard addressed to Harry's sister Nan.

was a cesspit underneath the toilet block and the effluent was pumped out every day into a large metal tank which sat on a cart. There was no horse to pull the cart so, each day, the guards delegated six men to pull it up to the fields, where it was emptied into the drills dug by other prisoners. They covered the effluent with clay, and brought the cart back to the camp. It was like emptying the midden for the whole of Derry! I always made sure I was nowhere near the toilet block when I knew it was time for the cesspit to be emptied. We called that cart 'Smelly Nellie'.

Every day we lined up in fives and were counted by the guards. The first morning those of us who had just arrived were told to stay in the square after the head count. We had a formal group photograph taken by a German photographer and in it we all looked healthy and well dressed, in British uniforms, which was exactly the way the Germans wanted the outside world to see us. In October 1941, we were relatively well fed and were still getting our Red Cross parcels, but as the war went on there were more and more food shortages. This photograph was made into postcards for us to send a message home to our families, albeit a censored one.

The other men explained to me that after the sinking of *Afric Star*, Father would have received a telegram telling him that I was missing, presumed dead. I sent a postcard to my sister Nan to let my family know I was still alive; she kept it with her all her life. I sent just the one. I could have sent other postcards but what more could I say? I only remember receiving one letter, from a woman called Cassie, who introduced herself as my new stepmother. She and my father had married while Edgar and I were at sea.

The German guards, who were all veteran Navy men, gave the three priests from Stalag XB a room to use as a church and ensured that there was bread and wine available for each Mass. They shared it with a Church of England minister. There were three Masses every morning. Fr Juno said the first one at 6 a.m., which I regularly attended. On Sundays, the Church of England minister held his service before Fr Juno said the first Mass. Once again, I approached him about serving Mass – it felt wrong for the priest to have no server – *but* this time made sure I did not touch him. He accepted my offer politely. I do not think he remembered me at all.

Every morning, I got up early, washed, fasted and served at Fr Juno's 6 a.m. Mass. I prayed for God to get me home and for Joan Evans and her baby to be repatriated. Some of the older guards came to Mass too. In those days, an altar boy held the small paten under the chin of the communicants as they received Holy Communion; I didn't like getting that close to guards, but I got used to it over time and wondered if we were all praying to get home. Fr Juno had no German, so one day, when a guard tried to speak to him and he could not understand, I went to get one of the prisoners who had learnt the language. The prisoner agreed to come. When Fr Juno realised that the guard, a man in his late fifties, wanted a priest to hear his confession, he dismissed the translator. I saw the guard kneel and receive absolution. That guard went to Mass regularly, and received Communion with the rest of us. It seemed very strange: we were supposed to be enemies, yet here we were praying and receiving Holy Communion together. Inside that little church we were just men.

As we settled in and reconnected with mates, it was possible to swap to other barracks as not all the barracks were full. I knew very few, but I met Billy English from the *Afric Star* and also the boxers Joe Walcott and Tom Keane and the others who had trained with me; I began boxing again. Two other boxers, by the names of Sharpe and Browne, helped with the training; Browne used to train with a cigarette dangling from his lips. When I had to fight an Egyptian, a big 6-foot-3-inch man with a long arm stretch, I turned to Sharpe and said, 'Cripes, how am I going to do this? He's huge!'

'Ah, don't box with him at all, just go in like a terrier and his arm won't reach you.'

I belted all around me and actually won my match! I got a little trophy – about the size of an eggcup; I lost it soon afterwards. I loved boxing. It was great training and it really kept me occupied.

We had a sports field where we played football and we made a track around it for running. In the winter, we helped the Americans and Canadians to make a small earth bank around the sports field, which we then filled with water. It did not take long for the field to freeze over and with makeshift sticks, the Canadians taught us how to play ice hockey. It was a very cold winter. Although each room in the barracks had a small wood-burning stove in the corner, there was a shortage of timber and it was impossible to get warm. We even took every second lath out of our bunks to burn, but it was no use.

We also had a library with over 3,000 books in it. I liked cowboy books and murder mysteries; they took my mind off things. Some of the other prisoners had other skills and were willing to teach us things like carpentry, languages, mathematics and lots of other subjects. It was a great way to ease the boredom. The Red Cross and the YMCA sent us textbooks, library books and sports equipment. We had the Milag Jockey Club, too, which held race meetings every Saturday evening. The 'horses' were wooden models that raced on a 36-foot track, controlled by the throw of dice. The men bet on the races.

I had never been to the theatre or a concert in Derry, but we had regular concerts in the camp. Some of the men who were musicians and had played in bands on cruise liners had managed to save their instruments; others were supplied by the Red Cross and YMCA. Some prisoners performed plays, which were always a good laugh. I could neither play nor sing, so I was always amazed by the talent these men had.

Every week or two we received Red Cross food parcels and every second month we got clothing, underwear, socks and gloves, which were all badly needed. Barter went on throughout the camp. Because I did not smoke, at first I used to share the cigarettes among the men in my barracks, just like I had in Stalag XB. Then I learnt about bartering and bartered some of my cigarettes for a watch. I had never owned a watch before. It had a big silver face with a black leather strap and I wore it until well after the war.

The food was better in Milag than it had been in Stalag XB. For breakfast, we got a cup of ersatz coffee, two slices of bread, and sometimes a small bit of cheese; for dinner, we had soup made out of turnips and potatoes; for tea, we were given three potatoes each. Occasionally, we were given a little horsemeat and some sugar. We made up a meal using these and our Red Cross food on the stove in our room. Christmas dinner 1941 is one I will never forget. We each had a big pork chop with plenty of fat on it, served with mashed potatoes and green peas. That was the last real dinner I had as a prisoner.

Sometimes, in our Red Cross parcels, we got a little bar of Cadbury's chocolate, or a little tin of real coffee. I soon learnt that these were worth more than gold. One of the men was sitting outside the barracks, slowly savouring his bar of chocolate, when he noticed the guard on watch duty looking enviously at him. Later that same day, the guard walked through the camp to speak to us. He asked if anyone would give him some chocolate. The lads started to barter with the guards for bread, cheese, milk and sometimes meat. The tins of real coffee were also bartered with the guards. I do not know how many tins of coffee or bars of chocolate it took, but one man exchanged his for a trombone!

Prisoners of war had freedom to move around the compounds, and it was possible to visit other shipmates in their barracks to exchange news. If darkness fell, they had no choice but to sleep where they were. One day, after a boxing match, we celebrated in another barracks and had to stay there for the night; that's how I met Valentine Harris. He had been behind me when our photograph was taken but this was the first time I had spoken to him. Valentine was from Dublin, in his twenties and married; he was always able to cheer people up and had a great sense of humour. When I returned to my own barracks, I was able to bring back stories, news and the jokes that he had told me.

Walter Skett, a prisoner in another barracks, regularly bartered with one of the guards. In mid-May 1942, he made arrangements to meet the guard after dark. Skett was breaking Rule Number 1. When we had all settled down for the night and the doors were closed, Skett slipped out. Unknown to him, the guard's shift had been changed and Skett was now being watched by another guard on duty. To reach the watchtower he had to cross the wire. Skett was now breaking Rule Number 2. Once he put his foot over the wire, a shot rang out. We all heard it. Next day, I heard Skett was dead. I was too scared to barter after that.

Prisoners of war were sent out to farms to help with food production. Farmers who needed help approached the guards to ask for volunteers. There was no supervision, but no one I knew ever tried to escape. The returning prisoners often brought produce with them and shared it with their barracks. By the end of 1942 there was a shortage of Red Cross parcels; sometimes we had to share one among four men. Goth, a Kent man from my barracks, regularly volunteered for field work. He was a solid character and I trusted him. One evening he called us together: he wanted to start a co-op in the barracks, well in our room, anyway. The idea was that we would pool all our Red Cross parcels and he would barter with the farmers for eggs, milk, cheese, bread and some meat, if he could get it.

'You can count me in,' I said.

Seven of us handed Goth what was left of our parcels. He made those Red Cross parcels work for us, all right!

In January 1943, I heard a guard calling numbers as he walked through our compound.

'90882, 90882, 90882!'

That was my number. I made myself known to him and he told me to go to the gate. As I walked there, I asked no one in particular, 'What am I being called for?'

One of the merchant seamen who overheard me said, 'Sure you're going home, son!'

'Well,' I replied, 'if I am, that's the first I've heard of it.'

When I got there, about thirty other men were standing around. None of us knew why we had been called; I started to get that sinking feeling in my stomach. What was going to happen now? The guards told us to go back to our barracks, pack our belongings and return immediately to the gate. All I had was underwear and socks, which were easy to pack into a rolled-up bundle and I returned as quickly as I could, thinking to myself, 'Have my prayers been answered? Maybe I am being sent home.'

Between the barracks and the gate, other prisoners came over to us and put notes and letters into our pockets, for their wives and families.

'Please call my wife, tell her where I am.'

'Call my mother …'

'My father …'

'My sweetheart …'

When I got to the gate, I spotted Billy English and stood beside him in the line; I felt safer with someone I knew and trusted. I recognised only two other men, Thomas Cooney from the *Portland* and Val Harris. Without ceremony, we were marched out the gate and into waiting lorries, fifteen in one and sixteen in the other. The canvas was dropped and tied down, the engines roared into life and we pulled out of Milag Camp. We had been told nothing. I felt sick again. One of the men, with an Irish accent, remarked,

'Don't think they're sending us home, lads.'

'What makes you say that?' asked another man, also Irish.

'Sure the Red Cross would have come and told us if we were going home.'

They were right. Any bit of hope I had was now gone.

9

ENTICEMENTS TO WORK

WE ALL STOOD FOR the duration of the journey, holding onto the frame for balance. It was a bumpy ride on what felt like country roads. We had no idea in what direction we were travelling. The only thing we knew was fear. I could smell it. I felt like a child again; I hated that feeling. I had so many questions and no answers. Where were we going? Why were there only thirty-one of us?

We had been singled out because we were Irishmen. This did not become clear until later. Was I an Irishman? As a Derry man, I was entitled to a British or Irish passport, but I knew nothing of this at the time. I lived in Northern Ireland, which as part of the United Kingdom was an enemy of Germany. On the other hand, as an Irishman I was a neutral and eligible for repatriation. If I was with other Irishmen, could it be that we were all going to be sent home? I did not think so, but I knew one thing – I was sticking with Billy English.

About an hour later, the lorries stopped and the engines were turned off. We heard German voices and footsteps approaching. The canvas cover was thrown back and for a moment, we were blinded by sunlight. There were five Gestapo guards with their guns by their sides. One spoke in English and asked us to get down from the lorries.

One of the Irishmen muttered, 'Not the usual reception, lads.'

I had to agree. The thirty-one of us climbed down:

Patrick Breen,	Thomas King,
Thomas C. Bryce,	William Knott,
Charles Byrne,	William H. Knox,
Harry Callan,	Michael Lawrie,
Edward Condon,	Peter Lydon,
Patrick J. Connor,	John J. Moffatt,
Thomas Cooney,	Thomas Murphy,
Owen Corr,	John Patrick O'Brien,
William (Billy) English,	Patrick J. O'Brien,
Richard Flynn,	Michael O'Dwyer,
James Furlong,	Gerald O'Hara,
James Gorman,	Patrick Reilly,
Bernard Goulding,	Robert Roseman,
Valentine Harris,	Daniel Ryan,
Patrick Kavanagh,	John J. Ryan.
William Kelly,	

We were in a big square concrete yard with a tall administration building in front of us. I could see the usual rows of barracks. Later, I found out that the building was a labour exchange office. The guards lined us up to give us our bed linen and to assign us quarters.

'Why were they being polite?' I wondered.

We did as we were asked. A man in a dark suit was sitting at a desk in the yard, with a big ledger in front of him and he was writing in it. The Gestapo guards standing nearby

Harry Callan's camp entry card, which was completed in Stalag XB, Sandbostel for the Red Cross in 1941.

were very relaxed. I stayed in line with Billy. The men up front had reached the desk and there was some conversation between them and the man in the suit. Then the voices got louder and the guards moved in closer to us.

I heard an Irish voice saying, 'We are not signing anything!'

'What are they talking about?' I wondered. 'Sign what?'

Then another voice joined in. 'No. We won't be signing for bed linen, either!'

Word came back down the line.

'They want us to sign something.'

'They say it's for the bed linen.'

'They want us to sign that we'll work for Germany.'

In Milag, the talk was that some prisoners had left to work for Germany. The Germans needed workers and so they targeted the 'neutrals' offering them 'working *frei*'. In return for their work, they would receive board and lodgings, and the freedom of Germany. The jobs were in shipbuilding, munitions factories and factories making parts for U-boats or planes. I hadn't believed what I heard in the camp. I mean, who would work for Germany? They were my enemy – they sank my ship! But it was all true. Now here they were asking us to work for them and to sign papers. How could we do that?

The men up front handed back the bed linen and moved away from the desk. The guards did not stop them. We went and sat together in the yard.

'What happens now?' I thought to myself.

I do not think the man in the suit was expecting us to refuse – certainly not all of us. He did not seem to know what to do and we sat there, waiting. It was all quiet; there was no one else in the yard. I found out afterwards that we were on a factory site, which worked around the clock and the barracks were for the workers, but I did not hear or see any of this.

We sat there all afternoon. It must have been around 5 p.m. when a guard arrived with a worker carrying a pot of soup, and we were each given a ladleful. Another guard spoke to one of the older men and told him that we would be given a bed for the night. Some Frenchmen came out of their barracks to go on night shift and while they were at work we slept in their beds. We never spoke to each other but we recognised their accents. We agreed among ourselves that we would keep the barracks clean while we were using it; it was the only way we could thank the Frenchmen. There was no heat from the January sun and I was glad we did not have to sleep outside. The toilet block and washrooms were smaller than those at Milag but they must have had more of them spread out over the site, because I never met anyone else in the block we used. It was as if they allocated them to us for our use alone. Having got used to life in Milag, this quietness was eerie.

When the guard came to wake us the next morning, we were already up and cleaning the barracks. He knocked on the door, which surprised us. He, however, was even more surprised when he saw us cleaning, and politely said,

'*Zeit aufzustehen.*' ('Time to get up.')

What was going on? If anything, this normal morning call made us more nervous. We finished cleaning, then went outside for a ladle of soup and a slice of bread.

A Gestapo guard addressed the whole group, in English. He suggested that while we were there, we should visit Bremen city, to see the sights. He gave us directions to follow the road up the hill but warned us to be back by 7 p.m.

Were they going to allow us walk into Bremen like free men? Would they shoot us before we got outside? I am sure the other men were thinking the same thing.

'Come on, Harry. You're not staying here,' Billy said. 'We'll see if we can get into the city. Let's go.'

Some of the older men stayed behind to mind our gear. I agreed to go with Billy. I was scared but I could not let him see it. The Gestapo guards were watching us. Had they their guns trained on us? Was it a trick? We were close to the gate now – two more steps. I stopped just outside it. There were no shots. I did not look back.

Off we went, up the hill and into the city. It was surreal. We walked around as though we were ghosts. We saw very few people; no one looked at us, no one spoke to us. We were in British Army uniforms, so the city people must have thought it strange to see us walking around. There was nothing in the shops and we had no money. Bremen, at that time, had no bomb damage, so we were able to admire the beautiful architecture. We walked back to the labour exchange yard and told the others what we had seen. At 8 p.m. we were given ersatz coffee and a slice of bread and we took over the Frenchmen's beds again. This was our routine for a week.

We found out that the factory was the Focke-Wulf factory – later, the Messerschmitt factory – which was making Fw190 fighter planes and parts; it must have been huge but we never saw around it while we were there.

At the end of the week, the guard told us to line up at the office where we were again asked to sign papers, to agree to work for Germany.

'You have seen how well you have been treated. You have had the freedom of the city. You are from a neutral country, so you can work for Germany, too, and you will still have this freedom.'

But we refused.

That night, at midnight, the door opened and the guard stormed in. '*Aufstehen!*' ('Get up!')

We were ordered to get into the waiting lorries. We hoped that we were going back to Milag. They had not persuaded us to work for them, how would they treat us now? After about two hours the lorries stopped, the tarpaulin was thrown back and we were in another city – this time it was Hamburg. We were taken into the labour exchange building and asked,

'Will you work *frei* for Germany?'

'No, we will not work for Germany.'

We were split up and each of us was taken separately to a room, where a guard and a labour exchange official questioned us. When my turn came my stomach churned, I was so frightened.

'No,' I kept saying, 'I won't work for Germany.'

'What's going to happen to me now?' I thought, 'will they send me back to Milag? Will they shoot me, or hang me?'

I was sure that they would kill me and I realised that I had stopped talking again.

Once more, we were allowed to walk freely around the city, but by then I was so traumatised that I could not even talk to Billy. I just stuck close to the men and went where they went, unable to take in any of my surroundings; I cannot say where we slept or ate. I know we were only there a couple of days and on the last day they brought an officer from the Kriegsmarine to talk to us. He said, in English, 'You are all seamen from a neutral country. You can work on our ships. We sail in and out of Sweden, and you can have as many girls as you like. Will you come and work for us on our ships?'

We still said no.

At midnight, the Gestapo guards came.

'*Raus! Raus!*' ('Out! Out!')

They were rougher with us this time; we had exhausted their patience. As we were loaded into the lorries, one of the men said, 'Can anyone see the North Star?'

I could not see the sky, let alone the North Star. It was impossible for us to work out where we were going.

10

BREMEN–FARGE MARINE CAMP

WHEN THE LORRIES stopped, the tarpaulin was thrown back and we were faced with five Gestapo guards training their guns on us. It was 2 a.m. and we didn't know where we were; we certainly were not back in Milag.

'*Raus! Raus!*' the guards shouted. '*Schnell! Schnell!*' ('Out! Out! Quick! Quick!')

We got out of the lorries as quickly as we could; all the time their guns were aimed at us. I thought that this was it. This time they were going to shoot us and no one would know anything about it.

I could see a barracks building to the right but not much else as the guards marched us towards it, shouting at us to move faster. They pushed us through the open door and into a small storeroom with no windows. Tired, shocked and disoriented, we hunkered down on the cold cement floor and huddled together for a bit of heat; even in my British Army uniform, I was still freezing. I heard the older men talking.

'The carrot is gone now, lads.'

'Don't know what they have in store for us but can't see us getting out of this one.'

I listened to them and felt hopeless. Would I ever get out of here?

Suddenly, the door burst open and two kapos stormed into the room. I found out later that kapos, or kallifactors as we called them, were also prisoners. They were handpicked by the Gestapo, put in charge of their fellow prisoners and given privileges, like extra clothing or rations. They were more brutal than the guards themselves. The kapos came armed with 2-foot-long rubber hoses, which they wielded like whips. They shouted at us.

'Aussteigen! Aussteigen!' ('Get out! Get out!')

I was at the back of the room, out of their way, but the men just inside the door were being lashed. We were not having any of that! Some of the men jumped the kapos. They grabbed the hoses and held onto them. The kapos did not know what to do. They were face to face with thirty-one men in British Army uniforms and there were only two of them. Both the kapos and the men held onto the hoses and stared at each other. Eventually, the Irishmen dropped their hold and the kapos backed out the door. We let them go.

We followed them outside and they ordered us to stand in the yard, in five rows of five men and one of six. It was only 3 a.m., we stood there with teeth chattering, cold, exhausted and afraid. A Gestapo guard came and looked us over. He seemed to be in charge because the other guards took orders from him. He was tall, over 6 foot. Something about him made me feel uneasy. I saw him many times after that. I never saw the colour of his hair because it was always covered by his military cap. He wore polished riding boots and he carried a riding crop, which he tapped constantly against his booted leg while he stood and watched us. He smiled but there was malice in that smile. I nicknamed him 'the Austrian' because he reminded me of an old photograph I had seen once, depicting an Austrian cavalryman. When he was around there was no doubting who was in charge.

We stood for an hour until the Austrian said, '*Morgen, Herr Doktor.*'

With a stethoscope, the doctor checked each of us, listening to our breathing and our hearts.

'Some men are unfit to work,' he told the Austrian. Gerald O'Hara was a bad asthmatic and Thomas Murphy had something wrong with his chest. It could have been his heart, but I do not know. The doctor left and we remained standing in the yard.

At 5 a.m., two men in prison clothing, with numbers on their backs, carried out a big pot of hot liquid and we were give a ladleful in a bowl. It was gritty, watery and the colour of maize; it tasted awful but at least it was hot. At 6 a.m., the Gestapo guards marched us through a small gate to a single rail line where there were a few flat bogies. Beside the rail line was a stack of rails. While the guards and kapos watched, we were ordered to load four rails onto each bogie. They were so heavy, it took seven of us to lift just one of them. We weren't allowed to take a break. The two kapos banged their hoses against the bogies and rails, shouting all the time, '*Schnell! Schnell!*'

When that was done, the guards ordered us to push the loaded bogies along the rail track. With every ounce of strength we had left, we pushed and strained to get them moving. The guards would not let us slow down at all; they were due to go off duty once we got to our destination. We pushed on for about 3 km through countryside but, because

I was bent over, my only view was of the track below me and the stones. The sweat ran off me, and my muscles screamed for rest. The rail track came to an end.

'Thank God,' I muttered and I could hear a few of the men praying the same.

Surely now we could take a break? But the guards changed shift and new guards came on duty.

The guards ordered us to unload the rails and to lay them, extending the railway into the green pastureland in front of us. From where I stood, there were fields all around and, in the distance, a river. At midday, we had a half-hour break for two slices of bread and a cup of ersatz coffee. I think it was made from crushed acorns but it could have been anything. It was dark in colour like coffee, hot, and served to us in delph, not tin, cups. We went back to laying rails again. At 6 p.m. we stopped. Then the guards ordered us to push the empty bogies back to the camp; after a full day's work, those empty bogies felt heavier than ever. My mind was numb and my muscles ached. I did not care if they put me in the little room with the cement floor: anywhere to lie down would do. Back in the camp we lined up. They counted us then they gave us a ladle of the same soup.

We were then marched to another building where there were several rooms leading off a corridor. Each room had two bunk beds to accommodate four men. The bunks were made of iron and there were mattresses, sheets, pillows, blankets and a 'tick' on them. When I was growing up, a 'tick' was filled with chaff, left over from the harvest and was used as a mattress by poorer families. The German 'tick' was like a duvet cover, which we used as an extra blanket. The 'Austrian' inspected the rooms and he insisted that the tick be folded very precisely, otherwise he stood over us as we refolded it, tapping his riding crop against his booted leg all the while.

There was just enough room to climb out of the bunks and get dressed in the space between them. At the end of the corridor there was a washroom with ten hand basins, two showers with cold water and separate toilet cubicles. The guards told us that this was where we were to stay. Trick or no trick, I was never so happy to crawl between those lovely sheets and into that comfortable bed. If it was this bad for me, it must have been much worse for the older men but I did not hear them complain.

Gerald and Thomas, who were unfit for work, were assigned to clean the toilets, washrooms and to sweep the yard. Gerald spoke some German, and between them they learned from the guards that we were in the *Marine Lager* or Marine camp. The Nazis had intended to use this camp as overnight accommodation for German U-boat crews, during crew swaps. We could not work out where the dock was, as we had seen no sign of one. I never saw any U-boat crews while I was there.

At 3 a.m. every morning, the kapos shouted at us to get up and to go to the washroom. They banged on the walls or the ends of the beds with their hoses, sometimes making contact with anyone who was in their way. Once washed, we tidied our bunks, put the sheets and blankets neatly into the tick; folded the tick up and laid it straight across the pillow. Sometimes the Austrian came into the room, to carry out an inspection. If that tick was not folded correctly, or not put straight across the pillow, he would throw all the bedding onto the floor and we had to start again.

Outside the barracks, we lined up and were counted; we waited there until 4 a.m. when we got our ladle of soup. All this time the Austrian stood in the doorway of the administration building, which we now knew was the first building we had been in, with that malicious smile on his face, watching us, tapping that riding crop against his leg. I hated being under his scrutiny. He was the boss and could do anything he liked with us. We stood in line until approximately 4.45 a.m., when we were all counted again. We were always counted in fives. At 5 a.m. we marched out the camp gate. That second morning, the guards gave us one hour to load the rails onto the bogies and push them to the end of the line, about 4 km away. Then, from 6 a.m. until 5 p.m. we laid rails, extending the line. We had no idea why we were laying track into a field and we certainly did not ask. Just like the first day, we had to push the empty bogies back to the starting point, to have them ready for the next morning. Every day, we got further and further from the camp.

A few days later, Billy English, Val Harris and I were pushing one of the bogies to the end of the line when we realised we were on a downward slope, which was great going down but not so good coming back. This day, we jumped on top of the bogie and freewheeled down the hill. The guard shouted at us, '*Halt! Halt!*'

He fired at us in the dark: twice he fired at us – but missed. We went on. We couldn't stop the bogie anyway. We had not planned this escapade but what a thrill! We started to laugh uncontrollably, but that was good, too. We arrived at the end of the line before anyone else. The kapos were already there and were surprised to see us so early. We just laughed and laughed at the look on their faces. Then we calmed ourselves and waited for the others. When the guard who had shot at us arrived, he looked relieved to see us

A sloped railway track at the construction site for Bunker Valentin.

there. We'd had no intention of making a run for it: where would we have gone and what would have happened to the others if we had tried? No, we were all in this together. After that, the guards never bothered about us, knowing we would be waiting at the end of the line.

A few weeks of rail-laying went by. One day, I thought a guard was watching me but I did not dare look around.

'You!'

He pointed at Billy English, too,

'You!'

I got a knot in my stomach while I stood in line, as he selected some of the others. He led us away from the rail track, further into the field, and I wondered if we were going to be punished for our bogie lark, but he had not picked Val Harris. The field was huge, about 8 acres, and the guard told us that our new job was to take the sods off it. I relaxed a little. The foreman, a big, lanky fella, came over to Billy English and me with a spade and a narrow rope coiled up in his hand. He handed Billy the spade and he handed me the rope. I asked Billy, 'What's the rope for?'

'Haven't a clue, Harry.'

So we just stood there. Five minutes later the foreman came back to us, looked at us and said, '*Dummköpfe.*' ('Idiots.')

He pulled the rope from my hand looped it around the bottom of the spade shaft and handed me the rope. He then took the spade from Billy and, holding it at a 45-degree angle to the soil, he told me to walk forward while keeping the tension on it.

'*Ziehen.*' ('Pull.')

The foreman kept the blade against the ground, while I pulled the rope. It started to slice through the soil, rolling

A bogie used from 1943–45 in the construction of Bunker Valentin, now on display in Denkort Bunker Valentin memorial.

A foreman oversees prisoners unloading supplies from a locomotive at the Bunker Valentin construction site, April 1944.

up the top sod. When we had a roll about 2 feet in length, the foreman shouted, '*Halt.*'

Then he cut the end of the roll with the spade. We went back to the start and began a second cut, beside the first. Handing the spade to Billy, we copied what he had shown us.

I said to Billy, 'Well, it's the first time I've ever seen two men working one spade!' We laughed.

All of us were now working in the field; some of us rolled sods, while others loaded them onto the bogies, which they pushed to the end of the line. They stacked the rolls in a pile and returned for another batch. We did this for the rest of January and into the middle of February; then we started digging.

We dug the soil and loaded it into tipping buckets that had been fitted to the bogies. Once full, they had to be pushed to the end of the rail and tipped out. Others shovelled the soil up into a mound. We had no idea what we were building. The field had become a pit and we cut out steps in the sides, to make it easier to climb in and out. A crane, erected on the site, lifted the buckets off the bogies and dropped them into the pit. When they were full, it lifted them back onto the bogies. Day after day, the mound grew to a height of nearly 10 feet; it ran the entire length of the field and was approximately 30 foot wide at the bottom. The rolls of sods were laid vertically against the mound, to stop the soil eroding.

We were hungry all the time. When midday came, it was really difficult not to bolt down the two slices of rye bread and ersatz coffee. I had to force myself to chew and drink slowly and to make this meal last as long as possible. Although our daily rations were similar to those we received in Milag, there we had received Red Cross parcels and did not have to work. Why had we received no Red Cross parcels in the Marine camp? Surely they knew where we were? When we showered, I could see that we were all losing weight. Like the others, my stomach was bloated.

'Why are our stomachs swelling up?' I asked Billy.

'We're being starved. We're not getting enough food for a working man. Try not to think about it.'

But it was hard not to; the pain of hunger was indescribable. We went to bed at 9 p.m. after the ladleful of soup and held our stomachs. If I listened, I heard the quiet groans from the others and I would start to cry. When I thought of the meals I had had at home, it made the pain worse. After a few weeks, the swelling in my stomach started to go down. I got used to the hunger pains, stopped thinking about them and just got on with living.

Gerald and Thomas found out that we were beside the River Weser and the village was Farge. Spring tides often flooded the land and the village, and we were building a dyke to stop this. Every day the work was the same, the only change was the weather. Digging kept us warm, especially in the cold weather, and we were lucky to have our British Army greatcoats.

11

BREMEN–FARGE LABOUR EDUCATION CAMP

ONE EVENING IN February 1943 as we returned from work, the guards marched us past the entrance to the Marine camp. A little further on, we were ordered in through another gate and into another camp. Above the gate, a sign read: *Arbeitserziehungslager* (*AEL*-Farge or 'labour education/punishment camp'). Inside the fence was a big square and what looked like an administration building. There was a small hut beside it, which I found out later was for delousing. We were never deloused.

Opposite the administration building was the barracks that was to become our new home. Gerald and Thomas had moved there during the day and they had all our belongings with them. The first thing John J. Moffatt asked them was, 'Did you bring my accordion?'

They had. He had not played it since he left Milag, however; he could not bear to and we did not want to hear music, either.

We stood in lines of five men, and were counted; the soup arrived at 8 p.m. Our emptied bowls were collected by a prisoner, and then we walked around until 9 p.m., when we followed Gerald and Thomas into our new barracks. We got a shock when we went inside. Gone were the lovely metal bunks, clean mattresses and bed linen. Now we each had a wooden bunk with a dirty mattress, pillow and blanket. The barracks was similar to the ones in Stalag XB and Milag. But this barracks had one large room on the left, which ran the length of the building, with a door at each end that opened onto the corridor. On the right there were more rooms but these doors were locked and during my time there, no one ever went into them. We no longer had our own washing facilities; instead, we had to use a dugout under the administration building, a large opening with no front wall or doorway, with hand basins, showers and toilets. There were no cubicles and no privacy.

We had been moved into one of Hitler's labour education/punishment camps in Bremen-Farge and a satellite of Neuengamme Concentration Camp. Isaac (Christy) Ryan arrived – the last of our group. He had been in Bremen Hospital when we left Milag in January because he was recovering from an appendix operation. As an Irish-born British Merchant seaman, he was sent to Bremen-Farge to join us. Now we were a group of thirty-two.

'Raus! Raus!'

At 3 a.m., the kapos were there with their rubber hoses, banging the walls and beds, shouting at us all the time. When they hit some of us with the rubber hoses, they could not believe it when the men turned on them, grabbed the hoses and held onto them as they had done previously. We stood together as a group and stared them down; after all, they were prisoners themselves. Then the men holding the ends of the hoses let go and the kapos backed away. I had no idea how much power these kapos had over other prisoners. We had been the only prisoners billeted at the Marine camp but we were not the only ones here.

There were Gestapo guards everywhere we looked. As we went down into the dugout for a shower, one of them gave each of us a rag for a towel and a small piece of soap, the size of a little butter patty, which felt like sandstone. I could never get it to lather but it did help to get the dirt off. One of us guarded our Army clothing while the others showered. The toilets were shared with other prisoners; there was no privacy. The other prisoners wore dark trousers and loose jackets with large numbers painted on the backs of them; we never saw them use the shower. We were allowed to leave our rags and soap back in our barracks but the kapos made sure we came straight out to the yard afterwards; we were not allowed back in again until 9 p.m.

At 4 a.m. we stood with the other prisoners, in lines of five men. A huge 30-gallon drum of soup was carried out into the square by four or six prisoners. We queued up for our ladle of soup but this time, instead of going back into our original positions, the older men moved to the back of the square and lined up behind the other prisoners. I followed them. It was then that I realised we were the only prisoners in army uniforms; all the others were in prison clothing. By moving to the back of the yard, we were making a statement; we were different – not criminals, but prisoners of war. We stayed in our lines until approximately 4.45 a.m., when we were counted again, then ordered to march out. Just as we started to march, a voice called out, *'Halt!'*

A Gestapo guard stood in front of us and in English said, 'You are Irish. Why will you not work for Germany?'

'We are prisoners of war and we will not work for Germany.'

'You are from Ireland – a neutral country – you worked for Britain, why will you not work for Germany?'

'We are prisoners of war and we will not work for Germany.'

His attitude changed. He shouted at us, 'You are civilians. Nobody knows where you are. You are our prisoners! You will work whether you like it or not.'

I suppose life would have been easier if we had said 'yes', but we were not going to do that – not ever. In unison we turned to the guard and said, 'We are prisoners of war, British Merchant seamen. We will not work for Germany.'

He turned on his heel while other guards ordered us to march on.

Gerald and Thomas were our main source of information. It was they who told us the *Arbeitserziehungslager* was a labour education/punishment camp where the German courts, or Gestapo, sent offenders. These prisoners also included German criminals, political prisoners, non-German civilian workers, Russian, Polish and French prisoners of war. When we were on the work detail, we British Merchant seamen were always put working together; we could not distinguish between criminal and prisoner of war, and so we kept our distance. For us, it was a slave labour camp.

When the spring came, the River Weser flooded the land where the dyke had not been completed. We stood knee deep in freezing water, digging up wet mucky soil. Over the months, our muscles had got used to the weight of the dry soil and we had built up a rhythm to our shovelling; now

Prisoners from the labour education camp, or *Arbeitserziehungslager*, working on the construction of Bunker Valentin.

our rhythm was gone. Our backs and shoulders ached by the end of each day. Then, in wet boots and trousers, we had to march the 5 km back to the *AEL*, pushing the bogies all the way. Our greatcoats were marvellous for keeping the top half of our bodies dry but they were quite a weight to carry when they were soaking wet. Eventually, when we got into our barracks, we hung our saturated clothes on the ends of our bunks and went to bed. By now, we were well used to putting our legs back into wet trousers and our feet into wet socks and boots; it was an awful feeling. Strangely, none of us ever got blisters on our feet.

One day, I noticed a prisoner slowly pushing a bogie by himself. The foreman, a German civilian, who was standing close by at the time, must have thought that the prisoner was slacking. He pulled a spade from another worker and hit the prisoner on the head with it. The man fell face down on the dyke, while the foreman ordered other prisoners to push the bogie.

I was horrified. 'Oh God, please don't let him be dead.'

The foreman moved away and we went back to our work; no one went to see if that man was dead or alive. I, too, turned away and continued digging. There was still no sign of him stirring when another loaded bogie arrived. The foreman ordered the prisoners to tip the soil over him. There are at least two or three bodies buried in that dyke.

That night I climbed into my bunk, put my coat over my head and cried. I was ashamed of myself; I cried because I had done nothing. Every time I closed my eyes, I could see the spade and hear it hitting the man's head and I would cry even more.

We were never beaten by the foremen but we witnessed the beatings. Sometimes they used hoses, sometimes a plank of wood or metal bar, whatever was close to hand. It was dreadful knowing that we could do nothing to stop them. I can still hear the cries of grown men being beaten to their knees. Many of them were middle-aged, office workers – they were not manual labourers. The kapos, too, lashed out with the rubber hoses, hitting prisoners for no reason. They never whipped us but lashed the air around us when they knew the foreman was nearby. I cried every night for the first two weeks in that hell of a camp. Every day there were acts of violence and when I closed my eyes, I relived them. One day, I realised that I had become acclimatised to the beatings: when I got into bed I could not cry for those men. That was awful. There were days when there were no beatings and we would say to each other, 'There must be something wrong. No beatings today.'

'We better watch out tomorrow, lads!'

The routine from Monday to Saturday never changed. On Sundays, we had a rest day. We were allowed to move freely in and out of our barracks. Meals, however, if you could call them that, were at the usual times and with the usual line-up. Every Sunday, the thirty-two of us got up, went to the showers, washed ourselves and then we scrubbed our underwear as best we could, with the little sandstone soap and cold water. One of the men had a piece of rope, which we strung up between our bunks as a clothes line. We made sweeping brushes out of twigs and swept the dust and dirt out of our barracks. Sunday was called our 'housework day'. The German guards were surprised when they saw us doing all this, even in the depths of winter, and some of them gave us little pieces of their own soap. None of the other prisoners showered or cleaned their barracks but we were different and we wanted them to know it; we had standards to keep.

The *AEL*-Farge camp expanded. Along with the administration building and our barracks, there were a couple of other barracks, and these housed the prisoners who were working on the site with us. The Austrian was still in charge and although he never beat us, I was always nervous of him; I was right to be – he was vicious with the other prisoners.

A lorry brought a new batch of prisoners. As they climbed down from the lorry and started to march to the delousing hut, the Austrian randomly kicked some men so hard on the backside that they fell over. Sometimes, he kicked them again as they got up. We had just finished our soup and were standing in line, waiting to go to the site. The Austrian wanted us to see this. The prisoners went to the administration building, where their names and places of employment were logged, their personal belongings were taken from them and they had to strip. They had to wear prison clothing. They were given old shoes, or wooden clogs which cut into their feet. Once in their prison clothing, they should have been marched straight to the site; but the Austrian was not finished with them yet. While we stood and watched, the poor unfortunates were marched into another room and he followed them in.

We listened as they were whipped and counted as each lash struck flesh; we heard their agonised screams. Thomas and Gerald found out that the new prisoners were made to bend over a table while guards pulled down their trousers and the Austrian then whipped them. Most of them were given twenty-five lashes. One was given fifty. We watched horrified as two guards came out, dragging his limp body – he didn't survive. I thought I had become immune to the beatings on the site but this jolted me back. It was more vicious and planned and I did not know how we had escaped the Austrian's whip. We were marched out to the site to work.

We now knew that we were digging the foundations for a huge building. It was going to be enormous. Some of the other prisoners were put digging with us but we kept to ourselves and did not speak to them.

Near the end of March, we had just gone to the washroom when there was a lot of activity around the gate. An Army jeep stopped at the entrance; the Austrian stood to attention and gave the Hitler salute as a Gestapo officer got out. We were ordered to line up in the square until the *kommandant* gave the order to leave. The Austrian had only been caretaking in Kommandant Walhorn's absence; it was the first time we saw him in a subordinate role. The doctor arrived and he and the *kommandant* spoke to each other. Then the doctor began to examine each prisoner, as before. When he came to our group, once more he declared Gerald and Thomas unfit for work.

12

BUNKER VALENTIN AND A LETTER TO THE IRISH CONSULATE

WHEN THE *kommandant* gave the order, we marched out the gate. While Kommandant Walhorn was at the camp, the whipping of incoming prisoners stopped. The Austrian must have been reassigned to another camp, because I never saw him again. A local policeman, Herr Gärtner, was put in charge of registering the prisoners. He was not quite as bad as the Austrian but he still treated the new arrivals dreadfully, kicking them on the backside, or drawing out a baton and hitting them.

Another policeman, Herr Hans Mayer, from the nearby village of Neuenkirchen, about 5 km from the *AEL*-Farge camp, came in every morning to ladle out the soup. He was also responsible for ensuring that the camp was kept clean and tidy. Anyone who was unable to work on the site, due to illness, was put working in the camp. They peeled

Top: Prisoners begin building the walls on this section of Bunker Valentin. *Below*: Huge reinforced steel structures are erected for the walls, dwarfing the prisoners on site.

Top: A prisoner climbs scaffolding. The three pipes to his left pump cement to the waiting prisoners above. *Below*: Prisoners building part of the steel structure of Bunker Valentin.

potatoes, cleaned the washroom and toilets with Gerald and Thomas, or swept the yard all day. Now they were joined by another of our number, Patrick Breen, as the doctor, who we found out was called Dr Heidbreder, had also declared Patrick unfit for work.

Consignments of steel bars arrived at the site on barges. Some of the prisoners were put to work unloading these and stacking them in huge piles. This was heavy work – as bad as lifting the rails. The twenty-nine of us were taken off digging foundations and the foreman detailed us to lay rails wherever they were needed. When this was done, we went back to digging.

I still got hunger cramps and it was hard not to think about food. The skin on my hands had toughened up and now there were fewer blisters. Sometimes, when we got back to the *AEL*, we had to wait for up to half an hour for our evening ladleful of soup. The waiting seemed like an eternity. I do not know if this was just a genuine delay or a deliberate tactic to show us that they were in control. On those nights, it was hard not to bolt the soup when it came. We were always exhausted and I could not get into the barracks quickly enough, to lie down and stretch out my weary body.

While we were busy laying rails, the monstrous steel building began to take shape. Gerald, Thomas and Patrick were able to share the information they gathered from the guards. We now knew that the project was code-named Bunker Valentin and would be a manufacturing plant for U-boats. Once it was completed, prefabricated U-boat sections would be welded together on a production line and then equipped. When constructed, the gigantic bunker was to be 426 metres long, 97 metres wide (the size of four soccer pitches), and 33 metres high. These dimensions are embedded in my brain, because of the hardship we endured for every centimetre.

We occupied one large room, on the left of our barracks; the rooms on the right were always locked and never occupied. Our section had been constructed as two rooms but before we arrived a dividing wall was removed. Although it was physically gone, we acted as if there was still a wall between us, using the original markings as a natural barrier. With me on my side of the room were Billy English, William Knott, Charlie Byrne, Thomas Cooney, Tom King, William Kelly, John P. Connor, Michael O'Dwyer, Val Harris, Richard (Dick) Flynn, Peter Lydon, James Gorman, John J. Moffatt, Bernard Goulding and William Knox. The rest of the men were down the other end of the room. We carried on as if we were two families living in the one house, and rarely mixed while in the barracks. When we were on the ships, we had shore leave and some of the older men had their own cabins; now we were in each other's company twenty-four hours a day. It was hard being together all the time but there were no arguments: we were too busy trying to stay alive.

There were eight bunk beds in each section and I can still see where each member of my 'family' slept. In the first top bunk was Charlie Byrne, from Arklow, County Wicklow, a bosun's mate on the *Orama*; he was a quiet-spoken man who mixed well with everyone. Below him, Val Harris, from Pearse House, Dublin, was an able seaman on the *Craftsman*. He was a great character, only a few years older than me, and always tried to find something to make us laugh and lighten our spirits. I boxed with him in Stalag XB and Milag.

John J. Moffatt, from New Ross, Wexford, was a second radio officer on the *Barveld*, another quiet-spoken man;

he got a bad chest while we were there. Dr Heidbreder declared him unfit for work and he joined Gerald and Thomas. Bernard Goulding from Skibbereen, County Cork, was a fireman and trimmer on the *Charante*. He was a slow speaker but always pleasant: a hell of a nice man. He and John J. Moffatt looked out for each other.

Richard Flynn, whom we called Dick, from Tramore, County Waterford, was an able seaman and had also been on the *Orama* with Charlie Byrne. He was a big fella, over 6 foot tall. Thomas Cooney from Wexford was a greaser on the *Port Wellington*. I remembered him from the MV *Portland*. He had been a big, heavy man then, but he was not heavy now. A very nice, elderly gentleman, he loved to talk.

Thomas King, from Clifden, County Galway, was an able seaman on the *Kantara*. The poor man went off his head. He used to flare up and have loud conversations with himself. He would shout and try to pick fights with us. Thomas Cooney looked after him. Cooney was the only one able to calm him down. He stuck with him when we were working to make sure that he did not get into trouble. Peter Lydon, from Tralee, County Kerry, was a bosun on the *Delambre*. Peter was moody and mixed with no one; he would speak to us if any of us started a conversation but he mostly kept to himself.

Patrick John Connor, from Carlingford, County Louth, was a mess-room boy on the AD *Huff*; he was known to us as 'J.P.'. He and Michael O'Dwyer were great mates, but he was always arguing with O'Dwyer – J.P. would have argued with a fly on the wall! Michael O'Dwyer, from Cork, was an ordinary seaman on the *Kantara* and sailed with Thomas King. He was a nice fella, only three years older than me, and a tailor by trade before the war. He had a head of ginger hair so of course we only ever called him Ginger. In Milag, he had a small room where he and a few other tailors carried out clothing repairs. One of my strongest memories of him was in Stalag XB, with a pair of shorts over his shoulder and a needle in his hand; he made boxing shorts for us.

William Kelly from Waterford was an apprentice on the SS *Silverfir*. He was only a few years older than me and was a very friendly fella. James (Jimmy) Gorman, from Clogherhead, County Louth, was an ordinary seaman on the *Rangitane*, and was a light-hearted person. As far as I know, he was only one year older than me. Jimmy and Val Harris were great pals – put the two of them together and they were sure to come up with some story that would make us all laugh.

William Knott, from Ringsend, Dublin, was an able seaman on the SS *British Commander*. He was another sad case: he retreated into himself and never came back. Charlie Byrne looked after him. When he found Knott standing at his bunk, Charlie would talk to him; he also kept close to the older man when we were working, with Knott copying whatever Charlie showed him to do. William H. Knox, from Dun Laoghaire, County Dublin, was an able seaman on the SS *British Commander* with William Knott. He was an argumentative man with no real friend there, and he made sure that we all left him alone. None of us liked him but, poor man, we didn't know that he was very ill at the time.

Then there was Billy English and myself. Tall with dark hair, he was a few years older than me and he had the top bunk. We watched out for each other.

At the other end of the room were the others: James Furlong, from Wexford, was a fourth engineer on the *Duquesa*. He was an elderly gentleman and very quiet, only speaking when necessary. Patrick Kavanagh, from Wicklow, an able seaman on the SS *Athelfoam*, was, like James, very quiet.

Thomas Murphy, from Dublin, an able seaman on the SS *Earlston*, was a small, quiet man who had chest or heart problems and had been declared unfit for work by the doctor. He was of great value to the group, because he was able to pick up information from our guards and some of the *Arbeitserziehungslager* prisoners during the day, so we had something to talk about in the evenings.

Isaac Christy Ryan, who was always known to us as Christy, from Tramore, County Waterford, was a fourth engineer on the *Speybank*. He knew his rights and constantly talked about repatriation and the Geneva Convention. It was he who wrote the second letter to the Irish Consulate. Thomas Bryce from Clontarf, Dublin, was another quiet fella. Although born and bred in Ireland, Bryce had emigrated to Australia as a young man. Working as a fourth engineer on the British Merchant Navy ship *Triona*, he considered himself to be Australian. He was one of the men who had not signed Christy's letter, perhaps because he thought he was no longer Irish.

Patrick J. O'Brien, whom we called Patrick, from Armagh, Northern Ireland, was an assistant steward and was also from the *Orama*. He was very chatty and friendly. Something happened in the washroom near the end of the summer of 1944 for which Patrick got into trouble. He was arrested and sent to Bremen Prison for a week before being brought back to us. He was lucky not to be shot. Robert Roseman, a bosun on the *Empire Industry*, was from Bray, County Wicklow, and a really friendly man who would chat with anyone. Kommandant Walhorn would, jokingly, ask him if he was Jewish and Robert would always exclaim, 'No, I'm Irish!'

Patrick Breen, from Blackwater, County Wexford, was an able seaman on the SS *Athelfoam* with Patrick Kavanagh. He liked to sit and listen to the men talking. Owen Corr, from Rush, County Dublin, was an able seaman on the MV *Silverfir* with William Kelly. He was a chatty fella who was only a few years older than me.

Gerald O'Hara, from Ballina, County Mayo, first radio officer on the SS *Devon*, another really nice gentleman, was well respected by everyone. He suffered badly with asthma and Dr Heidbreder would not allow him work on the site so he was in the *AEL* all the time. He, like Thomas Murphy, was very valuable to the group. On Sundays, in order to stop us getting maudlin, he would start up conversations about football, hurling or politics, anything to get us talking to each other. It was he who encouraged us to keep as clean as possible and to carry out our 'housekeeping' tasks in the barracks. He was the glue that kept us together as a group.

John J. Ryan, from Waterford, was third officer on the *Empire Ranger*; Patrick Reilly, from Wicklow, was an able seaman on the *Athelfoam*; Michael Lawrie, from Williamstown, County Galway, was a steward on the *Granli*; Daniel Ryan, from County Clare, was an able seaman on the *Natia*; Edward Condon, from Passage West, County Cork, was a second officer on the *Kohinur*; and John P. (always called P.J. by us) O'Brien from Kinsale, County Cork, was a steward on the *Tottenham*. It was he who wrote the first letter to the Irish consul.

Dick Flynn, Thomas Cooney and Peter Lydon were very religious. Every night, no matter how tired, hungry, cold or wet they were, they knelt on their bunks, facing the wall, and said their Rosaries. By this time, most of us had given up praying. I gave up on God. I had prayed to him to get us out of here, but we were still here. The Gestapo guards kept telling us that no one knew where we were; no Red Cross parcels or letters came. I felt I had been deserted by God. I think these men prayed for all of us, as well as for themselves and their families.

By March 1943, the construction had gathered such pace that it was necessary to bring in extra workers. One morning when we arrived at the site, there were over 1,000 new prisoners already there. These were different from the *AEL*-Farge prisoners: their heads were shaved, they wore ill-fitting, striped uniforms and the kapos worked them even harder than the rest of us. I felt the tension from the other Irishmen. We must have stood out in the British Army uniforms. There were so many of them and so few of us. Where had they all come from? Their vacant stares frightened me. Would we end up like them? It was a relief when the foreman detailed us to lay rails. I stuck closely to the older seamen.

That evening we found out that they were prisoners from Neuengamme Concentration Camp. Both these and the *AEL* prisoners were put to work moving the huge steel bars and girders and manually erecting them into place. The steel-framed walls grew higher and higher; it was really brutal work. There was constant noise and shouting. Men were beaten for the slightest thing; a glance in the wrong direction could elicit a blow from the foremen. It was worse when the Gestapo guards set their dogs on the concentration camp prisoners. The Alsatians were usually quiet but when a guard clicked his fingers and gave a command the dogs became aggressive, growling and snarling. Sometimes, for no reason that I could see, a guard would set the dogs on an unfortunate prisoner, biting him and pinning him to the ground, until the Alsatian was commanded to stand down.

The foremen had other distractions now and did not pay too much attention to us. We returned to digging the foundations and building the dyke, as we had done before. I was in constant fear of being beaten, or having the dogs set on me. We no longer had to push the bogies back to camp for the next morning. Instead, at the end of the day, we formed into three distinct groups to march back. The twenty-nine of us and the *AEL* prisoners entered the gate of our camp, while the concentration camp prisoners were marched around the perimeter to another fenced-in area, completely separate from us. I could not see any barracks there and did not know where they slept. All I cared about was that my own group of British Merchant seamen had survived another day. That was all that mattered.

This all changed in early May 1943 when we returned from the site to find Patrick Breen lying injured, bloody and bruised, on the ground between the barracks. He had been badly beaten by someone with a bar or heavy stick and was unconscious. Even though Gerald and Thomas had been in the *AEL* that day, they had not seen or heard anything and they were extremely shocked and angered. Why would anyone want to beat him up? I was horrified, confused and panicked. The other prisoners were in line but the guards stood there, watching us and waiting. We were all angry then. Gerald and Thomas stormed into the administration building and knocked on the *kommandant*'s door. They told him that we were prisoners of war, British Merchant seamen and demanded that he find out who had

The vast scale of the construction site of Bunker Valentin is clear in this official photograph. When completed, it would cover the area of four soccer pitches.

beaten Patrick Breen. The *kommandant* had a little English and he understood the words 'prisoner of war' and 'British Merchant seamen'. Gerald and Thomas followed him, as he came out into the square. The rest of us had stayed with Patrick but were afraid to move him. Kommandant Walhorn was shocked when he saw the state of him. He turned and roared orders at the Gestapo guards who came running. He pointed to Patrick on the ground, told them that he wanted a report and that he wanted to know who was responsible for this beating. Then he told us to get a stretcher and take Patrick to the sickbay. He gave another order to the Gestapo guards, '*Finden Sie die doktor und bringen ihn hier.*' ('Find the doctor and bring him here.')

The sickbay was a small barracks that had a large room with bunks, a smaller room, also with bunks, and another room where the doctor could carry out procedures when required. There were wood-burning stoves in the large room but I never saw smoke from a chimney. There were no medicines. The only first-aid items were a jar of white ointment, a jar of black ointment and paper bandages. One ointment was used for really bad wounds and the other was used when the worst of the injury was healed. All we could do for Patrick was to put him on a bunk to wait for the doctor; we were not allowed to stay with him. We had just finished our soup and were standing in the square when Dr Heidbreder arrived and went straight to the sickbay. Minutes later, the door suddenly opened, and a kapo ran across to the administration building to fetch Kommandant Walhorn. We later learned that Dr Heidbreder had been horrified at the injuries inflicted on Patrick and wanted the *kommandant* to report the incident. Someone had to answer for treating a prisoner of war this way; he insisted that Patrick be taken immediately to Bremen Hospital. To our astonishment, the *kommandant* arranged this. Sadly, Patrick died in Bremen Hospital on 13 May 1943. We never found out which one of the Gestapo guards was responsible. This time I did not lose my voice or shed any tears. We had no idea where Patrick was buried. We did not talk about him; we had to shut down our feelings to survive.

When a prisoner of war died in hospital, the Red Cross was notified in order for them to claim the body and advise his next of kin. I have often wondered if Patrick's tag was lost in the beating or removed? Bremen Hospital staff did not notify the Red Cross. The *kommandant* told us that Patrick had died and was buried. We assumed then that without his prisoner-of-war number Patrick's body was returned to the *AEL*-Farge camp and buried in the mass grave as a common prisoner.

Summer came. The ground dried up and the soil hardened. We were hot, sticky and covered in dust. It was every bit as difficult to dig the compacted dry earth as the wet mucky soil in winter; the good thing was we were no longer cold at night. Some of the men suffered dreadfully with sunburn. I was lucky: my skin just tanned. We were thirsty all the time but we got nothing to drink. We used to take up small pebbles, roll them around in our mouths, sucking on them, to help make a bit of spittle.

Near the end of summer, Kinsale man P.J. O'Brien asked Hans Mayer, the policeman, for some paper, a pen and ink, so that he could write a letter. We were surprised when he returned with the items but as P.J. explained, Mayer understood that as prisoners of war we were entitled to write and receive letters. P.J. wrote to the Irish consulate in Berlin, explaining what had happened to us and asked that the consul arrange to have us repatriated, or returned to Milag. We all signed the letter. Herr Mayer took the letter from P.J. but we do not know what happened to it; we never got a response. From the time P.J. wrote, we dared to hope that something would be done for us.

We could not understand how no one seemed to know where we were. The Red Cross knew when we were in Stalag XB and Milag, so they must have known where we were taken. Years after the war, I found out that both the Irish and British Governments knew that the Irish-born British merchant seamen had been moved to Bremen-Farge. The fate of Irishmen captured on British merchant ships and held in internment camps had become an issue for both

Official propoganda photograph of concentration camp
prisoners lifting the roof struts for Bunker Valentin, summer 1944.

the German Foreign Office and the Irish government. A
policy had been agreed between the two governments on
how to identify Irish nationals in order to repatriate them.
We had been identified as Irish seamen and therefore Irish
nationals. But the Germans needed labour for their war
effort, and actively recruited from neutral countries. To
refuse to work *frei* for Germany was punishable by a spell
of two to eight weeks in an *AEL* camp. We had been asked

to work *frei* for Germany and refused. Following our term of eight weeks in Bremen-Farge *Arbeitserziehungslager*, we should have been repatriated. To return us to Milag would mean acknowledging that we were prisoners of war and that the Germans had made a mistake. However, to repatriate us to our country of origin, we had to have passports and merchant seamen did not have passports. By now, we were almost eight months in Bremen-Farge.

As it turned out, the Department of External Affairs in Dublin knew only that we had been sent to Bremen, as the following extract from a letter dated 18 June 1943 shows:

```
18 Meitheamh [June] 1943


Department of External Affairs, Dublin to
the Irish Chargé d'Affaires, Berlin.


With reference to your minute 9/40 of the
12th April setting out a list of Irish seamen
who were stated to be interned in Germany,
I have to inform you that shortly after the
receipt of your minute, we received evidence
from various quarters that an unascertained
number of Irish seamen who had formerly
been interned in Marlag and Milag Nord had
been released from there and had been sent
to Bremen on January the 27th last.
```

That word 'released' in a prisoner-of-war camp could mean two things: first, that a prisoner was being repatriated; or secondly, that a prisoner was working *frei* for Germany. If someone was working *frei* for Germany, they were a traitor

The bunker in an advanced stage of construction.

to Britain. No one was looking for us.

In early summer, a German officer came to our barracks with passport application forms. I saw the older men taking and reading them. They did not throw these forms back but took them to the officer, who typed them up. Each man signed the typed form. I was very suspicious and confused, so I turned to see what Billy was doing. He explained to me, 'If you say you're British, Harry, you'll never get out of here. If you say you're Irish – which you are – you need to fill in this application form for an Irish passport. Then we can get out of here and go home.'

I trusted Billy so I completed the form. We all did. When I went to the officer, it may have been my Derry accent, or his lack of English, but my date of birth was wrongly recorded as 19 November 1925, and my address was

Londonderry, Ireland. Billy's address was County Wicklow, Éire.

All during that summer we worked on the foundations while the concentration camp prisoners worked on the building. By the end of summer, only half of the original Neuengamme prisoners had survived. They were quickly replaced; there was no shortage of prisoners in Germany. More and more pyjama-clad prisoners arrived on the site.

13

SECOND LETTER TO THE IRISH CONSULATE

ONE NIGHT IN October as we were getting ready for bed, Christy Ryan whispered that he was writing another letter. This time, he was sure that the letter would get to our consulate in Berlin. He had made contact with one of the prisoners, a Swiss, who was being repatriated. I do not know how he and Christy Ryan got to meet, nor do I know what that man's name was, but he had agreed to take a letter out for us. Christy said we could trust him. Some of the men were sceptical, others cautious – the risks were great.

'What will happen if they find the letter?'

'What if he betrays us and hands the letter over?'

'They'll put us in the punishment cell, or worse, shoot us!'

'We have to try.'

'Don't want to build our hopes up again.'

I did not care, one way or the other. I agreed with the older men: we were never going to get out alive. Christy must have been planning this for a while because he had managed to obtain paper and hidden it. He wrote the letter by moonlight and then he went around us all.

'Quick! Sign here. The more of us that sign, the better. I have to get this to our man first thing in the morning.'

SS Arbeitserziehungs Lager

2nd October 1943

(Stamped 'Received by: Schweizer, Consulat Bremen, 4.OKT.1943 * 005394')

Dear Sir,

This is our second appeal to you for assistance. We are Irish seamen captured from sunken English ships and brought to Germany as 'Prisoners of War'.

On the 7th of January of this year, while in the camp known as Marlag und Milag Nord, we were informed that we were being repatriated, and taken from the Prisoner-of-War camp and brought to Bremen Labour Exchange. We were there informed that we were released from captivity and were ordered to sign a Free Workers' Paper and go to the Railways where we would be given employment.

This we refused to do and demanded to be returned to a registered camp if not repatriated. Our request was ignored and threats were employed. We were then taken to a factory and again asked to sign the paper, which we again refused.

Here we remained for three days exposed to the dangers of Air Raids. Our next destination was Hamburg where we stayed for two days. We were interviewed by a Captain Müller who requested us to sail in German ships. We again refused and were returned to Bremen under the impression that we were going back to the camp. We arrived instead in a Gestapo punishment camp. Immediately on arrival at this place some of our comrades were kicked and beaten. The next morning the same thing was repeated without any cause. We then had to follow the same procedure as any other Straf Prisoner. Our hair was shaved off and numbers put on our backs. Everything that we had was taken from us including cigarettes and Tobacco.

From this time on we followed the same routine as the Straf Prisoners. We were forced to work the same number of hours and under the same conditions in all weathers as the other prisoners. As a result of this treatment one man died and there are a few cases of Tuberculosis. We are now all in a poor state of health, and not fit to face another winter here. The position is made worse on account of having a number of old and sick men amongst us.

On June the 4th we had a visit from an Officer attached to Marlag und Milag Nord. He is the first English speaking German we had met since we left the camp. He told us that a great mistake had been made and that we were now about to be repatriated. He produced Irish Passport Application Forms for us to fill and sign. These forms appeared to be genuine and everyone signed with the exception of five men who did not consider themselves eligible. From that time to the present date we have heard nothing and our conditions have only improved slightly. We will state however that the Lager Commandant has treated us with some consideration since his return.

Since leaving the camp, we have received no Red Cross Parcels or any other Red Cross comforts which we are entitled to. We receive very few letters from home and in all this time have only received about six letters to write home. We were not allowed to use this address. We are however still receiving private clothing and cigarette parcels.

On September the 21st fifteen of us were photographed. We believe the object is to supply us with identity cards with a view to forcing us to work again. This we are determined not to do and consequently are in doubt as to what our future treatment will be.

Some of us have received word from relatives at home stating that the Red Cross informed them that we were on our way home. Others that nothing is known of us and that the Red Cross cannot send parcels as we are out of reach. Any letters or parcels that we get are addressed to Marlag und Milag Nord our old camp.

We appeal to you, as Irishmen and Prisoners of War to be returned to a registered P.O.W. camp or repatriated without further delay. If we are to be repatriated why punish us in a punishment camp like this? We feel that some of our members will not survive the winter especially the old and the sick.

I wish to state that none of us at any time before we left the camp, or since signed any forms except the application for a passport. We have at all times refused to work for Germany or accept freedom under those conditions.

Will you kindly send one copy of this letter to the Irish Consul and another to the British Red Cross in Geneva or whoever should be responsible for us.

We should like you to co-operate in this matter with the Irish Consul. There are a few amongst us who have resided in England for a number of years before capture and there is a doubt as to their nationality.

You will no doubt find it necessary to quote all these facts to the Germans.

If you are asked the source of your information of course say that these facts were all contained in the first letter of P.J. O'Brien. This will prevent further trouble and do not send any reply to this

camp or we will be punished severely if
this is discovered.

It might interest the Irish Consul to
know that J.J. Ryan of Waterford, P.J.
Little's friend, the man whose repatriation
he was instructed to secure is a prisoner
here.

We remain yours faithfully
The Irishmen in Farge

P.S. Haste is necessary.

Signed:

J.J. Ryan	W. Knott	W.H. Knox
I.C. Ryan	O. Corr	Gerald O'Hara
J. Gorman	T. Cooney	Peter Lydon
W. English	R. Roseman	
H. Callan	J. O'Brien	
J.J. Moffatt	M. O'Dwyer	
C. Byrne	P. Kavanagh	
W. Kelly	D. Ryan	
V. Harris	M. Lawrie	
B. Goulding	James Furlong	
T. Murphy	P. John Connor	
R. Flynn	P. Reilly	
T. King	I.T. Bryce	

P.J. O'Brien (from Kinsale) and Edward Condon did not
sign the letter; I do not know why. I signed it so that Christy
would leave me alone and I could sleep. It was hopeless
anyway. Next morning, Christy managed to pass it to the
Swiss prisoner who delivered it to the Swiss consul.

It is a pity that we did not have the time or energy to read the letter. Our heads were never shaved and we never had numbers painted on our jackets, like the *strafe*, or punishment, prisoners. The only number we had was our prisoner-of-war number, which we wore around our necks on a disc and never took off. When we left Milag on 27 January, Christy was in hospital with appendicitis. While we were in the Marine camp, Christy was detained in Bremen Prison. It is possible that his head was shaved and he had to wear a number on his jacket. While the other prisoners were deloused on their arrival, we were not. Again, it is possible, that Christy was deloused, as he came directly to the *AEL* camp from prison. Christy may have continued to receive mail and Red Cross parcels, the remains of which he brought with him to Bremen-Farge and these may have been taken from him on his arrival. The rest of us did not receive mail or Red Cross Parcels in the *AEL* camp. Our parcels were used up by the time we arrived at Bremen-Farge. Once the Red Cross were notified that we had been 'released', they would have removed our names from the parcel list. Mail received by them for us could not be forwarded, as they had no forwarding address. It is possible that Christy's family were informed that Christy had been released and expected him to be repatriated.

Christy, referring to the working conditions in all weathers, wrote: 'As a result of this treatment one man died and there are a few cases of Tuberculosis.' But Patrick Breen died from a beating. For Irish people, there was a stigma attached to tuberculosis as it was a killer disease and not talked about in families. If there was tuberculosis among some of the men, it is unlikely that it would be spoken about. Christy may have confused Gerald O'Hara's asthma with the disease.

I do not know why fifteen were photographed in September, as Christy says in his letter. We had all been photographed in Stalag XB, but perhaps these fifteen had been brought straight to Milag and had not been photographed at the time. The photographs used on Billy's and my passport forms were those taken in Stalag XB.

The Swiss Consul contacted the Irish Consul. Now the Irish government knew where we were. The Irish chargé d'affaires in Berlin, Con Cremin, made arrangements with the German authorities to visit the *AEL* camp in Bremen-Farge. That Swiss man took great risks for us. We owe him a lot.

The work never changed, the routine never changed, the weather was miserable and we were miserable. Just before 4.45 a.m., on a snowy, freezing day in December 1943, Kommandant Walhorn ordered a kapo to instruct Christy Ryan not to go to the site but to remain in the camp. The kapo said that someone important was coming to speak to him. We left Christy Ryan, Gerald O'Hara and Thomas Murphy behind us. The rest of us marched out to the site with hope in our hearts.

We had to wait until we were allowed into our barracks for the night before we could find out what had transpired. Christy told us that a big, black limousine arrived and the Gestapo accompanied a civilian into the administration building, to meet Kommandant Walhorn. Shortly afterwards, Christy, Gerald and Thomas were summoned to the *kommandant*'s office, where they were introduced to Con Cremin, the Irish chargé d'affaires from Berlin. Christy was delighted with this as he had expected a member of the Red

Cross. Kommandant Walhorn left but two Gestapo officers remained in the room. Cremin sat on one side of the table while Christy, Gerald and Thomas sat on the other. He questioned them about our accommodation, food and the treatment we were receiving in the *AEL*. Christy said that when he leaned in towards Cremin, to complain quietly, the chargé d'affaires pulled back and cautioned him that he did not want to hear complaints. He explained that he was there to improve our conditions, have us returned to Milag, or repatriated, but to do that, he had to stay on good terms with the German authorities – there were to be no complaints.

'What did he mean by that?' one of the lads asked.

Christy had to admit that he did not really know but Gerald and Thomas agreed that that was what he said. They all said that it was very intimidating having the two Gestapo officers in the room watching them.

One of the men asked, 'What do you think, Christy? What are our chances?'

Christy replied that he thought we had a good chance now. Mr Cremin would have to make a report and once the Irish authorities knew where we were, we would be released. I went to bed that night and even though I was exhausted, it took me a while to fall asleep. I dared to hope. We were so excited when two deliveries of Red Cross parcels came not long after Mr Cremin's visit. However, they would be the last Red Cross parcels we ever got.

Many years after the war, I found out that Con Cremin had pursued our repatriation for two years and had come close to it on two occasions, but he never got us out. (Deirdre Donnelly of BBC Radio Foyle found out in her research for her documentary, *Journey through Time*.) The following is an excerpt from a memo that was filed in Berlin, in March 1943.

```
From:
Gestapo Office, Bremen to Reich Security
Head Office, Berlin. 31st March 1943
Re: The application for protective custody
of the 32 Irish Nationals following their
refusal to work, at present in the workcamp
Farge. Their return to Ireland is not
permitted on the grounds that the Local
Labour Office may seek to place them in
employment. A re-entry to the Internment
Camp is not to be considered.
```

We had refused to work for the Nazis, so they could not send us back to Milag, where all the other prisoners of war would find out what had happened to us. They could not, or would not, send us home, either. By refusing to work *frei* for Germany we had won our own battle; they were not happy, and we were paying the price for it. We, however, were confident and hopeful.

The winter of 1943 was bitterly cold and made the work even harder. There were lots of accidents on the site: prisoners slipped on ice; fell from the building works; got cuts and abrasions on frozen hands, legs and feet which became infected and there was an outbreak of diphtheria. There were many prisoners in the sickbay. Each time I tried to get the shovel through the frozen earth, it jarred my numb hands with pain. Some of the others found pieces of sacking, which they wrapped around their hands, to try to warm them. It was just as cold in our barracks, too. Even wearing the army clothing in bed, with our feet wrapped in the jacket, and putting the greatcoat over us, we still shivered ourselves to sleep each night. Without those British Army jackets and greatcoats, we would have frozen to death – many prisoners did.

One day, the policeman Hans Mayer told me to work in the sickbay and not to go to the site. I did not want to catch diphtheria or be sick but I had no choice. Dr Heidbreder told me to put ointment on wounds and to use paper bandages if needed. He showed me what to do, and so I worked in the smaller room all day, treating the lesser injuries. If I saw a broken bone or a wound that needed stitches, I was to keep the prisoner there until the doctor could examine him. A German civilian, employed as a sanitiser, came to the sickbay each day to clean it. I was not expected to do this work. Over the next few weeks and into January 1944, I was called on a few times to work in the sickbay.

I was always starving, and the cold weather made it worse. One day, when working in the sickbay, I realised that there were patients who, when given their ration of bread in the middle of the day, were unable to eat it and instead hid it under their pillow or in their jacket pocket. I went into the bigger room, no longer caring about getting sick, but thinking of one thing only: food. On one bed lay a man who was dying: I could tell by his eyes and his breathing. I reached out and felt under his pillow – nothing. I put my hand into his pocket and found it – a slice of bread! For a split second, I stopped: this was stealing.

But then I reasoned that the man was dying and did not need the bread. I went outside and ate it. Not long afterwards, the guilt hit me. What had I done? I had deprived a man of his last meal; I had killed him. It was one thing to rob the dead to live, but I had robbed a dying man to live. That is a fact, true as God; it is terrible, but it is the truth. I was nothing but the lowest form of animal and the guilt was dreadful. I was as bad as the Gestapo guards, or the kapos. I felt as guilty as if I had killed him myself and was deeply ashamed. What would my father think of his son now?

'Father, I stole bread from a dying man because I was starving.'

No, I would never be able to tell him that. I could not forgive myself for what I had done. I was definitely in Hell. I was relying on our three 'Rosary men' to pray for my soul.

There were about 200 prisoners in each work group, with one or two kapos in charge of them. One day, an *AEL* camp prisoner escaped and the kapos panicked when they realised what had happened. If the prisoner was not recaptured, they would be punished and lose their status and privileges. They would return to prisoner status themselves and would receive punishment payback from the other prisoners for all their brutality while they had been kapos. For three days that work group got nothing to eat. They still had to work but they had to stand and watch while we received our bread and ersatz coffee in the middle of the day. It did not bother me: after all, they were only *AEL* prisoners and could go home in a number of weeks. The escapee was recaptured four days later and returned to the camp. The Gestapo guards did not punish him. Instead, they brought him into the square and the rest of his work group were called out of their barracks. We heard the commotion and went to watch from our window. They formed a circle, while the guards threw the recaptured prisoner into the centre of the circle.

'Jetzt gehört er ganz Ihnen, es ist seine Schuld, dass Sie keine Nahrung bekamen.' ('Now he's all yours. It's his fault that you got no food.')

There was silence for a couple of minutes and then they started to kick the prisoner. They kicked that poor man to death. When he was dead, he was stripped, carried out of the camp, tossed into the mass grave and a bucket of quicklime was thrown over him. When they came back into the square they lined up in fives. They were each given a ladle of soup.

14

PUNISHMENT AND TYPHUS

IT WAS SPRINGTIME 1944. Early one Sunday morning, Kommandant Walhorn asked for volunteers to help a local farmer to clear the ditches on his land; fifteen of us volunteered. Clearing ditches was easy work in comparison to what we had been doing. We had no kapos or Gestapo guards with us, just the farmer, who was an old man. We could work at our own pace. At 10 a.m., the farmer gave us a mug of ersatz coffee and a slice of bread. When dinnertime came we got a big pot of soup with potatoes and vegetables in it, and the farmer did not limit us to one ladleful. We were allowed to eat until the pot was empty. At 3 p.m. we had to stop work because we were all vomiting into the ditches. The farmer's wife had thought she was doing the best for us but it was too much for our deprived stomachs. We worked another few Sundays on the farm but the soup was never as rich as that first time. Finally, there were no more ditches to clear and the work ended.

Outside the *AEL* camp, a huge area of ground had been excavated and seventeen oil refinery-size tanks were set down. A large pipe ran from these to the River Weser, to where the Germans planned to refuel ships and U-boats. One day, in late spring, the twenty-nine of us were ordered to cover the tanks with soil. They had been covered with cement, but now they were to be camouflaged so that they could not be seen from the air. Some of the tanks had doors inserted into them. I glanced in and regretted it immediately. I cannot get the vision out of my head. There were rows and rows of bunks. This was where the concentration camp prisoners slept. I had to block the picture from my head and keep telling myself – like a mantra: 'I don't care, I don't care, so long as it's not us.'

The concentration camp prisoners were marched out to the site in the morning, and we were marched in to cover up the tanks. Later, in August, another two barracks were erected at the tank site to house extra Neuengamme Concentration Camp prisoners.

When we finished the task of covering the tanks, we were sent back to the site to continue digging, moving tracks, filling and emptying bogies. Loose lime and clay arrived on barges and was unloaded by some prisoners who brought it to the line of cement mixers where other prisoners made the cement. Wooden scaffolding was erected around the steel walls and both groups of prisoners had to wheel barrowloads of wet cement up wooden ramps onto the scaffolding and then pour it into the steel walls. This was heavy work. There was constant noise and the cement dust was everywhere. Whipping and beatings still went on, even though the prisoners were exhausted. Some collapsed and fell to their deaths. They fell down into the foundations or into the walls. No one checked if they were alive, but if they did not get up, no one was told to pull them out and they were left there while cement was poured over them. There are a lot of bodies in that building.

After the war, Raymond Portefaix, a French survivor of Bunker Valentin, recorded his experiences, writing that 'the dust from the cement was torture … During the night, it settled on nasal hairs, became encrusted and made breathing difficult.' When he coughed, he spat out white balls, which all but tore his chest apart. I thanked God we were never put on cement duty.

The heaviest and most dangerous work was on the *Eisenkommandos* (iron detachments). Prisoners had to manually lift and haul iron and steel girders into place on the building. These detachments were known as *Himelfahrtskommandos* (suicide squads): prisoners died from exhaustion or heart failure. Their bodies were moved by other prisoners and piled up at the edge of the site. There were times when we were told to move them. When we did this, we checked their pockets for bread. Sometimes we were lucky. If prisoners collapsed, but were not dead, they were also shifted to the pile. By the end of the day, there were men, still alive, piled in with dead men. I could only imagine the horror of opening my eyes and finding dead men all around me. We never had to pull these poor wretches out but other prisoners had to; then they put them on stretchers and carried them back to camp. If they did not die on the way, they usually died in the sickbay.

The German engineering company in charge of building Bunker Valentin ensured that the whole project was photographed. They were careful, however, not to photograph us – after all, we were not supposed to be there. Under the Geneva Convention, as prisoners of war, we could not work on anything dangerous or on anything that supported the German war effort. Prisoners of war, hired out to civilian contractors, were supposed to receive pay, get one rest day in a week and live in adequately heated and lit buildings where conditions were the same as those for German troops.

Looking back, I believe that Kommandant Walhorn himself recognised us as prisoners of war and tried to adhere to the Geneva Convention as well as he could. He was a Gestapo officer, in charge of criminals and political dissidents but he never treated us as *AEL* prisoners. Officially, we were not listed as prisoners of war in Bremen-Farge. Yes, we got a day of rest on Sunday but we were never paid. We had no heating, tick or clean linen. We had no light after 9 p.m. Our barracks was clean only because we kept it that way. Our conditions were not the same as those of German troops: we had experienced those barracks in the Marine camp. But we did not have to share with anyone else and even though the camp became overcrowded, the rooms opposite ours remained empty. We were never deloused, nor were our heads shaved; no numbers were painted on our clothing and we wore British Army uniforms. We were like no other prisoners in the *AEL*-Farge camp.

We Irishmen were never put in the punishment cell in the camp. It was so small that a bunk of about 2 foot 6 inches long filled the back wall. A prisoner had no room to stand up in it and when he sat on the bunk, with his feet on the floor, his knees hit the opposite wall. He could spend three or four days in that cell, in complete darkness, with no food or water; in the summer he baked and in the winter he froze. Once, I saw a prisoner put in the cell. He marched to it, saying nothing; three days later, I saw the Gestapo guard open the door to let him out. An old man came out, cramped and blinded by the sunlight. After that, I did my best to avoid it when prisoners were going or coming from the punishment cell.

There was a mass grave outside the perimeter of the camp in which some 3,500 men were buried. Most of them died from malnutrition, exhaustion, dysentery, typhus or heart attack. When a prisoner died in the camp, he was stripped and his naked body was put in a room beside the administration building where it was kept for a week while the prisoner's employers or family were notified. If the body was not claimed, it was disposed of by other prisoners, who were ordered to throw it into the mass grave and then cover it with quicklime. The mass grave was a large hole which was left open for all of us to see. We had to pass it twice a day; it was impossible to avoid. When the open grave was full, earth was put over it and another hole dug in preparation for the next batch of bodies.

We never tried to escape because the risks were too great. A few of the *AEL* prisoners tried, but they were always caught and shot. Once Gerald and Thomas heard whispers that there was going to be an escape attempt, which made us all very nervous; there was no knowing how the guards would react, or who would be punished. We lay in our bunks that night with our heads covered, hoping to hear nothing. In the morning as we marched to the site, they were there, shot dead, lying in a tangled heap outside the gate. It was a warning to all of us. After a few days, they too were stripped and dumped in the mass grave with the other bodies.

I saw all these terrible, dreadful things and I lived in fear all the time. The *AEL* prisoners, many of them Germans, meant nothing to the Gestapo guards. Even to us, they were no longer men, no longer human beings – they were just prisoners. Walking by the hole filled with bodies, to keep sane, I repeated the mantra 'just prisoners … just prisoners … just prisoners'. To this day, I still have nightmares about those prisoners.

One night, while we were in bed, we heard the sound of vehicles and the noise of posts being driven into the ground. We fell back asleep and at 3 a.m. the kapo woke us. As usual, we headed to the washroom before going to the square to join the other prisoners for our ladle of soup. As I walked out the door, I glanced to my right to see what was going on.

I had never seen a hanged man before and I never want to see one again. The Gestapo had portable hanging posts, with nooses and ropes attached, which they erected when they arrived in the *AEL* camps. They were judge, jury and executioner; not just for camp prisoners but for anyone in or outside the camps. The bodies were left hanging for a few hours to ensure that as many of us as possible saw them. There were five men hanged. As far as I know, three were French and two were Polish. I never saw or heard of any other hangings. I didn't think I would be able to eat my soup that morning but we were alive and starving. We forgot about those prisoners swinging from the ropes just beside us in the square, ate our soup and marched out to the site.

Gerald O'Hara was a very well-educated man. He and Dr Heidbreder had many conversations when the doctor visited the camp. When Gerald O'Hara's breathing became really laboured, Dr Heidbreder, worried about his state of health, moved him to Bremen Hospital. Gerald died of typhus in March 1944. He was fifty. I thought I had got used to death but this was different and it really upset me. I looked for Gerald in his bunk and wanted to hear his gentle voice again. Why did he have to die now, just when Mr Cremin was working to get us out? Our days continued on as before. No one but us missed Patrick or Gerald.

One day, towards the end of March, Thomas Murphy, our information gatherer, stopped me and said, 'Harry, you're from Derry, aren't you?'

'Yeah.'

'Well, I heard today that the Germans bombed Derry in 1941 and destroyed the city. Sorry, Harry. I hope your people are okay.'

I was numb. I had no way of knowing if my family were safe. The older men told me not to dwell on it or I would go mad. I crawled into my bunk that night, thought of my sisters, brothers, Father and Aunt Ellen and cried myself to sleep.

By April, we had heard nothing from Con Cremin and I lost all hope. I began to feel really unwell. I had pains in my back and could not breathe. Marching to the work site was very difficult and I worried that I would not be able keep up with the others. One evening, back in our barracks, the others told me to go to the sickbay and report to Dr Heidbreder.

'He will look after you, Harry.'

'You can't work like that.'

'What if one of the foremen just thinks you're slacking? No, Harry, you have to report into sickbay in the morning.'

They did not have to say any more. If a foreman thought I was slacking, I could be the one lying dead in the dyke or foundations; if I was going to die, I certainly did not want it to be like that. I was afraid to sleep in case I did not wake up again.

15

WORKING OUTSIDE THE CAMP

THE NEXT MORNING, I had a temperature. After I had my ladle of soup, I went to the sickbay and waited for Dr Heidbreder. He examined me and declared me unfit to work for two weeks. I lay down on a bunk in the small room off the main sickbay. I do not remember him telling me what was wrong with me; in fact, I don't remember the first week very well because I had a fever and was delirious. I had dreadful nightmares but I also dreamt about home; sometimes I woke up crying. Dr Heidbreder checked in on me every day and by the second week he arranged for me to have extra rations. At 11 a.m., every morning, I got half a bowl of cold porridge with a cold potato in it. There was no milk, or anything else on it, but it tasted heavenly. I knew I was getting better.

Dr Heidbreder had very good English. On one visit, he told me he was pleased with my progress and that he had spoken to Kommandant Walhorn about me.

'Harry, would you like to come and work in my wife's garden?'

Did I hear him correctly? Was I still delirious? He asked if I would '*like* to …' I hesitated.

'Well, Harry, would you like to?'

I was going to be taken off the site? I was going to work in a garden? Of course I wanted to work for his wife! In my head, I said, 'Oh yes, I'll have that,' but what I actually said was, 'Yes, Herr Doktor. Thank you.'

'Go and wait in my car.'

I left the sickbay and climbed nervously into the front passenger seat, expecting a guard to stop me or shoot me. A few minutes later, Dr Heidbreder got into the driver's seat and away we went. There was silence in the car as we drove the short distance to his home. I wondered if this was some sort of trick.

It was a big house, standing on its own with a garden at the front and a huge garden, the size of a football pitch, at the rear. Dr Heidbreder parked the car and got out. I followed him to the back door and into the kitchen but I was petrified. It was forbidden for prisoners to enter a German's home. Frau Doktor was there, with three of their children and the housemaid; I later learned that there was also a baby boy in the house. The children were afraid when they saw me. I did not know what I looked like but I knew my clothes were hanging loosely. Later, when Dr Heidbreder weighed me, I was 6 stone – just under half my weight before I was captured. The housemaid said, '*Der arme Mann, wie die Toten zu Fuß*'. ('The poor man, like the dead walking.')

I can only imagine what those three children thought as they clung to their mother's skirt.

'*Mama, wie sollen wir ihn nennen?*' ('Mama, what name do we call him?')

Frau and Dr Heidbreder, 1944.

The Heidbreder children in their garden, 1944: *(l–r)* Mareike, Enno and Uwe.

She looked at me, smiled, then turned to them and said, 'Harry.' Then she corrected herself and said, '*Nein. Onkel Harry.*' ('No. Uncle Harry.')

And that is what Mareike, Uwe and Enno called me from that day on. It felt wonderful at that moment!

I just stood there, looking around me, while the family went into another room. There was a small table with two chairs, some cupboards, a sink and a range, not unlike the one we had at home. Then I realised that there were two women in the kitchen and there was no sign of the doctor; it made me very nervous. What if someone came in and saw me standing there? I had just decided that it was safer to go outside and stay in the garden, when the housemaid spoke.

'*Setzen Sie sich und trinken Sie eine Tasse Kaffee.*' ('Sit down and have a cup of coffee.')

I did not move. I had not sat down in a year and a half. She pulled out a chair, and then very gently, taking me by the arm, led me to it and sat me down. She gave me a cup of hot coffee and one of her rationed biscuits.

'*Mein Name ist Katie, und das ist Anna, die Köchin.*' ('My name is Katie, and that is Anna, the cook.')

Anna did not turn around but that did not matter. I was no longer an animal. I was given back my dignity and humanity by those Christian gestures. My mind was in turmoil. Did I dare enjoy this moment?

When I had finished, Katie brought me outside and showed me where Frau Doktor wanted to grow her vegetables. I started to turn the soil and dig the vegetable patch. It was a warm day and working in the garden was very peaceful. There was no one threatening me and I took my time. At midday Katie called me, 'Harry, *Essen.*' ('Harry, eat.')

She waved at me to come to the house, so I went to the back door and waited. I noticed that Dr Heidbreder's car was gone and I wondered fleetingly how I would get back to the camp. When I went into the kitchen, on the table were a cup of hot coffee and a plate of sandwiches made with home-baked bread and filled with *wurst*. She indicated that I was to sit at the table, which I did. I wanted to bolt the food before it was taken away but Katie just smiled at me and I smiled back. I was going to make this meal last. When I finished the last crumb and drained the coffee cup, I said, '*Danke, Katie, und Anna.*'

I went back outside to continue digging. Dr Heidbreder returned and drove me back to the camp. Although it was my first day's work after my spell in the sickbay, it had not been hard labour. I was tired, but not exhausted like the rest of the Irishmen. I quietly said 'hello' and went to my bunk.

It was hard to believe that the Irish chargé d'affaires was still working on our case but Christy Ryan was confident that we would hear from him soon. We did not know that Cremin was having difficulties because we had no passports. Instead, we Merchant Navy men had Discharge Books, which were held in the relevant marine office where a seaman signed on a ship; mine was held in the Marine Office in Liverpool Docks. So the first thing he had to do was to establish our identities and confirm that we were all Irish born, and therefore, Irish nationals.

Kommandant Walhorn had overall responsibility for the prisoners in the *AEL*-Farge camp where prisoners were sentenced to hard labour for a maximum of eight weeks. We Irishmen had now been in the Bremen-Farge camp for fourteen months. We wore British Army uniforms and POW numbers. We were known to the Red Cross and now had the Irish consulate working on our repatriation to a neutral country. Although we did not know it at the time, Kommandant Walhorn had queried our presence in the camp with the authorities in Berlin and was very uneasy when he received a memorandum instructing him to send us to Neuengamme Concentration Camp and certain death. One morning, he ordered the kapo to tell us to stay in the yard when the other prisoners marched out. We stood in our rows of five and waited until Kommandant Walhorn and Dr Heidbreder came out of the administration building. The doctor examined us and declared some of us unfit to work on the site; I was one of them. A few days later, the same thing happened and some more Irishmen were declared unfit. By this time, we were all very undernourished and some of the men suffered from typhus, diphtheria and other illnesses. Within a short time all of us had been declared unfit to work on the site, even though not all of us were sick. In April 1944, Owen Corr and Thomas Murphy were sent to Bremen Hospital with symptoms like those suffered by Gerald O'Hara. We lost them to typhus, too. When they died, Owen was twenty-nine and Thomas was fifty-three. We were now down to twenty-eight Irishmen.

In Bremen-Farge the prisoners in the concentration camp and the *AEL* camp died from typhus, dysentery, malnutrition, heart attacks, lung diseases, infected wounds, overwork and beatings. We Irishmen were lucky that Dr Heidbreder sent us to Bremen Hospital. The other prisoners only had the sickbay and as for the concentration camp prisoners, well, I don't know if they had anything at all. Typhus was caused by lice on humans and there was no treatment for it. The poor fellas had fever, dreadful headaches, a blistery, red rash, even on the soles of their feet, and pains in their joints. It was a terrible way to die.

One morning at the end of April, in the square, Hans Mayer selected me from the group. I was always afraid of the guards and tried not to draw attention to myself but Hans Mayer was different, being the local policeman and not one of the Gestapo. So when he called me I stepped forward and hoped that I was not wrong about him. He spoke no English but I spoke a little German by this time. Günther's Nursery in Neuenkirchen needed some workers and he told me to pick another man to go with me. I picked Billy English. He gave me directions in German to go straight down the road to the main street, turn right and keep walking. Opposite a church on the left-hand side, with a clock on it, we would see a big gateway. We were to go in there.

Billy and I headed off. I understood the words for 'straight', 'turn right', 'church' and 'clock' so I hoped that we would find the place. It was a brisk 8 km walk and I pointed out Dr Heidbreder's house to Billy as we passed it. We found the nursery and went in. The house was a very wide red-bricked two-storey building, which had exposed wooden beams crossing over each other on the top storey. The name on the building was 'Friedrich Wätjen' but the nursery was known as 'Wätjen und Günther'. We were met by a small elderly gentleman whom we called Herr Günther. He brought us into a field and showed us that he wanted us to dig a piece of ground about 12 foot by 24 foot. He got a spade, dug it into the ground, lifted the sod and turned it over. He gave each of us a spade and left us to it.

At 10.30 a.m. we were called to the house. I had never seen a conservatory before and did not even know the word for it then but attached to the back of the house was a large timber-framed glass room with a table and bench where Herr Günther indicated we were to sit. He disappeared and returned with a tray of coffee and wurst sandwiches; we really enjoyed them. It was years later before I found out that they were sharing their rations with us. As soon as we finished we thanked him and returned to our digging. Later in the day we were called to the house for our dinner. This time we were brought into the kitchen, where we sat by ourselves at the table. There was a range, like the one at home, and the stove fire was burning brightly; it made the room warm and cosy. It had been a long time since either of us had experienced the luxury of a home fire. A young woman served us a bowl of vegetable and potato soup with lovely freshly baked bread. It was delicious and we thanked her for it. She rewarded us with a lovely smile. As we went back to the garden to work I jokingly said to Billy, 'Hey, maybe we'd better slow down or else we'll be finished too early and I don't know about you, but I wouldn't mind having another cup of coffee.'

But we could not do that; they were nice people and so we worked on at a good pace. Herr Günther had broad beans growing there and he pulled one pod off, opened it up and gave a bean to each of us as he said, '*Das ist besser als jede Rindersteak.*' ('That's better than any beef steak.')

I understood and said, '*Geben Sie mir die Rindersteak ersten.*' ('Give me the beef steak first.')

He hesitated, looked at us both and started to laugh. We joined in. Oh, it was so good to laugh!

That evening, Herr Günther had a visit from the Gestapo. Somehow they heard that we had been served our food in the kitchen and he was warned that we were to be

Herr Fredrich Wätjen and Frau Wätjen of Günthers Nursery, 1944.

fed outside. For the rest of the week and Billy and I worked there, we were served our food in the conservatory – we were not brought into the house again.

The man we called Herr Günther was in fact Herr Wätjen, the original owner of the nursery and father-in-law of Herr Günther. He and his wife lived with their daughter and her husband and son, Wilfried. Wilfried Günther was a grand lad, about four or five years old. He followed his grandfather everywhere and eventually took to following Billy around too. Billy played with him. Wilfried would squeal with laughter when Billy sat him in the wheelbarrow and ran through the nursery with him. Richard Günther had been called up in 1940 and his father-in-law was managing the nursery in his absence. Due to bad health Richard was discharged from the army and returned home to work in his nursery. I do not recall meeting Richard Günther. Herr Wätjen never corrected us and never seemed to mind being called Herr Günther. He was a kind and good man. He grew tree saplings which the prisoners from the many camps in the area were sent to collect. The German guards planted trees everywhere to hide what they were doing. Herr Wätjen used to place a piece of bread in the bottom of one pot and then put another pot containing the sapling on top of it. The German guards eventually spotted the double pot and one day he was warned that he too would end up in the *AEL* if he persisted. What the Gestapo did not know and never found out was that Frau Wätjen and Frau Günther boiled pots of potatoes during the day and then at night, together with Herr Wätjen, hid the potatoes in the walls and hedges along the fields and the routes that the prisoners took.

16

'IRLÄNDER' AND A TYPHUS EPIDEMIC

THE CONCENTRATION CAMP and *AEL*-Farge prisoners continued building Bunker Valentin without us. We Irishmen had been declared unfit to work on the site but having nothing to do all day in the camp was nearly worse. I would think about home and family, and would get melancholic. It was worse for the married men, especially if they had children. They had no way of knowing how their families were coping. The Merchant Navy's policy was that when a ship was sunk or captured, the owners stopped paying the crew. A seaman was considered no longer in their employment if he was not on board his ship. The men knew that their wives would not have received any pay from the day they were captured.

It was Hans Mayer's responsibility to keep the camp clean and, because we had nothing to do, he told us that we should apply ourselves. So we joined our comrades sweeping the square and cleaning the washroom; we were not guarded doing this work. Herr Gärtner, the other local policeman, still came up from the village whenever a new consignment of prisoners arrived. I was put working with him on a couple of occasions. He registered the prisoners coming into the camp and released those being sent home. He still treated them dreadfully whenever he knew the *kommandant* was not around, often hitting or kicking them. The prisoners who were going home lined up while their civilian clothing, shoes and personal items were returned to them. They dressed and waited for the lorry to arrive. The incoming prisoners alighted from the lorry and were immediately sent for delousing. They gathered in the square, stripped off their shirts and pants and were given the prison clothing handed back by the released prisoners. They were given worn shoes or wooden clogs to wear. The new prisoners' civilian clothes were then given to me to fold. Herr Gärtner showed me the professional way of folding clothes as though I was putting them on display in a man's shop; I had to pay particular attention to jackets and jumpers. The bundle was put into a brown bag sealed with three brass fasteners and then Herr Gärtner wrote the prisoner's name on it. It was my job to store it on shelves set aside for the purpose in the administration building.

Billy continued to work for Herr Günther and I worked for Dr Heidbreder but, apart from these households, nobody outside the camp spoke to us. Here were two young men in enemy uniforms freely walking down the village street. We must have caused quite a stir. The Gestapo had shouted at the villagers in Bremervörde when they tried to give us food and poor Herr Günther had been reported by a local to the Gestapo for bringing us into the kitchen to feed us; no wonder no one dared to speak to us! In wartime it was difficult for neighbour to trust neighbour. I was surprised one morning while on my way to Dr Heidbreder's house to hear

'*Morgen, Irländer!*'

I replied '*Morgen*' and kept walking. After that, the villagers regularly greeted us.

At the doctor's house, the children talked to me in German and, with lessons from Katie, I was picking up the language. For a few hours I could forget about war, forget about the camp and imagine that this was my real life. In the evening I went back to the camp to stand in line for my ladle of soup. Billy and I were not the only ones in our group working outside the camp. We never talked about the work we did nor what we got to eat. We were living two lives and it was rather confusing.

One evening in April when I arrived back at the camp I found the gate locked and a sign on it which read 'TYPHUS'.

I was so shocked that I stood there for a few minutes, wondering what to do. I was supposed to be in my barracks by dark and knew the consequences if I was found outside by the Gestapo guards. I was not just outside the barracks but outside the camp! I turned and headed back to Dr Heidbreder's house. I felt sure that he would know what to do.

The doctor's car was not there so I hid in the garden until he got home. I hoped no one would see me because I didn't want the family to get into trouble. Dr Heidbreder was surprised to see me when I called out to him, but I quickly explained what had happened. However, he said that the camp was closed because of a typhus epidemic and nobody was allowed in or out of the camp. He brought me around

Katie Sause and Mareike Heidbreder, c. 1944.

to the side door of his house and led me down a flight of steps into the basement, where he pulled out a trestle bed. He warned me that no one was to know I was there: not

Anna, not Katie and especially not the children. I would have to be up early in the morning, tidy everything away and hide in the garage until 6 a.m. I agreed and thanked him.

Each morning, I very quietly put away the trestle bed, crept up the basement steps and let myself into the garage where there was a bucket of fresh water and a towel, which I used to wash myself. After 6 a.m. I checked that there was nobody about, let myself out of the garage and walked up the drive as normal. After a cup of coffee and bread, I carried out whatever tasks Frau Doktor needed me to do and in the middle of the day I ate my soup, which was like the stews Aunt Ellen made at home, with plenty of vegetables and potatoes in it.

Herr Doktor allowed Katie to practise her teaching skills so he gave me permission to stay later in the evening. I had coffee and home-made bread for tea and when it was dark, I said goodbye and left to walk to the camp, but turned back to wait in the garage until the house went quiet and everyone was in bed; then I sneaked into the basement for the night. I lived that life for two weeks. One morning, as the doctor was leaving in his car, he called me over and spoke to me in English. 'Harry, the camp is now open again. So this evening after work you go back to the *Arbeitserziehungslager*. Do you understand?'

I swallowed my disappointment. '*Ja, Herr Doktor, und Danke.*'

That evening when I finished work in the garden, I told Katie that I had to get back to the camp and that I could not stay late any more. I walked back hoping that I would find the gate locked but it was open. As I stood outside the door of my barracks fear hit me. What was I going to find inside? Were the others okay – had anyone died? When I walked into the room I did a quick head count; no one else had died. What would I say if any of them asked me where I had been? But no one did. Voices called out.

'There you are, Harry.'

'Harry.'

I said 'hello' and climbed into my bunk. I wondered how many of us had stayed outside the camp. Had Billy stayed at Herr Günther's? Just as I never told anyone where I had been, nobody else said anything either. Loose talk could bring the Gestapo down on innocent people and we were not going to be responsible for that. So those two weeks became lost and we carried on as if they never happened.

Kommandant Walhorn nicknamed me '*Blackie Wandermann*' ('Blackie the Traveller'). My skin was tanned and I had a head of bushy, wild black hair. I must have reminded him of a gypsy.

'*Ich brauche dich und ein anderen Mann. Suche jemanden aus.*' ('I need you and another man. Pick someone.')

I understood and replied, 'Billy English, Herr Kommandant.'

There was a merchant farmer from Blumenthal waiting for us at the gate. He imported vegetables from Spain, which supplemented what he farmed on his own land, and supplied them to local grocery shops. We climbed into the back of his lorry and went with him. Approximately half an hour later he drove up a long driveway to a big shed to the right of a farmhouse similar to Herr Günther's. The merchant farmer parked and gestured to us to load up the lorry with wooden boxes, which were like the ones we used at home for 'pitting' potatoes (that is, layering them in boxes until they sprouted and were ready for planting).

Once we had the lorry loaded we climbed into the back with the boxes and he drove for an hour into the railway station in Bremen. He led us to a boxcar. When I saw it my body and mind froze. I do not know what Billy was thinking. What was going on? What were we doing here? My legs were shaking, my mouth was dry and my stomach was knotted in fear. He stretched out his hand to the lock on the door to open it. My mind saw everything in slow motion. He started to slide open the door ... Were we going to face more people like ourselves? Were we going to be told to get into the boxcar? The one thing I did not expect to be faced with was – a boxcar full of onions.

Oh, the relief! I didn't know whether to laugh or cry. We started to load those onions into the boxes and stack them in the lorry; we only got half the boxcar emptied that day. On the return journey to the farm we had to sit in the cab with him, but he never spoke to us at any stage. When we got to the farm in Blumenthal we had to take the boxes out of the lorry, stack them in the shed, sweep out the back of the lorry and the yard. The farmer then brought us back to the camp. It was after 9 p.m. and we had missed our ladle of soup; we were starving. We had had nothing to eat or drink since our ladle of soup at 4 a.m. I said to Billy that I was going to see Kommandant Walhorn to ask him for some food.

'No, Harry, don't! You'll get shot if you go in there complaining.'

'Sure Billy, aren't we dying anyway? If he shoots us it would be quicker.'

I knocked on Kommandant Walhorn's door.

'*Kommen.*'

Kommandant Walhorn was sitting behind his desk. He looked up at me and said, '*Was willst du, Blackie?*' ('What do you want, Blackie?')

So I told him that we had worked all day without water and without food. He called one of the cooks and asked if there was anything left. To our surprise, we each got a bowl – not a ladle – of soup and a slice of bread. It had never tasted so good!

The next day when the merchant farmer came to collect us, he was summoned into Kommandant Walhorn's office while we waited beside his lorry. After a short time the farmer came out of the administration building with a thunderous expression. Without a word, he gestured for us to climb on the back of the lorry and drove us to the farm in Blumenthal. He pointed to a little covered-in area that linked the house to the shed, indicated that we were to sit there and then went into the house. His wife came out with a tray of sandwiches and coffee. We could hardly believe it. When we were finished eating and drinking, we stacked more empty boxes into the lorry, climbed in and went to the *Bahnhof* in Bremen to finish the job we had started. We packed the last of the onions into boxes and got back to the farm at about 5 p.m. where we unloaded them and stacked them in the shed. Once we had tidied up, we sat in the covered-in area and were given another tray of sandwiches and coffee. When we were finished, the farmer drove us back to the camp where Kommandant Walhorn was waiting at the gate. He asked me, '*Haben Sie Speisen und Getränke bekommen heute, Blackie?*' ('Did you get food and drink today, Blackie?')

'*Ja, danke, Herr Kommandant.*' ('Yes, thank you, Kommandant.')

That merchant farmer never called for any of us again.

When the ships' officers among us no longer had to work on Bunker Valentin, Kommandant Walhorn gave them a separate small hut to use as a work area. They were told to attend to any repairs required around the camp and received the proper tools needed. They repaired doors, windows, replaced damaged timbers and other such jobs. One of the men, James Furlong, used to whittle away on pieces of wood to occupy himself. I asked if he could make a little sailing boat and he did. James took pride in his work and made a beautifully finished boat with a mast and sail. I was delighted with it so the next day I went with Billy to Günther's Nursery and brought it with me for young Wilfried who had just had a birthday. His eyes lit up. He had never had a toy boat before.

'Danke, Harry! Danke, Billy!'

He ran off to show the gift to his mother and grandparents. Herr Wätjen was surprised and came out to thank us. Billy stayed there while I headed back to Dr Heidbreder's house to work in the garden. I walked with a bit of a spring in my step. Some of the Gestapo guards who had seen James making the little boat for me asked if he would make some for them too. They wanted to give them to their children so they brought him the pieces of timber he needed and he made a few little boats for them.

Because I was working in Dr Heidbreder's house I did not at first notice Kommandant Walhorn's absence in spring 1944. He was involved in an accident around that time and returned to his bungalow outside the camp to recuperate. Kommandant Schipper took over for six months. He had no dealings with the Irishmen so we continued to work for the villagers and local famers, coming and going as we pleased, and in that way Kommandant Schipper recognised our prisoner-of-war status. However, we still got no Red Cross parcels.

Kommandant Walhorn was not a well man; he always appeared to be in a lot of pain and walked with difficulty. His wife and two small daughters came to spend some time with him during the summer of 1944 and stayed in his small bungalow. I was on my way to Dr Heidbreder's house and I could not believe it when I saw two lovely little girls with the *kommandant*. I would not have wanted my sisters anywhere near all that pain and suffering. The *kommandant's* family stayed in that house for about two weeks. I never saw them again.

17

THE HEIDBREDER FAMILY

IN THE SUMMER OF 1944, I worked at Dr Heidbreder's nearly every day. My main job was gardening, which I loved. I kept the vegetable patch, cut the grass with a scythe – just like I had done in Granduncle James's fields – and raked the pebbles on the driveway. Frau Doktor was very strict about this. Herr and Frau Doktor were important people in the village and had the biggest house. Appearances had to be kept up. I realise now that some days Frau Doktor just gave me jobs to do so that I would be there and not in the camp. No one reported me for eating my meals in their kitchen.

Anna, the cook, never spoke to me, but each day I joined Katie at the kitchen table for my meal and coffee. Katie continued to give me German lessons when Frau Doktor had no other jobs for me to do. I was a model pupil! In Germany in those days, young girls were required to work as a housemaid in another woman's home to learn the skills necessary to be a good German housewife. When Katie completed her year with Frau Doktor, she was going to attend teaching college in Poland. Frau Doktor allowed her to work part-time in the village school too. Katie diligently corrected my bad German. One day when I was struggling with the language, in temper she picked up the dictionary and threw it at me shouting, 'Harry, *studier dies!*' ('Harry, go study it!')

It really felt like being at home with my sisters and brothers!

Mareike, a lively, blonde nine-year-old with long pigtails tied in bows, and Uwe, a typical eight-year-old boy full of mischief, were at school. Little Enno, who was five, followed me around while I did my jobs. The two-year-old baby spent his days in his pram on the balcony upstairs, so I never saw him. The older children also helped me with my German. They laughed at my mistakes and felt very important teaching a grown-up.

Tiger, the family pet, was a big, black shaggy-coated mongrel but he had a gentle nature and the children loved him. Frau Doktor often sent me to walk to Blumenthal to buy offal for the dog, an 8 km round trip. One day, Frau Doktor gave me a bicycle for this journey but I never rode it. If I got back early and Frau Doktor had no jobs for me I would have no choice but to go back to camp. Instead I put the bucket on the handlebars and walked the 8 km. Frau Doktor made no comment.

The basement was divided into three rooms. One was used to wash and wring out the clothes, a second was used for storing food and the third held the winter and summer furnaces, which I kept clean. The large, empty space beside the furnaces was used for drying clothes in winter. There was also the trestle bed where the previous labourer had slept before the war and where a young Irishman had secretly stayed for two weeks. A door led up to the yard from the basement. On Tuesday mornings Frau Doktor would be in the basement early, to supervise Katie and another girl

Harry Callan wearing one of Dr Heidbreder's shirts in 1944 and wearing the watch he bartered for in Milag und Marlag in 1941.

from the village who helped with the washing. My job was to wring out the clothes, go to the garden and erect the clothes-line poles.

One day, Frau Doktor told me to bring along my underclothes and said she would wash them for me. When I arrived the following Tuesday, she asked me for them. I was embarrassed and said that I had dropped them on the way; in reality, I was wearing the only underwear I had. She must have guessed the real reason because the following Tuesday she gave me an old shirt and underwear belonging to Herr Doktor to change into while mine were being washed. The doctor was not a big man but his old clothes were huge on me; my ribs were sticking out and it made me realise just how skinny I had become. In the evening I changed into my own shirt and underwear before returning to the camp. When Sunday came, the older men could see that my clothes were clean and that I was still showering, so they were satisfied. We maintained our standards of cleanliness.

When the doctor's parents came for a holiday, Frau Doktor introduced me to her in-laws. I didn't see much of Frau Heidbreder, who mainly kept to the house. Herr Heidbreder was different though. He was a small, neat man with a goatee beard. He was a keen gardener and joined me while I was planting apple trees. He told me that he had pear trees in his own garden and we talked about fruit trees and gardening in general. He asked me where I had learnt to use a scythe so I told him about my work in Granduncle James's fields and about the vegetables that were grown at home. I was glad that I had some German or I would have missed out on these conversations. The children were sad when they left and I missed Herr Heidbreder's company too.

Before Katie left to go to university, she asked me if I knew anyone who would chop wood for the old teacher and his wife to have it ready for winter. I told her I would get someone for her and so that evening I told the lads and one of them said he would do it. When Katie left in midsummer, another girl from the village took her place. I missed her and especially missed my German lessons with her. She had been a very good friend to me. Anna, the cook, continued to ignore me. Her boyfriend (a Luftwaffe pilot and Katie's brother) would call for Anna but never went into the house. He must have found it strange to see me sitting at the kitchen table with his sister but he said nothing; in fact, he totally ignored my presence too.

The days were warm and sunny. Frau Doktor asked me to go with the children and the new 'daily' to the River Weser, which flowed by the end of their land and where there was a little beach. It was a favourite spot for the children who loved to play and swim there. They were good swimmers, as was the new maid. One day at the beach she said to me, '*Meine Mutter erzählte mir wenn die Tommies kommen ich bin nach Hause laufen.*' ('My mother told me if the Tommies come I am to run home.')

Had they heard something on the radio? Were the Allies near? Maybe we would get out of here after all. I stayed on the beach while the children and the young maid swam, hoping they would be safe. I never told Frau Doktor that I could not swim.

On a lovely still autumn morning I was heading to the doctor's house at about 4.30 a.m., taking my time. It was dark and the village had not yet stirred. The only sound was my own footsteps. Suddenly, I thought I heard someone behind me. When I quickened my pace, the other footsteps quickened too. My heart missed a beat. Then a woman's voice called out, '*Irländer!*'

I stopped, turned around and saw a figure standing a few yards away from me. There did not seem to be anybody else with her.

'*Morgen, meine Dame.*'

'*Morgen, Irländer.*'

She asked me if I would chop wood for her as she had no one to do this work. I explained that I was on my way to Dr Heidbreder's house but that I would try to do it for her later. She pointed out her house to me and I walked on. That evening on my back to the camp I stopped at her house.

'*Irländer, komm herein.*' ('Irishman, come in.')

'*Nein, meine Dame. Ich bin hier um das Holz zu hacken.*' ('No, Mam. I am here to chop the wood.')

She seemed to have forgotten that she had asked me to chop the wood for her but she came out of the house and I followed her around to the back where she gave me an axe. There was already a good pile of wood there but I did not ask any questions: I just chopped what was left, which did not take me long. As I put away the axe, she called from the house, '*Irländer, Kaffee und Essen?*'

I was not going to refuse coffee or food so I went to the kitchen door but there was no one in the kitchen. A voice called out from a room beside the kitchen, '*Hier drinnen.*' ('In here.')

I stepped into the room and saw a pot of coffee and a plate of biscuits on the table. As she handed me a cup of it she pointed to the chaise longue and told me to sit down.

I walked over and sat down. She sat at the other end of it. Now I was getting worried. I really was an innocent and I knew nothing about women's wiles. But it suddenly dawned on me the woman was lonely; there were no other young men in the village. I was not at home. I was not free. I was still a prisoner of war and I definitely should not have been where I was. The coffee went sour in my stomach. I thought to myself, 'This is a trick to get me caught.'

I got up, put the cup on the table and made for the door, thanking her. She told me that just beyond her house there was a track that ran across the fields and was a short cut to the camp. I thanked her, left as fast as I could and found the well-trodden piece of ground just where she said it would be. I started down it when a man's voice called out '*Halt!*'

I stopped and waited. If this was a Gestapo guard, what would I tell him? An old man came out from the darkness right beside me. I had passed him and had not seen him.

'*Wo kommen Sie her?*' ('Where are you coming from?')

'*Dr Heidbreder Haus.*'

He looked at me.

'*Wo gehen Sie hin?*' ('Where are you going?')

'*Arbeitserziehungslager.*'

He grunted at me and walked away. My heart started beating again. Obviously, I had given the correct answer and this was indeed a shortcut to the camp.

While I walked, it dawned on me that the old man must have seen me come out of the woman's house; if he had and reported it, I would be in serious trouble. No one would believe that I had not taken advantage of an opportunity like that. I had been brought up to respect women. It was a really stupid thing to have done; I knew the law. I felt sick as I thought about it.

Kommandant Walhorn had returned to work part-time. My only hope was to speak to him before the old man did. The track eventually led me to the back of the Farge camp where the concentration camp prisoners were. I did not look in, but walked around by the fence until I got to the gate of the *AEL*. I went straight to the administration building and asked to speak to Kommandant Walhorn. I explained what had happened and he heard me out. He asked me to tell him where the shortcut was then he took pen and paper and wrote a note, which he handed to me.

'*Wenn Sie wieder gestoppt, wird zeigen diese Notiz.*' ('If you are stopped again, show this note.')

I did not know what the note said because my German was not good enough for that but I put it in my pocket and left the administration building.

The next day when I got to the shortcut the old man stepped out. This time I took the note from my pocket and passed it to him. He read it, looked at me and smiled as he handed it back to me. He gave me a friendly salute and walked away. It was not much of a shortcut so I decided not to bother with it after that. I never saw the old man again.

When the weather was bad, Frau Heidbreder found jobs for me to do in the house. For instance, I had to clean the parquet flooring in the dining room using wire wool. The wire wool was hard on the fingers but it was an easier job than scrubbing the cement kitchen floor at home. Another job was to scrape down the varnish on the hardwood windows and doors; I used a piece of glass for this. The doctor kept a rabbit and one of my jobs was to take the rabbit to a local farmer who had a buck, to mate them. The offspring went into the pot for Sunday dinner. On Sundays, the Irishmen were allowed to go for walks in the local area. The villagers greeted me as I walked, with a nod and '*Irländer*'. When I called to Dr Heidbreder's house, Frau Doktor always ensured that there was a portion of stew with a small piece of rabbit in it for me.

18

HELL CAMP, BREMEN FARGE

IN DECEMBER 1944, Kommandanten Walhorn and Schipper were replaced by Kommandant Schauwacker. Talk in the camp was that he had been the leader of a Nazi extermination unit that, in one night in November 1941, murdered more than 3,000 people in Kerch, Crimea. On his orders, people were marched out into the streets – men, women and children – and were used for target practice.

During his time in the *AEL*-Farge camp, he was an inhuman, cruel and brutal man, especially to the Polish and Russians prisoners. He beat one Polish prisoner with a hose, shot him in the leg and then rubbed salt into the wound. The wound went gangrenous so Schauwacker told the guard to shoot the poor man. Schauwacker used some of the camp prisoners for target practice, making them run backwards and forwards while he shot at them – like ducks at a fairground shooting gallery. We watched this dreadful sight from our barracks window, utterly helpless. I climbed into my bunk and put my jacket over my head but I could still hear the shots. I do not know if he killed any of them.

Everyone was on their guard; there was no place to hide and no one was safe in the square. Yet we had to stand there in line, for counting, feeding and marching to and from work. He could appear calm, just watching, then pounce on a poor man for no reason. Schauwacker never touched any of the Irishmen, as though there was some sort of protective shield around us. He must have known from the records that the Irish chargé d'affaires was working on our behalf and that the authorities in Berlin were aware of us. This seemed to frustrate him because he appeared to be even more vicious to the *AEL* prisoners when we were around.

Schauwacker was, some would say, an ordinary, pleasant-looking man, dark-haired and of average height. In peacetime, he would have been lost in a crowd, but in a Nazi uniform, he was a monster. I was on edge all the time. I made it my business never to be on my own when he was near and to get out of the camp as quickly as possible each morning to the safety of Dr Heidbreder's house. I noticed that Dr Heidbreder was spending less time at home. Once Schauwacker arrived, the doctor's workload in the camps increased. He looked tired all the time.

Schauwacker drowned one prisoner by holding him upside down in the overnight barrel. This barrel was carried out every morning by six prisoners from each barracks, to be emptied into the cesspit. We were in the square when he caught the prisoner by the ankles, turned him upside down and pushed him head first into the barrel. He smiled all the time and held the struggling man until he stopped moving. The other prisoners stood, like us, unable to do anything. When the prisoner stopped struggling, Schauwacker sauntered off to the administration building.

Two Russian *AEL* prisoners tried to escape but were captured. Schauwacker ordered them into the administration building where they were made to drop their pants. Two guards held them while Schauwacker whipped them until they were skinned. Then he rubbed salt into their raw, bleeding wounds and made them walk out of the administration building. I heard their screams and saw them stagger towards the sickbay when he released them. But they did not make it. He shot them dead before they reached the door.

While Schauwacker was in the *AEL*-Farge camp, I was in a state of constant fear. When would he start shooting us? We Irishmen were luckier than other prisoners: any of us working for the villagers or farmers legged it out of the camp as soon as we got our ladle of soup and did not return until the end of the day. The others in our group who stayed made repairs or kept the camp clean so that they did not draw attention to themselves.

The food had always been meagre but now the portions were smaller and the soup was like dishwater. The *AEL* camp prisoners were starving. Some of those who were put on kitchen duty tried to sneak potato skins from the scrapheap or eat raw potatoes. If the *AEL* prisoners were reduced to this, what were the concentration camp prisoners eating?

One day as I was going out the gate, Hans Mayer pointed out one of these prisoners to me. The man was rolling on the ground, groaning and holding his swollen stomach.

'*Er hat rohen Kartoffeln gegessen. Er ist vergiftet und sterben wird.*' ('He has eaten raw potatoes. He is poisoned and is going to die.')

His body was in the mass grave when I returned later that day.

Schauwacker killed men he caught scavenging for potato skins on the scrapheap. When he caught a Russian *AEL* camp prisoner scavenging he held him down with one hand. He stuffed potato and filth into the man's mouth and then, using a piece of wire which he found on the scrapheap, he shoved the filth down that prisoner's throat until he was dead. We stopped looking out the window after that. The feeling of rage and helplessness was dreadful. We could do nothing.

Schauwacker enjoyed playing cat and mouse with the prisoners. I watched him from the yard.

'Will I shoot you? … No I won't … Move. I shoot you … Don't move. I shoot you …'

He pulled the trigger. Click, click – no bullet! He pulled the trigger again. Click, click – bang! It was horrific. I turned away. An elderly Pole was picked on by Schauwacker. He made him run back and forth across the yard, back and forth, back and forth, while he shot at him. He did not kill him – he just destroyed his mind. That poor man was left babbling like a child. When Mayer arrived in the camp, he found the man in the square. He was absolutely shocked and horrified when he saw the condition of the prisoner. The policeman took the Pole to the sickbay where he died later that day.

I went out to Herr Doktor's house on Christmas Eve. It was snowing heavily and was bitterly cold. The village looked wonderful: people had put wreaths made with twigs, berries and colourful ribbons on their doors. I was greeted excitedly by the Heidbreder children.

'*Fröhliche Weihnachten, Onkel Harry.*' ('Merry Christmas, Uncle Harry.')

I was brought into the kitchen to the warmth of the lit stove and lovely aromas. In Germany, unlike Ireland, Christmas dinner is eaten on Christmas Eve, and the Heidbreders invited me to stay for it. I sat in the kitchen with Anna, who kept her silence, while we ate the delicious rabbit stew, followed by coffee. Frau Doktor gave me a gift – one leather glove. I found out afterwards that it was considered unlucky to give a pair of gloves as a present. Her heart was in the right place. They were lovely people and the children were wonderful but I missed Katie. I thought of her and wondered where she was this Christmas and I thought, too, of home and my family and dared to hope that they were all safe. I said goodnight, donned my coat and put on my glove. I stuffed my other hand into my coat pocket and headed back through the snow to the camp. January and February 1945 were among the coldest winter months of the twentieth century in Europe, with blizzards and temperatures as low as minus 25 degrees Celsius. Temperatures were well below freezing until the middle of March. Even though our army greatcoats were well worn by this stage, we were very glad of them. My one glove was a boon, too.

During the Christmas period I had an opportunity to speak to Dr Heidbreder about the terrible things that were happening in the camp. I confirmed his suspicions. His workload had increased and the type of injury he was treating in the sickbay was no longer work related so what I told him did not come as a surprise.

Kommandant Schauwacker was in the camp two months. During Kommandant Walhorn's time, there had been deaths in the camp, mostly from illness or work accidents. However, under Schauwacker there was a huge increase in deaths, most of them violent. The bodies were left lying where they died as a warning to us all; after a few days they were thrown naked into the mass grave. Dr Heidbreder, as the *AEL* camp doctor, had to report to Berlin to inform them of casualty numbers or epidemics. He reported the increase in deaths at the camp and at the end of February the Gestapo arrived, arrested Kommandant Schauwacker and took him away.

When I returned from Dr Heidbreder's house that night, all the men were talking about it and there was great speculation as to how it had come about. Our officers, who were in their work hut, saw the Gestapo arrive and said they could not believe their eyes when they saw Schauwacker being marched away. He was replaced by Kommandant Voss who stayed at the camp for approximately two weeks; he was followed by Kommandant Schrader. As far as I know, there were no prisoners shot once Kommandant Schauwacker was taken away.

The new *kommandanten* were not violent men but, although the fear abated, we were still prisoners at their mercy. There was no word from Con Cremin and I had given up hope. Even though the Irish and German authorities knew of our whereabouts, no one appeared to be doing anything to repatriate us. Bremen had been bombed and there had been several sorties over us. We were in danger of being killed by our own bombs.

We did not know that the war had turned against Germany; the Allies were getting closer and Russia was regaining ground. In Bremen-Farge the pace of work on Bunker Valentin had increased significantly; every day there seemed to be more and more concentration camp prisoners on the site. From the farthest end of the doctor's garden

I could see the bunker in the distance and the prisoners working on the roof. They were like ants swarming everywhere. I was very thankful that we no were no longer working on the site.

William Hutchinson Knox, who had been ill for some time, became worse; his swollen stomach gave him great pain. Herr Doktor came on a Sunday to operate on him. Four of us moved him to a lower bunk and held him down for the operation. Knox never said a word. Dr Heidbreder made an incision in his side and put a very fine funnel in under a rib. Fluid gushed out. Knox seemed to be more comfortable afterwards. At the end of February Knox developed the same symptoms as before. I asked Dr Heidbreder if he could do anything for him but he told me that Knox had cancer and that there was nothing more he could do for him; he had no medicine or painkillers. The doctor was telling the truth: there really was no medicine by that time; neither the black nor white jars of ointment were of any use to Knox.

Dr Heidbreder told me what to do to give Knox some relief. He was on his bed, the top bunk up against the wall. I turned him on his side while two of the other men held him. Again, he never spoke. I found the spot, just as Herr Doktor had told me, and as I had seen him do previously, took the funnel and punctured the skin just below one of his ribs to release the fluid. Knox's breathing became easier and less laboured. Unfortunately, it was not a cure. The next day Dr Heidbreder sent Knox to Bremen Hospital. Two days later, on 2 March 1945, he died.

Towards dusk one evening, the doctor had just arrived home and the family were in the dining room. Anna had prepared the evening meal and the young maid and I were in the kitchen with her. We heard planes and then explosions. The house shook. The young maid was terrified but could not run home. The Allies were trying to bomb Bunker Valentin. Dr Heidbreder rushed all of us down into the cellar. He gave me a candle to hold and was surprised that my hand did not shake. Nobody said anything. I turned and went upstairs to the yard to see the bombs and young Uwe ran up after me. I watched with mixed emotions as they bounced off that monster. Of course I wanted our lads to destroy it but at the same time I was proud of the work all the slave labourers had done. Those bombs made only small dents. I remember thinking that if it could not be destroyed, then all of us would be remembered and also thinking that our lads were close and that surely we would be found soon and repatriated. It was 27 March.

Then the Allies dropped two massive bombs which penetrated the thinnest part of the roof. They did not manage to destroy Bunker Valentin fully but they ensured that it would never be used for its purpose. We were approximately 1.5 km from the bunker so those huge bombs might as well have been in the back garden. Herr Doktor pulled the two of us back down into the cellar where we stayed until the bombing ended. It was not too long a wait for me but I am sure that for the doctor and his household it felt like a lifetime. While Doktor and Frau Heidbreder comforted Mareike, Enno and the baby, Uwe stayed with me. When it became quiet, we all went back up to the kitchen. Frau Heidbreder was pleased to see that there was no damage done to her home, not even a broken pane of glass. I was happy for her. Later, back in the camp, there was plenty of speculation in the barracks. We wondered how close the Allies were and if they knew that we were here.

When Katie came back from university in April, she was in a terrible state. She had made the 1,000 km trek from Poland on foot. Her parents brought her to Dr Heidbreder's where she stayed so that he could keep an eye on her recovery. One afternoon, when Frau Doktor went to visit a neighbour, I took the opportunity to sneak upstairs to Katie's room. I knocked on the door and looked in. Katie looked awful. Her feet were sticking out from under the blankets and they were heavily bandaged. Katie was very upset when she saw me for two reasons: it was against the law and, more importantly, she did not want me to see her in that state. I did not want to upset my friend so I promised her that I would not sneak into the house again, that I would wait until she was better to talk to her. I crept out of the house.

That same day when I arrived back in the camp, a Latvian Gestapo guard came into the barracks.

'*Holen Sie sich Ihre Sachen und außen schnellwas!*' ('Get your belongings and outside quickly!')

We did not know that in other camps all over Europe, German troops were pulling out and marching back to Germany; they took the prisoners of war with them for protection. We grabbed what belongings we had, which were precious little, and went out into the square. We were the only prisoners there. I looked at Billy and could feel the familiar knot of fear in my stomach. A Gestapo guard approached us and ordered us to march out of the camp. As we marched he told us that we were going back to Milag.

Milag. Had I heard him correctly? Were we really going back to Milag?

The guard was not intimidating in any way; in fact, his gun was hung loosely over his shoulder and he was trying to make conversation with us as we marched. This made me even more nervous. Billy seemed to be lost in his thoughts, too. Some of the older men were trying to work out what was going on.

'Reckon our lads must be close if we're going back to Milag.'

It sounded great but no one seemed to be convinced.

We were marched past the doctor's house but I did not see anyone there. I thought of the children and how I would miss them. I never got to say 'goodbye' or thank the Heidbreders or Katie. Many years later I was told that little Mareike had cried for three days and that the children kept asking, '*Wo ist Onkel Harry?*' ('Where is Uncle Harry?') Dr Heidbreder told them that I had gone home. We had disappeared again and all traces of us at the *AEL*-Farge camp were gone too.

As we were marched past Herr Günther's Nursery in Neuenkirchen, a lorry came along and our guard flagged it down. Ginger O'Dwyer recognised a driver who delivered building materials to the bunker site. Our guard told him to take us to Milag, but he refused. There was an exchange of words between the two of them. No civilian would dare refuse a command from an armed Gestapo guard but that was what had just happened. I looked at the others, who had noticed it, too. To our surprise, the guard never pulled his gun.

The officers in our group realised that there had been a shift in power. They called out to the guard and showed him the few cigarettes they had bartered for with the little boats they had made. The guard understood. He offered the cigarettes to the driver who eventually agreed to take us the whole way to Milag. We climbed into the back of the lorry and our guard climbed into the cab with the driver. It was necessary for him to stay with us as we had no papers and we were wearing British Army uniforms. Without written Gestapo orders, any German troops we met along the way would shoot us and our driver. The guard had been ordered to deliver twenty-seven prisoners of war to the camp authorities in Milag and to complete the transfer papers in triplicate, before he could take up his duties. He, too, was being transferred to Milag. The journey took about an hour and finally, after twenty-seven months, we were back at the gate of Milag Camp.

19

RETURN TO WESTERTIMKE AND LIBERATION

THE TRUCK STOPPED at the gate of Milag. We helped each other climb down and thanked our driver, who gave us a friendly wave as he turned and drove back to Neuenkirchen. It was late afternoon when we walked into Milag with our guard. I do not know what the others expected by way of a welcome but I expected some of the Merchant Navy POWs to ask us what had happened; we were like skeletons. The POWs in Milag had reduced rations but had not had to work like us. No one asked what had happened to their letters, which we had taken with us when left in January 1943. There was no one calling out like they had the first time we arrived in Milag und Marlag Nord, 'Over here, lads. There's a free bunk here.'

Instead, as we went further into the camp, merchant seamen jostled us as we walked by, calling out, 'Here's the fucking Irish … look at them.'

'Serves them right. Whatever happened to them, they deserved it.'

'No sympathy here for you lot.'

It was awful. The men around us were angry and resentful, cursing and saying spiteful things. I could not understand it at all. I actually felt that I had been safer in the *Arbeitserziehungslager*. We did not know that a rumour had spread throughout the camp after we left that we had signed up to work *frei* for Germany. In their minds, we were traitors.

Billy and I stuck together. With over 4,000 prisoners of war in Milag alone, it was very difficult to find merchant seamen we knew. Billy eventually found us bunks in one of the barracks and we moved in. The other lads sent us to Coventry. Christy Ryan found some of his old mates and it was through them that we heard about the rumour. Christy explained to them that we had never signed up or worked *frei* for Germany. He told them that we were twenty-seven months in a slave labour camp, starved, beaten and worked into the ground. He told them about the deaths of our five comrades and that we had worked for the villagers and farmers in recent months during our captivity, just like some of them did in Milag. This information was passed throughout the camp.

When we went to the shower block and stripped off, it was obvious we had not had a good time. Some of the lads wanted to talk to us but Billy and I refused. I wanted to forget the horrors and the person I had become for some of that time.

John Hipton, a British Merchant seaman and prisoner of war in Milag, had seen us go and return. Years after the war he was interviewed and asked about the treatment meted out to the Irish and British by the Nazis. He is recorded as saying: 'I do think the Irish were given worse treatment by the Nazis than the British were. And how these Irish seamen from a neutral country were able to survive for as long as they did in that slave labour camp is just a credit to the human spirit.'

When Sunday came around, I saw men going to Mass but I did not join them. How could I go? How could I receive Holy Communion? I had not been to Confession. How could I tell a priest that I had stolen bread from a dying man? I knew that there were three priests in the camp but I did not know if Fr Juno was one of them; if he was, he did not come looking for me.

By listening to the rumours, we found out that several escape tunnels had been dug in Milag. The first was built between March and August 1943 and was about 12 metres long. Twelve prisoners escaped but were recaptured within two weeks. The second tunnel about 40 metres long and was built between April and August 1944. Five prisoners escaped but were soon recaptured. The third tunnel, which was built by Norwegian prisoners of war, was discovered before its completion and the fourth was dug to store contraband, such as wireless parts.

Prisoners of war from other camps had been arriving constantly since Christmas 1944. The numbers in Marlag Camp had nearly doubled, causing serious overcrowding. Food rations were reduced to cater for the increased numbers. Prisoners from different camps had different experiences; it was through these survivors that we heard the stories of what later became known as 'the Long March', which made our own transfer seem like a Sunday outing. As the Russian Army advanced, the Gestapo evacuated POW camps and forced over 80,000 POWs to march west towards Germany, using them as human shields. Farm wagons were used to carry those unable to walk and were pulled by other prisoners in blinding blizzards, often sinking knee deep in snow. Villagers reacted differently. Some threw bricks and stones while others shared the last of their food with prisoners. Those who tried to escape were shot. Those who could not keep up were left to die at the side of the road.

Many German civilians joined these groups of prisoners because they, too, were fleeing from the advancing Russians. I thought about Katie then. Because of food shortages, prisoners on the Long March were reduced to eating dogs, cats, rats and grass – anything they could find. Thousands of prisoners of war died along the way, from exhaustion, pneumonia, diphtheria and typhus. Sleeping outside on frozen ground in temperatures of minus 25 degrees Celsius resulted in frostbite, often requiring amputation of extremities. The prisoners of war were also vulnerable to air attacks by Allied forces who mistook them for retreating columns of German troops, which, of course, was what the German authorities had planned. Allied forces advancing from the west liberated the prisoners they met. However, not all were so lucky. In some cases, the German troops changed direction and marched the prisoners towards the Baltic Sea. By the time they were liberated, some prisoners of war had marched over 800 km while others had marched nearly nearly twice that distance.

On 2 April 1945 the *kommandant* of Marlag Nord announced to the Navy prisoners there that he had orders from Berlin to abandon the camp. He was to leave a small detachment of guards behind to hand over to the Allies, who were already in Bremen. There was a great buzz in the Milag

Camp on hearing this news. However, that same afternoon over 100 *SS-Feldgendarmerie*, or German military police, arrived at Marlag. They rounded up 3,000 Navy prisoners of war and marched them out of the camp, heading east. Mistaking them for retreating German troops, the RAF attacked them several times over the next couple of days and many prisoners were killed.

On 9 April the last of the German guards left both Milag and Marlag and were replaced by much older men, the *Volkssturm* or Home Guard. Although not threatening, they were responsible for keeping order and the day-to-day running of the camps. On 19 April the rumours were confirmed: Germany was losing the war and the Allies were close by. The many skilled engineers and craftsmen in the Merchant Navy and the Navy had bartered their Red Cross cigarettes, 100 of which were worth 250 marks, for the parts needed to make old-fashioned crystal wireless sets. Tuned to the BBC broadcasts, they kept us informed of the war's progress and this information was passed from barracks to barracks. Of course, there were regular raids by the camp guards who found and confiscated a few of the wireless sets, but not all of them. The prisoners sold more cigarettes to buy back the parts and start all over again.

That same day, word was sent to us in Milag from the Navy in Marlag that there were German tanks lining up outside the wire fence at the back of their camp. Wave after wave of tanks rolled up; we could hear the rumbling in the distance. The 15th *Panzergrenadier* Division positioned themselves outside Marlag Camp. In the meantime, word was sent rapidly through both camps that the Allies were advancing at the Milag side.

'Quickly, lads. Start digging trenches.'

We did not have to be told twice. We set to with whatever we could get our hands on – pieces of wood, even our hands – to dig trenches between the barracks. These trenches were about 2 foot deep and not very long. They could accommodate two men hunkered down together. We didn't have time, energy or equipment to dig anything deeper or longer. Then the shooting started.

We dived into those trenches, crouched down and covered our heads with our arms, trying to make ourselves as small as possible. The Germans fired over and through the camp at the approaching Allied troops. There were bullets flying everywhere and there were explosions, too. I did not stick my head up to see what was happening but just stayed down in that trench and hoped that I would survive. After what must have been a few hours, but what felt like an eternity, the firing stopped and there was silence. We all stayed where we were in case the shooting started up again. The men's voices could be heard now:

'Are they finished?'

'Our lads must be close.'

'Can we move yet? My legs are cramping.'

'What's happening now?'

'Can anyone hear anything?'

Then word came through the camp from Marlag Nord: 'The German tanks are leaving!'

A cheer went up.

We climbed out of our trenches and stretched our legs, then slowly walked around to check where the mortars had landed and if any damage had been done. Miraculously, there was no damage and, better still, no one had been injured. The firing had gone over us and the battle moved elsewhere.

There was a nervous energy in Milag now. We gathered around the wireless sets as much as possible while always keeping a watch out for the *Volkssturm*. The British Guards Armoured Division was getting closer. The division was made up of the Grenadier Guards, Coldstream Guards, Scots Guards, Irish Guards and the Welsh Guards. On 27 April 1945 at 2 a.m., we heard the rumbling noise of a tank and other vehicles approaching our camp.

'Not again,' I thought, running out of the barracks and heading for the slit trenches.

We did not care about Rule Number 1 any more: we were all outside after dark and we had no fear of the *Volkssturm*. Then a roar went up from those nearest the gate.

'It's our lads. They're here!'

We climbed out of the trenches and from all over the camp men were walking quickly to the gates of Milag. Then they started running and I joined them in the charge. When I got to the square, I saw a big tank at the entrance to the camp. Men were cheering, laughing and crying. I was cheering with the rest of them. This was no dream: the Allies were here and we were going to be freed! Then the top of the tank opened and a head appeared. It was an Irish Guard and he called out.

'Is there a Richard Flynn here? … Has anyone seen a Richard Flynn? … My father, Richard Flynn?'

I could not believe it. Dick, who had been with me in the *AEL* camp? Could it be the same man? One or two voices started calling out, 'Dick Flynn? Richard Flynn?'

Then the Irish Guard shouted out, 'Dick Flynn from Waterford. He was on the *Orama.*'

It *was* our Dick Flynn! He was here somewhere. Imagine, his own son here at the gate! I was shouting 'YES! YES!'

I could hear some of my comrades from the *AEL* camp calling out too. Now everyone was calling back through the crowd, 'Richard Flynn … Dick Flynn … Waterford … *Orama*.'

'HERE! He's here!'

There was Dick being pushed forward. The crowd was like a curtain opening to let him through, then closing back in behind him. The joy and excitement were electrifying. It felt like every one of us at that moment was part of Dick Flynn. The Irish Guard jumped down from the tank and gathered his father into his arms. They stood there in the middle of that huge crowd, locked in an embrace. There was a hushed silence for a few seconds. Tears streamed down my face. There were grown men all around me in that square, with big grins on their faces and tears running down their cheeks.

The silence ended and a huge cheer went up. Hats were thrown into the air. Men hugged each other and jumped up and down. The tank at the gate was the reconnaissance unit of the Guards Armoured Division. I was so proud that it was the Irish Guards who had rescued us. It was later that day before the rest of the Guards Armoured Division arrived. The bar was wrenched off the gates as the square filled with vehicles and our khaki-uniformed troops. The excitement was overwhelming. We climbed up on the tanks as they drove around and cheered our heads off, waving hats and jackets, laughing and crying. We were like children again and there was a madness in the air. We had survived. Then things went quiet. It was as if every prisoner suddenly realised that he was free and remembered missing friends who had not made it.

A voice started to sing. Others joined him. Another man danced and others just jumped about cheering. Then the crowd was off again, joining in the mayhem. One man who still had his bagpipes was joined by a Welsh Guard. The two of them marched through the camp playing those bagpipes; it was a wonderful sound to hear. Grown men would suddenly jump up and start dancing a reel or a jig when the bagpipe players were near. Yes, it was madness – but what a joyful madness it was!

Towards evening, some of the men who worked on nearby farms went off to get more food. There was not much available because the local people had very little left. They had vegetables, however, and one of the farms had a couple of pigs. The men arrived back with their bounty and a huge fire was built in the square. Two spits were made and the pigs were roasted over the flames. Smaller fires were built all over the camp and vegetable soup was made. Darkness arrived. Out of habit, I started to move towards my barracks. Then I stopped. No one was moving. The spotlights on the watchtowers still shone and the lights in the camp were still lit. I sat down again beside a fire and joined in the talk and laughter. There were no more rules: we stayed out after dark and crossed the fence just to show that we could and we left the lights on as we partied all night long. Next morning, the remains of the pigs were still on the spits. I had not eaten any: I remembered only too well what had happened when I had gorged myself on the rich soup out on the farm. The smell of that cooking pig made me nauseous.

The liberation of over 6,000 men was not an easy task. The Allies had not expected to find so many of us and there were food shortages until provisions were sent from the rear. The elation was gone and replaced with discontent, which at times spilled over into angry outbursts.

'At least the Germans fed us.'

'Where's the food?'

'We're free men. Why can't we go home?'

It took nearly two weeks for the supplies to arrive. I had been eating potato or rye bread since 1941, some of the men since the beginning of the war. When we finally got some white bread, it was like eating cake.

By now the Guards Armoured Division were better organised and they sorted us into groups. Those who had arrived at the camp first were to leave first, and so on. The Allies intended to use Milag und Marlag Nord as a prison camp for those Germans accused of war crimes who were awaiting trial. Their fate would be decided by Allied judges. Because of this, the Guards Armoured Division were anxious to get all of us out of the camp. Priority was given to the sick and injured. The medics walked around the camp, and in and out of the barracks, identifying injured and sick men, who they directed to the square where they had set up tables.

A medic spotted me and told me to follow him. In February I had shown Dr Heidbreder a sore on the left side of my face. He had apologised for having nothing to give me for it and told me to leave it alone. It became scabbed, septic and very sore and had now reached my eye. When we got to the square a medic asked me to lie on one of the tables. Then, using tweezers, he pulled off the scab and cleaned the area with methylated spirits. I clenched my teeth and groaned; I will never forget the pain of that sting. They told me that my face would heal and I went back to my barracks, trying not to feel sorry for myself; there were far worse cases than mine.

Billy and I watched as more and more of our merchant seamen were sent home. Finally, it was our turn. The Allies had a roster of capture dates and names of ships and their crew; they also had prisoner-of-war numbers which they matched with the tags around our necks. An Allied guard walked through the camp calling out prisoner-of-war numbers and eventually I heard 90882 called.

We lined up with the others to be moved that day. I wore my army clothes and in my pocket was my piece of soap and one glove. I had no other possessions.

This time we were happy to climb into the waiting British Army lorries. There were at least a couple of hundred men moved out on each run. Because Billy and I were captured at the same time, we were moved out of Milag on the same day. Although we were crammed into the lorries, this time the canvas covers were not pulled down. We were able to see the countryside and the atmosphere was light-hearted. After a two-hour drive we arrived at a field camp. I groaned and said to Billy, 'Not another bloody camp. I thought we were going home.'

'We're back where we started, Harry. Another holding camp.'

We were disheartened when we looked around and saw tents everywhere. At least we had some shelter. We formed a long line and the Army officer in charge said, 'You'll be billeted here for a week or two and will be flown home as soon as possible. When you get your blanket, find yourselves room.'

There were rows and rows of white canvas tents and eventually we found room in one of them. There were no beds, just a ground sheet; we rolled into our blankets and slept on the ground. The Army fed us a bowl of soup and white bread three times a day.

The first couple of days were not too bad. It was early May and the weather was mild. But then it started to rain. It was raining when we went to sleep and it was raining when we woke up. It poured down in torrents and did not let up. We were all miserable and some of the tents started to leak. Then there was a shortage of food and rations were reduced. The men began to grumble. There were angry scenes when the merchant seamen confronted the officers in charge.

'What are we doing here in the middle of nowhere?'

'Where are the planes that are supposed to be getting us home?'

'What the hell did you take us out of our barracks for? We're drowning here.'

'Yeah, at least we were dry in our barracks.'

'We need food. Where's the food?'

Tensions mounted. The crowd became a mob and finally the officer on watch reported what was happening. The Army trained their guns on us. It was an awful thing to see our own Army pointing their guns at us. The mob quietened down. Thankfully no one was shot. People backed away and went into their tents out of the relentless rain. A few days later, having sat in our tent for most of the day trying to keep dry, I looked at Billy and said, 'I don't know about you, but I'm out of here.'

'Where are you going?'

'We're in the countryside. There has to be a farmhouse with a barn around here somewhere. At least we'd be in out of this awful rain and we'd be dry.'

'Well, I'm with you, Harry. We've been here five days and it doesn't look like we're leaving here for another week anyway. So let's go.'

There were thousands of men in that field, but there was no roll call and no one checked us as we walked out. We walked through the rain and mud for a few miles until we came to a farm. There was a yard with sheds and a big barn attached to the farmhouse; there was no sign of anyone about.

'What do you think, Billy?'

'I think there's someone watching us from the farmhouse. We'd better be careful.'

An elderly man approached from the barn, smiling.

'Over to you, Harry. Say something to him.'

'*Guten Tag.*'

The man stopped and continued to smile at us.

'*Dürften wir für ein paar Nächte in Ihrem Stall bleiben?*' ('May we stay in your barn for a few nights?')

'*Sie sind Tommies. Sie müssen ins Haus kommen. Bitte, bitte.*' ('You are Tommies. You must come into the house. Please, please.')

We followed him through the barn and into the farmhouse; there was no sign of any livestock. His wife stood at the kitchen table nervously waiting for him. The old man told her that we were Tommies, that we had asked to use the barn for a few nights and that she was to get food quickly. Soon there was the smell of coffee brewing and there was delicious bread and jam too. We told them that we were *Irländers* and not Tommies; British Merchant seamen – liberated prisoners of war – and on our way home. They never told us their names, but bade us sleep in the house. They led us upstairs to a spare bedroom in which there was a huge bed. We could not believe our luck. We fell onto that bed and were asleep in minutes. It was heaven.

We woke the next morning to a knock on the bedroom door and breakfast in bed: bacon and egg and a cup of coffee each. I had to be dreaming! They waited while we ate, smiling at us all the time. We did not want to be rude and so we made ourselves take our time. Later that day, we walked around the farmland with the elderly man and afterwards, sitting at the kitchen table, he told us that there had been a lot of theft in the area and the livestock was gone. Vegetables had been stolen from the fields too. Now he was happy because, if there was anyone hiding out in the fields, they would see the 'Tommies' with him and hopefully leave his farm alone. We stayed a second night at the farmhouse.

Then Billy said, 'Harry, we can't stay any longer. They're sharing what food they have with us. We don't want to miss the plane. We'd better leave soon.'

He was right. So in the morning when we went downstairs, we told the farmer and his wife that we had to leave.

'*Wir sind bereits fast fünf Jahre hier wir haben jetzt nach Irland zurückzukehren. Vielen Dank für Ihre Gastfreundschaft.*' ('We've been here nearly five years, we have to return to Ireland now. Thank you for your hospitality.')

The elderly lady threw her arms around us and hugged us. Her husband shook our hands and they both wished us a safe journey home.

20

GOING HOME

WE HAD NOT BEEN MISSED. Two days after we returned
to the field camp, we were told to assemble at the gate
where Army lorries were waiting for us. The rain had finally
stopped. They told us that they were taking us to an airfield
about an hour's drive away.

I had never seen a plane on the ground or up close. There
were a lot of them. I heard some of the men say that they
were either DC-3s or Dakotas. The RAF rushed us along,
dividing us into groups of fifty. Billy and I managed to
stick together. A crew member directed us to the steps and
we quickly climbed on board as the engines fired up. The
whole plane began to vibrate and the noise was deafening.
The only thing I could see was a long wooden bench on
each side of the plane and we sat down promptly. We were
told that these were the planes the paratroopers jumped
from and not to worry, we were in safe hands. To be honest,
I was more excited than nervous; for a little while I was
sixteen again and this was an adventure.

There were no windows. They told us that we were
going to Brussels and that it would take about two hours.

We bumped across the airfield. The engines revved up, the plane shook and the benches vibrated. This really hurt my bony backside, but I was not going to complain. We were lost in our own thoughts when the captain sent back word that we were coming in to land and to hang onto our seats. The plane touched the ground. I thought we were never going to stop. I realised that I was holding my breath. We landed at Brussels Airport on 5 May 1945.

In the terminal building, an RAF crew member led us to a row of tables behind which sat British civilian men. There were queues of former prisoners of war at each table, some more dishevelled than others and all looking a lot older than they really were. Most of us were dazed and confused. I stood behind Billy as the line shuffled forward. When he reached the table I could not hear what was being said except 'Billy English' and 'Thanks'. Then it was my turn. All I was asked for was my name. They handed me 500 Belgian francs and a sterling ten-shilling note and told me to enjoy myself in Brussels, saying they would call me when it was time to move out. I did not know how they would find me but I turned around and saw Billy waiting for me, and we walked out of the airport to the waiting British Army lorries.

British forces had freed Brussels and now there were Allied troops everywhere we looked. There was no sign of Gestapo and I could feel a giddiness building up inside me; I wanted to burst out laughing and cheering but I knew that if I started I would probably end up crying. I bottled up my emotions and just absorbed the sights and sounds around me. The driver stopped outside a hotel where there were rooms for us and where we were to stay each night until we were called to go home.

'Enjoy yourselves, lads. You're free now.'

With a wave he climbed into the cab and drove back to the airport.

When the porter showed us to our room all I could focus on was the two beds in it. They were dressed with a mattress, clean linen, a pillow and blankets. I ran my hand over the blankets and grinned at Billy who had already thrown himself onto his bed. I followed his example. We slept soundly, waking automatically at 3 a.m. We had to remind ourselves that we did not have to get up and go outside. We could stay in our beds all day if we wanted to, so we each rolled over and went back to sleep for another few hours. Hunger woke us. There was a toilet and washroom at the end of the corridor but no hot water, although we were used to that. We stepped outside into the bustle of city life.

Like us, there were men in uniform everywhere. There were bars and cafés on every street, theatres, cinemas and dance halls; we walked around in a daze. Eventually, we stopped for a coffee and sandwich and got talking to some British soldiers in the café. They invited us to join them at another café where we could get a beer and meet some girls, so we joined them. Billy really enjoyed his first beer and I enjoyed my lemonade. (I was having enough trouble coming to terms with everything so I was not about to start drinking alcohol.) There was no talk of war, yet we were all scarred by it. After a few beers Billy and I decided to leave and have a walk around the city to get our bearings.

Just outside our hotel we saw two girls coming towards us. Billy decided to ask them where we could find a cheap café. They were Belgian but spoke a little English and told us that they would show us where there was one. We walked with them through the city up a side street until we came to the café, where the girls ordered for us. I was trying to take in everything: the place, the people and the sounds of talking and laughing. I definitely had hot coffee but the rest of the meal was a blur. I realised that once again I could not talk. My stomach was knotted and my body felt like a coiled spring. I kept reminding myself that I was not in Germany and that these were not German girls but I kept glancing towards the door, expecting to see Gestapo guards. Billy was totally relaxed and talked easily with the girls; every now and then he glanced my way to check that I was okay.

'Get a grip of yourself, Harry!' I told myself. 'Get a grip. Say something. Anything!'

So I looked at Billy and managed to say, 'Where are we going to next?'

We paid the bill and the girls agreed to show us around. Some of the cafés had music and we stopped to listen. Later on, they invited us back to their hotel. Billy accepted their invitation and so I went along with them. We went upstairs. Billy said as he disappeared into one of the rooms with his girl, 'See you later, Harry!'

The other girl stood watching me. I was twenty-one and did not know what to do. I had never been with a girl. I was terribly nervous and conscious of the scarring on my face. I stood in the corridor wondering, 'What now?' She opened the door and I went into her room; she put her arms around me and kissed me on the lips. I closed the door.

Later, I went back to my own hotel because I did not want to be missing if the Army called for us. I fell into a deep sleep so I do not know when Billy came back. The following day we went out on the town again. There were lots of soldiers and girls in all the cafés and we joined them.

Impromptu sing-songs started up and we grabbed partners for a dance; it was one big, wild party. The dancing spilled out onto the streets. When calmness descended we moved on to another café. We met plenty of girls that day and when another girl invited me back to her hotel room, there was no hesitation.

'See you later, Billy!'

Billy was in his bed when I got back to our room. Next morning once more we headed off to the cafés where we met two more girls and treated them to coffee and cake. Our Belgian money was running out so Billy suggested that we go for a walk. We linked arms with the girls and set off to walk around the city. We did not get too far. A British army lorry pulled up beside us and the driver called out, 'Are you prisoners of war?'

'We are,' we replied.

'Climb aboard, lads. You're going home!'

In my pocket was the last of my soap and the single glove. Neither of us had any other luggage. So we kissed the girls and climbed into the back of the Army lorry. I looked back once but they were already out of sight.

We picked up other prisoners of war and when the lorry was full we headed back to the airport. The planes on the airfield were not Dakotas but Lancaster Bombers. These were the same type of aircraft that had bombed Bunker Valentin. Once again, everything was very rushed. The pilots needed to get in and out of Brussels as quickly as possible. The planes could carry only up to twenty-five of us at a time. There were no seats at all – we filled the empty spaces where the bombs had been.

On board we hunkered down with knees interlocked with the men opposite us, for balance, and linked arms with the men each side of us. Our backs pressed against the sides of the plane. Billy and I could not see the gunner up top at the tail of the plane but the other men could see his gun constantly turning, keeping watch for German fighters. We were still at war. Also on board were the captain and six other crew. One of them told us that we could not move about and that if we needed to use the toilet bucket at the back of the plane, we had to call the gunner who would contact the crew up front. One of them would have to take our place to let us go. I never knew if this was a joke or not but none of us was moving, that was for sure! We stayed on our hunkers for the whole journey.

We were back in danger, back in the war and we could be blown out of the sky at any moment. There were no windows in the plane but maybe that was just as well. We were not flying very high but we were freezing. The crew wore fur-lined jackets and boots but they felt the cold too; our Army uniforms were tattered and threadbare by this stage. Then we heard the up-top gunner's voice. He sounded excited. He left his post, stuck his head down and shouted at us, 'We've won! The war is over. Germany has capitulated!'

There was stunned silence. No one said anything. We just looked at him.

'Did you hear me? We've won. The war is over!'

We found our voices then and started to cheer and sing. We wanted to jump up and down but we could not.

'Where are we now?' someone shouted.

'Over the River Rhine,' the gunner replied, before reminding us not to move. He climbed back into his position and we continued our journey. We sensed each other's excitement and there were prayers, tears and laughter but no one moved. It was 8 May 1945.

I turned to Billy and leaned my head in towards his ear, 'I hope the German pilots heard that news or else we're sitting ducks.'

The journey took approximately four hours then one of the crew shouted, 'We're coming into land, lads. Brace yourselves.'

We just held onto each other, no longer on our hunkers now but sitting on the floor of the plane still with our knees interlocked. It was early evening when we landed in RAF Base Westcott Buckinghamshire. We were among one of the first groups of prisoners of war to land there. The door opened and a voice said, 'Right, lads. You're home now. You're on British soil.'

We got to our feet and staggered to the door with pins and needles in our legs. RAF crewmen were waiting for us.

'Take it easy, lads. You'll be all right soon.'

At last we were on British soil. I had survived. I was nearly home. There were no wild celebrations. We were just a lot of ordinary men, all traumatised, hungry and exhausted, who could not believe that we were finally free and safe.

A crewman led us to the RAF administration area where a civilian clerk sat behind a table. We queued in single file, waiting our turn. This time Billy was behind me. When I got to the table I was asked for my name and home address.

'Harry Callan, 7 Derryview Terrace, Waterside, Derry.'

Then I was asked for my prisoner-of-war number.

'90882.'

The clerk checked his records. I do not know what the lists were but they could have been ships' records, missing persons, Red Cross prisoners-of-war records or a combination of all three; there were a lot of papers on his table. He ticked me off a couple of lists.

'Right, I have you here, Harry. I need your prisoner-of-war tag.'

I had put that tag around my neck in Stalag XB in April 1941 and had never taken it off. Now I handed it to the clerk who matched it against his records. He ticked off his list and placed my tag in a box with a lot of other tags.

'Are you all right for money?' he asked.

I assured him that I still had the ten-shilling note that I had been given in Brussels.

'Good man. Now if you just wait over there for a while, the doctor will see you and then we will get you sorted for the night.'

He put out his hand to me and I shook it.

'Welcome home.'

I waited for Billy. The doctor came along and asked us to strip off our jackets and shirts. Just like Dr Heidbreder, the doctor used a stethoscope and sounded our chests front and back. That was that. He did not comment on our protruding ribs or our weight loss. He did not comment on anyone's scars nor ask us what we had been eating during our captivity.

'You're fine. Just eat little and often.'

An Army lorry took us to a small hotel in Oxford, about an hour's drive away, where we spent the night. We were fed and then went to our rooms. There was a hand basin with hot and cold water but I was so exhausted that I just fell into bed. I kept reaching for my missing cord and tag. I could not stop myself from thinking that at any moment there would be a knock on the door and I would have to explain why it was missing. But there was no knock. Without my prisoner-of-war tag I had no proof. Who was going to believe what had happened to me? I slept badly. It was a long time since I had slept in a room by myself and I missed the sounds of the other men.

> *It is night. I know I'm in England but the Gestapo are here and I'm being marched out of the camp. How can this be? What's happening? I haven't crossed the wire. It's after midnight but I've been in my barracks. Why am I here? I look around for Billy or the others but there's no one there. I'm being marched out to the mass grave. I'm shouting, 'But I am alive, not dead.' The Gestapo don't hear me. I'm screaming, 'I'm a prisoner of war. Look at my tag. I have to be sent back to the Red Cross.' My hand goes to my neck but there's no tag. They're going to throw me into the mass grave. Can they not see that I'm alive? 'I'm not dead. I'm alive. Do you hear me?'*

I woke shouting out the word 'Alive.' Tears were running down my face.

For a few moments I did not know where I was. I did not sleep after that. I sat in my room waiting for morning to come and for Billy to knock on the door. He knocked at 6 a.m. I was already washed and dressed.

'All right, Harry?'

'All right, Billy.'

'Let's get our food and go home,' he said, grinning.

We went downstairs and joined the others in the dining room where we were given hot porridge, bread, jam and tea. A clerk gave us directions to the railway station and special passes for the trains. Because Billy and I were leaving the mainland to go to Ireland, we also received special boat passes and passes to travel on the Irish railways. He wished us good luck and then left.

We got a direct train to Liverpool. From there we could get a boat to Belfast and Billy could use his Irish rail ticket to get a train to Arklow in County Wicklow. We spent the three-hour journey in a comfortable silence and were able to buy a cup of tea from the tea trolley. It was a ten-minute walk to the docks but the boat to Belfast had left the previous night and only sailed on alternate nights. We were told that a boat from Holyhead to Dublin would sail later that evening and we agreed that we would try to catch a train to make the Holyhead sailing.

We saw the damage caused by the Luftwaffe to Liverpool Docks, which were very changed; there were many new buildings. There were stalls at the port selling tea and buns but we bought nothing: our breakfast had been like a full day's ration to us. We arrived in Holyhead around 2 p.m., went straight to the ticket office and showed our passes. The ticket clerk glanced at the passes then at us and said, 'Welcome home, lads!'

It felt good to walk up the gangplank and board the boat. We stood out on deck facing into the wind and listened to the familiar sounds of a busy harbour until finally the engines fired up and we pulled away from the quayside. It felt strange not having a job to do. We did not speak to anyone. We just stood there looking out to sea.

'Okay, Harry?'

'Not feeling too good, Billy.'

'I'm not feeling so good myself. Guess we need to get our sea legs back again.'

To our surprise and dismay, Billy and I were both seasick on that three-hour crossing. We were glad to walk on dry land when we reached Dublin port. We walked to the nearby railway station at Amiens Street and again presented our passes the ticket office. It was time to go our separate ways. Billy was getting the train south-east to Arklow and I was heading north-west to Derry city. This time there was no welcome from the ticket clerk, who just glanced at our passes and handed us our tickets.

We made our way towards the platforms and stood there for a minute. This was it. I had known Billy for five years and for most of that time in captivity when we had watched each other's back. Who would do that now? I had to remind myself that the war was over that we were now safe. But how to say goodbye? Embrace? Shake hands? Billy broke the silence.

'Here, Harry, let's exchange addresses. We'll get settled in at home and I'll contact you then. Maybe I'll come visit you in Derry or you could come down to Arklow to visit me?'

We verbally exchanged addresses and walked away to our respective platforms. I was on my own now. I did not look back.

I had a shock of bushy black hair that had not been cut for five years; my face was thin and bony like a skeleton's with a scar that covered a third of it; my clothes were ragged, shabby and filthy. I must have looked like a tramp. There were other people in the carriage but they just glanced at me and looked away. No wonder. They probably did not know what to make of me travelling through neutral territory in a British Army uniform. I kept my head down and did not make eye contact with anyone. At the railway station in Dundalk the train stopped and I heard someone mutter, 'Border control.'

Armed soldiers in green Irish Army uniforms came on board. They walked through the train and stopped when they saw me. I was nervous. I did not look at them and they did not ask me anything. They passed through the carriage and shortly afterwards the train left the station. Between Dundalk and Newry was the actual Border crossing. The train stopped again and this time armed British soldiers boarded. They too walked through the train but they did not stop when they saw me; to them, I was one of their own.

The train pulled into the Great Northern station in Derry city and I climbed out of the carriage. I had not written home so I was not expecting anyone to meet me but my father was standing on the platform. He stood there looking at me with a strange look on his face like he was seeing a ghost. I walked slowly towards him. He threw out his arms and I walked into that embrace.

'Son! Son!'

Father had never hugged me like that before and I did not want that hug to end.

'Come on now, son. I have a taxi waiting. We were sure that you'd get the boat from Liverpool and the train from Belfast so we were all over at the Waterside station. When you did not get off the Belfast train I came over here. Will we stop off at the station on the way in case there's anyone still there?'

'If you like, Father. I don't mind.'

I did not feel up to meeting a lot of people but Father had hired a taxi – a huge expense – just to bring me home so what could I do? My mind was reeling. Who had told him I was coming home? It did not matter. I was just glad he was there. We were heading to the taxi when we met a man who had known me as a boy. He stopped and stared at me, shocked. I was surprised when he did not say hello, but just nodded his head in my direction and walked by. I did not realise how wretched I looked. The taxi crossed the bridge and stopped at the Waterside station but there was no one there; Father was disappointed. All I wanted to do was get to Derryview Terrace.

'Come on, son. Let's get you home to the family.'

Those words gladdened my heart. We climbed back into the taxi and Father and I sat in companionable silence for the short drive.

There is an old Irish custom to put a lighted candle in the window to guide people home. The house seemed smaller than I remembered but although it was still daylight there were candles in every window; it was a very welcoming sight. As the taxi pulled away, Father turned to me and said, 'Right, son. Let's get you inside. Cassie will be waiting for us.'

For a moment I thought, 'Who's Cassie?' but then I remembered that Father had married Cassie Cusack in 1941. I took a deep breath, followed Father in the door down the hall and into the kitchen; Father left the front door open.

I noticed that the range still warmed the kitchen but my eyes were drawn to the table, which was laden with cakes and sandwiches, a big jug of milk and a bowl full of sugar; it was the first sugar I had seen since 1941. There was a young woman standing beside it: Cassie. Father introduced us and Cassie came around the table and gave me a hug.

'Welcome home, Harry!'

Before I could catch my breath I heard footsteps in the hall and then there seemed to be a unending stream of people coming through the house. All my old neighbours and their families came to say hello, shake my hand and welcome me home: the Moores, McLoughlins, Allens, McGinns, Cannings, Murphys, Hegartys and Elliotts, the

McCaffertys, Stewards and Cannings from Corrody Road, and the Gillespies from Half Mile Hill. I was stunned. I had been captured at sea and survived. I was no hero. But this was a hero's welcome.

I expected to see Aunt Ellen but she was not there. Later, I could not remember seeing Nan, George, John or Gerry but I was told afterwards that they were there with their children. As far as I knew, Edgar was still at sea. Cassie was busy at the range making numerous pots of tea while some of the ladies helped her to hand out plates of food. I could not touch a thing. The smell of sugar and sweet cake made me feel ill. With everyone talking, the noise in the house was deafening. I was too tired to talk. Eventually they all went home and Father, Cassie and I were left in the kitchen.

'Where's Eileen?' I asked Cassie.

'At work, Harry. She'll be home shortly. She wanted to be at the station but she could not get off work.'

Just then the back door burst open and Eileen ran into the kitchen. She was calling out, 'Harry, Harry! Where is he? Where is he?'

I stood up and smiled at her. Always enthusiastic, full of fun and laughter, my baby sister was now a young woman. I put out my arms ready to catch her as she charged towards me. Suddenly she stopped and went silent. She stared at me and started to cry. As suddenly as she had arrived, she turned and ran out the back door, crying hysterically.

'Harry, oh Harry! Oh God!'

I went to run after her but Cassie put out her hand to me and said, 'Leave her, Harry. She'll be fine in a little while. She was so excited about you coming home, it's just emotion and shock.'

'If you're sure, Cassie?'

'I'm sure, Harry. Now we need to get you settled. You'll be in your old room at the front of the house. Robin and Drew, your two new brothers, are already in bed in that room. You met them earlier, if you remember? Eileen is now in the back room with your new baby sister, Yvonne, and your father and I are in the parlour. Have a good night's sleep, Harry. We'll see you whenever you get up.'

I went upstairs and fell exhausted into the big bed in the front room. It felt strange to be in this bed by myself. I could not settle. I lay there listening to my baby brothers asleep in the other bed. There were so many changes here at home. It was an awful lot to take in.

21

DEALING WITH THE CHANGES IN DERRY

I HAD BEEN AWAKE SINCE 4 a.m. but I lay there with my eyes closed listening to the sounds of the house. Robin, aged four, and Drew, aged three, were excited and wanted to know all about me. Father came in and told the boys to keep quiet. I got up and went into Eileen's room to look in the mirror. Like many prisoners of war, I had no beard but my hair had grown for a while and then stopped. It was a symptom of starvation. I did not recognise myself underneath my bushy hair. The bones were jutting out on my face and the whole left side looked badly burnt. Now I could understand why Eileen had been upset.

There had been many changes downstairs too. The privy was now a proper flushing toilet and was connected to the main sewage. The midden was gone. A new extension, which was called the scullery, had a sink with running water and a gas cooker. Cassie had left a bucket of warm water and a soft towel for me. I made a lather with the soap, scrubbed my hair with my hands and then rinsed myself with that lovely warm water. It was heaven! There was electric light in the hall, the parlour and the kitchen. Candles were still used in the bedrooms, the scullery and the new privy.

I ate the bowl of porridge Cassie gave me as my little brothers watched me. I needed time to myself so I told her that I was going for a walk. She understood. She shushed the boys and told them to go outside to play. I walked around all my old haunts where it was peaceful. I stopped at the Stewards' house on Corrody Road where I knew there would be a cup of tea and a slice of bread for me. Father had told them I had been a prisoner of war so they did not ask me anything about it. Instead, we talked about the time when I delivered the groceries to them. It felt like we were talking about someone else entirely.

I left the Stewards, headed off down past the Waterside railway station, crossed Craigavon Bridge and waited outside the shirt factory where Eileen worked. Eventually the horn blew and she came out chatting and laughing with other girls. She hesitated for a moment when she saw me, but said goodbye to her friends and came over to me.

'Sorry, Harry.'

'It's all right, Eileen. I was shocked when I saw myself too. It's only a scar and it's healing up nicely. Will I walk you home?'

She smiled up at me. It was going to be all right. She linked her arm in mine and we walked home together.

After tea, Father told me that I could go to Burton's where I would be given a suit of clothes. He also said that I was due back pay. Thanks to Mr Churchill, shipowners were obliged to deposit funds into what became known as the Pool, to cover back pay and wages for missing seamen

Cover of Harry's first
Discharge Book.

Inside pages of Discharge
Book, showing *Afric Star*
entry January 1941.

following the capture or sinking of their ship. This was all good news to me. I could not wait to change my clothes.

The next morning, Friday 11 May, I headed down to the Pool in Derry port where I signed on. Every port in the British Isles had a Pool and each had records of every ship captured or sunk during the war, a list of crew members for each ship and a list of prisoner-of-war numbers from the Ministry of Defence. The clerk asked me for my name, Discharge Book number and my prisoner-of-war number and he ticked all of these off his lists. My Discharge Book was still in Liverpool so the clerk completed the form for it to be returned to me via the Pool at Derry port. Then he gave me five years' back pay of £1,000. My wages had been increased from £2.10s to £3.8s.4d when I had taken on the position of assistant cook and butcher in 1941. So with money in my pocket I headed into Derry city to Burton's. The sales assistant took a look at me, sizing me up, and then he measured my inside leg, my chest and arm length and showed me into a cubicle.

'Prisoner of war, Sir?'

'Yes.'

'Right, I'll be with you shortly, Sir, if you would kindly wait here for a moment.'

True to his word, the assistant returned shortly afterwards with a full set of clothing: underwear, socks, white cotton shirt, striped tie and a grey suit. I stripped off the clothes I had worn for so long and it was good to feel cotton against my skin. The suit was not an old man's suit but a modern classic cut with well-fitting trousers with a double-breasted jacket, which felt really comfortable. I put on my new socks and my old army boots. Then I bent to pick up the old British Army clothing.

'Leave that, Sir. We'll look after that.'

I left the khaki which had served me so well over the past four years and I walked out of that cubicle in my new clothes. When I went to pay for them the assistant said, 'That's okay, Sir. The government is covering the cost. I just need you to give me your prisoner-of-war number and your name.'

'90882. Harry Callan.'

And I was written into another list. I left Burton's with a lighter feeling and headed for a shoe shop. I purchased a pair of shiny black leather laced shoes with leather soles. The only other pair of leather shoes I had owned were at the bottom of the sea in the *Afric Star*. The shoes felt strange on my feet but even if they had pinched every toe I would still have worn them! I left my old cracked worn-out Army boots behind me in the shop. I broke in my new shoes walking around the city. Later, I stopped at Eileen's workplace to walk her home. She was delighted when she saw my new clothes.

When Father married Cassie, Aunt Ellen had gone to live with Aunt Mary Jane and Uncle John Jarvis at the top of Fountain Hill. The next day I walked over to visit her. She threw her arms around me; she was just as I remembered her.

Aunt Mary Jane still had her job at the shirt factory and Aunt Ellen was keeping house for her. I had tea and a slice of Aunt Ellen's bread and I told her that I thought of her when I made bread on the ships; she smiled warmly. I hid some money in the tea caddy, knowing she would find it later. I walked over the bridge into the city and bought a bar of soap, a towel, some more underwear, socks and another shirt. It was good to have money to spend.

I received a letter from Billy on 17 May in which he told me that he was on his way to Dublin to visit his sister and if I met him there we could travel back to Arklow together; he included his sister's address in the letter.

'Cassie, I've had a letter from a friend of mine, Billy English. He was a prisoner of war with me. I've been invited to stay with him for a few days in Arklow but I'll be back soon.'

'That's fine, Harry.'

'Would it be okay if Billy came to stay here for a few days too?'

'Of course, Harry. He's welcome to stay here any time.'

I had never spoken about Billy to Father or Cassie. I had told them nothing.

I took the train across the Border to Dublin. As I was walked out of Amiens Street station I heard a voice calling, 'Harry, Harry!'

Billy was waving at me.

'Glad you could come, Harry. It's good to see you!'

'Good to see you too, Billy!'

It was early afternoon and the weather was fine, so we jumped on a tram to Howth. The village had a sizeable fishing fleet and harbour. We walked along the harbour wall in companionable silence and then stopped at a café for fish and chips. Later, we headed back on the tram along the coast road to Clontarf where Billy's sister lived. She was tall with dark hair like Billy and very friendly. That night Billy slept in the spare bedroom and I bunked down on the settee. The next morning we said our goodbyes, then walked the few miles to Busáras where we got the bus to Arklow.

The journey through lovely countryside and small villages took over three hours. I saw very few official bus stops along the way; it seemed to me that the bus driver stopped anywhere he saw a person with their hand stretched out. Passengers got off along the route, too, sometimes right outside their homes. There was a great buzz of conversation on the bus and I asked Billy if all the passengers knew each other. Billy said no, that country people were always ready for a chat and to share news. It was while we were on the bus that Billy told me that he had given an interview to *The Irish Times* newspaper a few days earlier. I was shocked.

'Why did you do that, Billy? I haven't spoken to anyone. What about the others? Did they give interviews too?'

'No, just me. The lads are not too happy; they don't want to talk about it but people keep asking them if it's true. No one wants to believe it. They think that I'm making it up.'

He handed me the article to read. The buzz of conversation faded into the background and I was back in Farge. I did not want to, but I had to read the article:

The Irish Times, 17 May 1945
… Mr English (Billy English on his return to Ireland) saw a naked Belgian prisoner beaten to death with rubber hose for attempting to escape. A Pole was shot in the thigh while trying to escape and the SS Guards rubbed salt into the wound and beat him with electric cable. He walked from the end of the camp to the hospital but a Russian doctor, also a prisoner, was refused permission to attend him and gangrene set in. The doctor said it would be more merciful to shoot the man. The guard did so. Next morning a French prisoner who refused

to give information was shot. A Russian
prisoner was thrown into the camp refuse
heap and the camp commandant Schauwacker
forced some of the muck from the heap into
his throat with a wire before throwing him
back on the heap. He was struck with a rifle
butt on the head and killed. His body was
left for three days on the heap …

All these things were from a previous time and I wanted
to forget them – I wanted to get on with my life. I did not
know what to say to my friend.

Charlie Byrne lived across the road from Billy; Patrick
Reilly and Patrick Kavanagh lived further up the road. I
could understand why they were upset. It would be hard for
them, knowing that their families and neighbours had read
the newspaper; not many of the people I knew bought *The
Irish Times*. I handed the article back to Billy.

'Sorry, I just can't talk about Farge.'

'That's all right, Harry.'

Slowly the banter and conversation of the other
passengers came back.

Billy's mother was a small woman in her fifties. She
and Billy lived in a two-up two-down cottage on Harbour
Road in Arklow. We walked around the town or on the
local sandy beaches and in the evenings we went to the
pub where Billy could have a few pints. I did not know
that people in southern Ireland had not known what was
going on in the war; between the Censorship Board and
the Catholic Church, very little of the truth reached the
ordinary Irish person. There had been a few comments
passed about the newspaper article. They did not believe

that guards would commit such atrocities on prisoners. It was a long time before people learned the truth.

I got restless. Whether it was the newspaper article, my Derry accent or a combination of both, after four days I had had enough of the sideways glances and whispers in the pubs. I asked Billy if he would like to come back up to Derry with me.

'Yeah, I'd like that, Harry.'

22

NIGHTMARES AND THE WAR AT HOME

FATHER AND CASSIE WELCOMED Billy. I think Father was hoping that we would talk about our war experiences but we never did. I slept with my brothers and gave Billy the big bed for himself. I left money in the tea caddy for Cassie so that she could get more food and anything else she needed. I took Billy around Derry city and the surrounding countryside and in the evenings he had his pint and I had my lemonade. Billy stayed five days and then, like me, he got restless.

'Time for me to get back to Arklow, Harry.'

I went with him to the Great Northern station and we shook hands.

'Good luck, Harry.'

'You too, Billy.'

He boarded the train. Ours had been a friendship born out of necessity in extremely difficult times. Now that we were free, there was not enough to hold the friendship together. We did not want to revisit the things we had in common. I hoped that someday I would sail on the same ship with him again and would be proud to do so.

Nightmares began to haunt me. Cassie and Father heard me shouting in my sleep but they never said anything. Father knew I needed time to heal. I paid my way in the house and the only thing Father asked me to do was to attend Sunday Mass with my family while I lived there. I went to please him but I did not pray, go to Confession or receive Holy Communion. Father noticed but did not pass any comment. One Sunday after Mass, I sat with Father reading the papers.

'Father, I need to ask you something.'

'Son?'

'Have you heard anything about Edgar?'

'Aye, son. He went down with his ship. The telegram arrived.'

With that, Father hid himself behind his newspaper while I fell silent, thinking about my older brother. What had it been like for Father in 1941? I never thought about my father receiving telegrams. He had received one to tell him my ship was captured and sunk; a few months later, he received one to tell him that Edgar was missing presumed dead; later that same year, there was one to say I was in a prisoner-of-war camp; in 1942 came the dreaded telegram to confirm that Edgar was dead; and then there was nothing more for three years until he was advised by telegram that I was on my way home.

'I got a letter, you know, from a prisoner …'

It was Father's voice.

'… a prisoner of war. He was sent home from Milag because he was ill. Seemingly he spent two years walking backwards so the Red Cross arranged for him to be sent home. Did you know him, Harry?'

'No, Father. I don't think so.'

'I took three days off work and travelled down to Tralee in Kerry to try and meet him, to find out about you – to see if you were still alive.'

Father was still behind his newspaper; it was as if he was talking to himself.

'I arrived at his house but there was no one home. I asked some of his neighbours if they knew where I could find him. I think they were suspicious of me and my Derry accent. Nobody seemed to know anything about him and if they did they were not going to tell me. I could not delay any longer. I had to get back to work.'

Father had never talked to me like this before.

'Do you remember the man now, Harry?'

'I can't remember his first name, Father, but I do remember him. I think it was Cahill. Cahill walked backwards all the time. The other lads in the barracks watched out for him. They used to link arms with him so that he didn't walk into anything. I didn't know that he had been sent home. I wonder, did he get all right? Excuse me, Father.'

With that I got up and left the house for a while; I did not want to be reminded. Father never brought up the subject again.

On Sunday afternoons, Cassie visited her mother. She brought Robin and Drew with her and asked if I would like to join them. Cassie's mother knew my mother and began to tell me about her: she had worked in one of the local shirt factories and boarded with Mrs Cusack from Monday to Saturday each week until she met and married Father. Cassie, who had been a baby at the time, had no memory of my mother. I could not wait to share this news with Eileen.

Cassie made sure that I was eating little and often. She always had porridge, bread and tea in the morning, soup and stews for dinner and bread and jam for supper. She was worried about me because I was not putting on weight. When I pushed my finger into my thigh it was like pushing soft dough; it left a dimple that took a while to go away. It felt like there was water under the skin, a weird sensation and very hard to describe. I did not tell her any of this.

At the end of June I went to Ballyshannon to visit my mother's sister, Auntie Mai. Granny Keenan was dead so Auntie Mai and her four children were living in the old cottage. It was a warm sunny day and the top half of the door was open so I knocked on the frame, calling out, 'Auntie Mai?'

'Come in, come in. Harry, what a surprise!'

She hugged me, then stood back from me, holding onto my hand.

'Let me look at you. Back from the dead, thank God. But Harry, your face: what has happened to your face?'

I told her about the sore, about the army medics cleaning it up but not about anything else. I stayed with her for two weeks and enjoyed myself, taking walks or lying out in the sunshine while my cousins swam or played on the beach. I tried hard not to think about the Heidbreder children. Auntie Mai made me promise that I would go to the doctor for a check-up when I went home.

'Harry,' she added, 'you need to tell the doctor about your nightmares.'

I was shocked. I had no idea that my nightmares had disturbed her and the children.

'You woke me every night but I didn't know what to do for you. It's all right, but you need to talk to the doctor.'

The doctor sent me to Belfast for an X-ray and a medical check-up but I did not tell him about my nightmares. I was told I had tuberculosis. But it was not all bad news: I was on the road to recovery. Seemingly, my holiday with Auntie Mai had done wonders for me. I stayed in the Seaman's Mission for another couple of weeks and took complete bed rest, only getting up to go to the nearest café for a meal. At the end of the two weeks I had another X-ray and examination. The doctors were happy with me and said that I could go home but that I could not work for a year: my body needed that time to heal fully. The letter they gave me for the Pool made no mention that I had been a prisoner of war and needed to recover from that; it spoke only about TB and the recovery period required.

When I got off the train in Derry I went straight to the Pool where I handed in the letter, and received my weekly pay after that. The second thing I did was to buy a car. George Taylor, a school pal, suggested that I go to Belfast for one. The following day he and I took the train to Belfast and I bought a Standard for £30. I had never driven a car before but Dr Heidbreder had made it look easy. George assured me that there was nothing to it and so I got behind the wheel, started the engine and drove back to Derry.

One evening I met my brother John on his way home from work. We walked and talked for a while.

'You know, when I was away, John, I was told that bombs had been dropped on Derry and that the city was destroyed. I thought you were all dead. I didn't know what I'd find when I got back.'

John thought about this for a moment:

'We were lucky, Harry. On 15 April 1941 the Jerries dropped two parachute mines over the Foyle. One of them exploded near Pennyburn Church and the second bomb exploded as it landed on Messines Park; that one killed fifteen people. On the same night the Jerries dropped 200 tons of bombs on Belfast city. They killed over 900 people and more than a thousand were injured. God help them and their families. During the war, Derry became a naval base which looked after half the escort vessels in the North Atlantic. Derry played an important role in the "Battle of the Atlantic". Harry, do you know that since 1940 there has been no unemployment in Derry? Imagine that! Anyone who was able to got work on the building sites in the docks, the factories and the farms.'

'Oh God, if I hadn't left I would have had a very different life!'

There was no point in thinking about that. I had enjoyed every minute of my life at sea before January 1941.

It was George who told me that there were now five airports in Northern Ireland: Eglinton served Derry; Maydown also served Derry and surrounding areas; Ballykelly was a command centre for all air crews; Mullaghmore was the base for the RAF and US Air Force; and Limavady near Belfast was another RAF base. It was the planes from Ballykelly that had flown ahead of us while we were in convoy and reported enemy sightings.

Then George said, 'Do you know, Harry, the Derry-to-Belfast railway line runs across the main runway of the Ballykelly Airfield? And do you know, the train has right of way.'

And there was I worrying about the Germans blowing us out of the sky! I could get killed on the railway line, by a Lancaster landing in Northern Ireland.

We had a great view from Derryview Terrace of Spitfires and other military aircraft flying over the Foyle. The first group of U-boats that had surrendered to the Allies were taken to Lisahally and tied up there. It was a novelty for people. They took picnics and had family days out on the quayside beside the U-boats. These were the killers from the deep, the ones that suddenly appeared in the middle of convoys and were able to cause such destruction, mayhem, pain and death. I had seen enough of them during the war and did not need to see them now. I went off in my car in the opposite direction. In winter 1945, twenty-eight of the U-boats, which were tied up at Lisahally, were taken out into the Atlantic by the British Navy and scuttled.

There were new cinemas and dance halls in Derry. I brought Eileen and her friends to the pictures in my car but I refused to go to war films. I started going to dance halls and was never short of a partner. I think the girls liked the fact that I did not drink and I wanted to dance all night long, and I always drove my dancing partner home afterwards.

23

CHRISTMAS 1945 AND GOING BACK TO SEA

AT CHRISTMAS 1945 Robin and Drew were very excited when Father brought home the Christmas tree, which we all helped to decorate with candles. The boys and even baby Yvonne were mesmerised by the flickering light and twinkling decorations. It brought back memories of other Christmases; when I thought of the Heidbreder family I stopped reminiscing.

'Father, will you hang our stockings now?' I asked.

Father looked at me and smiled. Cassie pulled out a sock for each child and we went upstairs where Father hung three of them on the back of the boys' bedroom door and two on the girls'. Eileen looked at me and smiled: Santa would still be coming to us this year.

The next morning I woke at 4 a.m. and lay in bed listening to the sounds of my home. The boys woke at 6 a.m. and, seeing that there was something in their socks, they jumped on my bed.

'Wake up, Harry! Wake up! Santa Claus has come!'

Of course I had to pretend that I was asleep and that they woke me up. Together we took our socks off the door. There they were: the apple, the orange and two shiny new pennies. Santa Claus had not forgotten.

I had bought myself a new shirt from Burton's for Christmas and felt very smart heading off to Mass with my family. Everybody was in their Sunday best, and was happy and smiling. There was a big turkey with potatoes, carrots, Brussels sprouts and gravy. Cassie had made cakes and pudding, and there were different-flavoured cordial drinks; it was a feast indeed!

After Christmas I met George Taylor and told him I wanted to sell the Standard and buy an Austin 10; it was easier to start the Austin on cold mornings. George brought me to another car dealer he knew, this time in Derry; I traded in the Standard and paid £50 for the Austin 10. I drove Cassie to the shops and to visit her mother, which delighted her. I wanted to take Aunt Ellen for a drive but she was too nervous.

I was getting better and had put on some weight but I was bored and restless. I wanted to go back to work. I had to wait until the medical examination in June and for the doctor to declare me fit for work. I went for long walks every day to try and build up the strength in my legs and I went dancing most nights. In May I returned to visit Auntie Mai. At the end of my visit I told her that I was heading back for my medical.

'You'll do fine, Harry and you're welcome to visit any time.'

'Thanks, Auntie Mai.'

We gave each other a big hug I climbed into my Austin 10 and drove home. I told Father that I was going to Belfast for my medical.

'Grand, son. It will be good for you to get back to work.'

I drove to Belfast and reported to the Belfast Clinic, then stayed at the Seaman's Mission for three days until I received their letter telling me to go to the TB clinic. I got a clean bill of health and drove back to Derry with my letter for the Pool. When I told Cassie the news, she baked a cake to have with our tea that evening.

'We're celebrating tonight: Harry is fully better!'

The next day I headed to the Pool with my letter but the clerk on duty said that there were not many ships looking for crew at that time. So I went back home and waited another two weeks, calling at the Pool each day. I still received my pay and I continued to leave money in the tea caddy for Cassie. Then one day, the clerk in the Pool said that he could not keep me on his books any longer as there were no ships running out of Derry looking for crew. I would have to go to the Belfast Pool. I drove to the garage where I had purchased my car and they bought her back for £40. I walked home to Derryview Terrace where I told my family that I would be heading to Belfast the following day and that I did not know when I would be back again.

I was up early the next morning to say goodbye to Father before he left for work. I met him in the kitchen.

'I'll be heading off now, Father. Thanks.'

'You take care of yourself, son, and thank you for being good to Cassie and the children.'

I put out my hand but my father pulled me into him and for the second time in my life I felt his embrace. Then, with a sniff and a 'Good luck, son', he turned and went out the door.

A little while later I, too, quietly left the house and headed for the Waterside Station. This time I carried a suitcase and not a paper bundle like I had in 1939. I was

Harry Callan in 1946
when he returned
to work at sea.

able to get a room in the new Seaman's Mission in College
Square East near Queen's University. From there I reported
to the Pool each day to see if there was any work and on
Fridays I got paid. After two months, at the beginning of
September, I was offered a job; finally, I was going back to
sea.

On 13 September 1946 I signed on as assistant steward on
the passenger ship, the *Princess Margaret*, which sailed from
Heysham to Belfast. I was the relief cover for the assistant
steward who was on sick leave. I took the overnight boat
from Belfast and arrived next morning in Heysham to take
up the job. My duties were to ensure that the cabin crew
kept the passengers' accommodation in order. I felt seasick
the minute I stood on the deck of the *Princess Margaret* but
thankfully it lasted only a few hours. Two days later the

assistant steward returned and I signed off. I travelled back to Belfast by boat and went back to the Seaman's Mission and the Pool.

On 25 September I signed on the SS *Dorothy Rose* as steward. Once again I was seasick until we were under way. I did not know then but I was to suffer like that every time I went on board a ship for the rest of my sea-going days. I worked by on *Dorothy Rose* as cook when in Ellesmere port or Belfast and I forgot about eating little and often. I began to take handfuls of butter, which I ate like ice cream; I smothered my potatoes in butter, and every time I passed the fridge I took spoonsful of raw mince and ate it. Deprivation makes a man do odd things. I started to put on weight. I really enjoyed my time on that ship. When the *Dorothy Rose* docked in Newcastle upon Tyne on 17 March 1947, I signed off.

I stayed in the Seaman's Mission in Liverpool, registered at the Pool and a month later I heard at the port office that the Headline Company were looking for crew. On 9 May 1947 I signed on with them as assistant steward on the MV *Inishowen Head*. There was a red hand painted on each side of the funnel on every one of their ships, the symbol of the province of Ulster, which they referred to as the 'Red Hands of O'Neill', the earl of Tyrone. We were never short-handed on a Headline Boat – there were always two extra hands!

When I showed my Discharge Book at the office I was quizzed about the gap in service. My book stated 'discharged 29 January 1941 – at sea'. I had to explain that my ship had been sunk by a German Raider, that I had been a prisoner of war until 1945 and had been recovering until 1946. From then on I pinned a short handwritten statement into my book to explain this and was never asked about it again.

We sailed to Montreal in Canada, the USA and other places. I particularly enjoyed the approach to Montreal from the St Lawrence River. It was magical at night, with all the churches and crosses lit up on the hillsides. Montreal was a predominately Catholic city and a lot of Catholics from Northern Ireland had emigrated there; Protestants tended to go to Toronto.

The Stella Maris Catholic Organization was situated in nearly every port and Montreal was no exception. The priests ran dances as fundraisers for the church and kept a wary eye on all seamen. Coffee and biscuits were served at the interval but no alcohol. Priests patrolled the streets to make sure that girls went home alone. We laughed about this. Those of us from Ireland were used to these patrols; at home the priest went around on a bicycle, beating the ditches with a stick. In Montreal, when we walked girls home we regularly had to jump over a garden wall until the priest passed; the girls would let us know when the coast was clear.

We returned to Belfast in August 1947 and a young lad from Belfast, Bobby Dallas, signed on as cabin boy. I remembered how Dick Knight had taken care of me and I made sure that Bobby was at the dances with us and got back safely to the ship. We sailed from there to Dublin port where we docked for the night. The National Ballroom in Parnell Square, which we nicknamed the 'Ballroom of Romance', was where some of the crew went to dance. Bobby and I joined them. I dressed in my suit, white shirt and a new tie that I had bought in Canada. It was wide with a yellow flower pattern. It was the latest style and made me feel smart.

At the National Ballroom, I saw a girl. She was gorgeous. She was petite with dark curly hair and when she laughed

Harry Callan wearing his Merchant Navy pin on his lapel, c.1950.

her eyes lit up; I could not stop looking at her. When the band struck up a waltz I plucked up my courage and crossed the floor.

'Would you like to dance?'

She smiled that wonderful smile.

'I'd like that.'

'I'm Harry.'

'Nice to meet you, Harry. I'm Anne.'

I held her in my arms and did not want that dance to end. At the interval I offered to buy her a cordial. After the war, rationing had continued so things like ice cream and chocolate were considered luxuries and cigarettes, too, were in short supply. I did not want Anne to go back to her friends or to dance with anyone else so I kept buying her ice creams – four or five of them!

A man was always popular if he had cigarettes to give away. Anne did not really smoke but as it was fashionable she liked to puff one just like the film stars did. She was there with her sister Sadie and some friends. I made sure to pass the cigarettes their way too. It worked! Anne danced with me all night.

I asked if I could walk her home and she agreed. Sadie and her friends followed behind. Anne lived in Ferguson Road in Drumcondra and as we walked I told her that I was a seaman.

'Could I call on you, Anne, when I'm back in Dublin?'

I could not believe it when she smiled and said, 'Yes.'

I had arranged to meet Bobby at Hopkins' Corner at the end of O'Connell Street; like Clery's clock it was a landmark for people to meet. I walked just over 4 miles from Ferguson Road through Drumcondra, along Dorset Street and Frederick Street to O'Connell Street. We walked from there down the quays to Alexander Basin where our ship was docked. It was the route I regularly walked once I started dating Anne. I never thought to ask her if there was a shorter way. Years later I found out that I could have walked via Richmond Road and East Wall Road, which would have cut nearly 2 miles off my journey!

24

LIFE MOVES ON

I SPENT CHRISTMAS in Belfast at the Seaman's Mission waiting to go back on the MV *Inishowen Head*. The company promoted Bobby to assistant steward and so we went to a local dance to celebrate. I dressed in my suit and headed to his house, which was just off York Road and not that far from Belfast Docks. His mother, a little stout woman, was very welcoming and she invited me into the kitchen.

'It's nice to meet you, Harry. I'm glad to be able to thank you for watching out for Bobby.'

'Sure it's nothing, Mrs Dallas.'

'Will you have a cup of tea while you're waiting?'

I did not get time to answer because the front door burst open and hit the wall with a bang. I heard heavy footsteps on the floorboards in the hall the kitchen door was flung open and a man shouted, 'Get you out here quick! There's a couple of Fenians down here want beating up!

The man stopped and looked at me. Bobby's father was as shocked as I was, having expected his son to be in his kitchen. Mrs Dallas blushed with embarrassment. I stood still, then nodded my head to him.

'Mr Dallas.'

Mrs Dallas moved to stand beside me as she said, 'This is Bobby's friend Harry Callan from his ship.'

Bobby came downstairs. He had heard what his father said but he did not make any comment, ignoring him as he walked past. He gave his mother a hug and kiss then, turning to me, said, 'I see you've met my mother and father, Harry. Let's go or we'll be late for the dance.'

I shook Mrs Dallas's hand and nodded to Mr Dallas as Bobby and I left the house.

'Fenian' was a derogatory term for Catholics, but we never spoke about the comment Mr Dallas had made; in fact, we never spoke about religion at all. Since the war I had noticed that there was now a religious divide, which I had never experienced before. I had aunts, uncles, cousins and friends who were Protestant; most families in Northern Ireland had. I could not hate them just because they had a different religion to me. I did not want anything to do with it. From then until the day I retired I wrote the letters POW opposite the word 'Religion' on any documents.

Another assistant steward on the MV *Inishowen* by the name of Kelly was promoted to chief steward on the SS *Fair Head* and he suggested that I sign on with him, as there would be a better chance of promotion for me on that ship, he said. The ship would be sailing out of 'Londonderry'. That's what my Protestant cousins called the city; we Catholics called it 'Derry'. So on 31 December I went home to see my family.

'Son, there you are! Everything okay?'

'Yes, Father. I'm sailing from Derry tomorrow and took the opportunity to come home to see you.'

'You'll stay the night, so?'

'I will, Father. Thanks.'

The next morning I left the house early, hiding some money in the tea caddy on my way out; it was the last time I stayed with Father and Cassie.

The SS *Fair Head* carried dry goods to Europe and was waiting for Route Approved Status, which meant that mines along the route had been cleared and it was deemed safe as a regular shipping route. Although the war had been over for nearly three years, there was still the threat of mines and no ship could travel to Europe without route approval. I sailed out of Derry on 2 January 1948 as assistant steward. The North Sea was a big change from the Atlantic, with biting winds, very rough seas and big swells. We eventually arrived at the mouth of the River Weser in Germany.

I was at my duties when I looked out the window to see Bremerhaven on my port side. Bremen was our destination. It suddenly stuck me where I was and where we were going. I felt sick, and this time it was not seasickness. I was sailing up the river that I had seen from the site; the river that overflowed into my boots as I dug. Something possessed me; I was no longer in control. Suddenly I was running up the stairs to go on deck and I stood with my knuckles turning white as I clenched the rail. There was the monster Bunker Valentin, huge, dark and silent. But there was no silence in my head; I was back there. I could not move. I could not say anything. The crew were watching me and it was not until we moved upriver where I could no longer see it that I slowly became aware of my surroundings and went back to my duties.

We were to dock overnight in Bremen, which gave me the chance to take the train to Farge, an hour's journey. The village had not changed much in the three years although I was surprised that I did not meet anyone I knew. I arrived at Dr Heidbreder's house, walked up the gravel driveway, headed to the kitchen door and knocked. A woman whom I had never seen before answered it. I greeted her in German and asked if Dr Heidbreder was at home. But the whole family was away for the day. She asked if I would like to leave a message. I asked her to say that Harry Callan had called.

She closed the door. Disappointed, I returned to my ship.

Shipping companies required all cooks and chief stewards to have the Nautical Cookery Certificate in order to be eligible for promotion. I had befriended the cook on the SS *Fair Head*, Johnny McCorry, who was also from Northern Ireland. The company registered both of us for a course in the National Sea Training School of Nautical Cookery, Glasgow, Scotland. I did not learn anything new, but I had the time of my life. We went dancing every night and, despite our late nights, on 20 April we managed to attain our Cook's Certificates. When I signed onto the SS *Fair Head* on 11 May I was promoted to second steward. When we arrived at Dublin port, I told Johnny that I was calling on a girlfriend and I would meet him later in the Ballroom of Romance. Anne's mother, Jude, answered the door.

While we sat in the kitchen drinking tea, she asked me about my family and work. I was delighted to be able to tell her that I had just been promoted.

'I was hoping that Anne would come to the dance with me to celebrate. I'm only in port for the night.'

Jude assured me that Anne would be delighted and that she and Sadie would meet me there.

I picked her out from the crowd immediately; she smiled when she saw me and I took her hand. We danced all night and when I took her home, I kissed her at the gate. She promised that she would be there the next time I docked

Harry Callan and Johnny McCorry in Scotland in 1948.

in Dublin. Johnny was late. I stood at Hopkins' Corner waiting for him until a Garda on his beat approached me.

'Move along there, Sir. Can't have you standing around. Move along now.'

'I'm waiting for my shipmate. He won't be long and we'll be walking together down the docks to our ship.'

'Well, we can't have you standing around here. Walk up and down, Sir. That would be all right, but if I catch you standing here again I'll have to do you for loitering.'

Eventually Johnny arrived.

I continued working on the SS *Fair Head* until January 1949. Each time we went up the River Weser I ran up on deck and stood at the rail as we passed Bunker Valentin; I could not help myself. I did not know it but the crew took bets: on how quickly I would go up on deck; how long I would stay in the one spot and at which point of the river I would leave to go back to my duties. Some of the crew asked me what was so interesting about the building. I could not tell them

'I'm just curious,' I said.

My nightmares haunted me. I woke myself up shouting out, drenched in sweat and tears. My cabin mates certainly heard me and saw me thrashing in my sleep but they never mentioned it to me.

In winter 1948 we docked again at Bremen port and I decided that this time I would try to find Katie. I took the train to Farge but there was no answer at her house. I asked some neighbours if they knew where Katie Sause now lived but they either did not know or would not tell me. Disappointed, I returned to my ship but promised myself that someday I would find out what had happened to her.

I signed off the SS *Fair Head* in Belfast and took the position of second cook on the SS *Fanad Head,* another Headline Ship, on 10 February 1949. She, too, brought dry goods to Germany. Unknown to me, word had spread and the crew on this ship also took bets when I went on deck as we passed Bunker Valentin. We docked in Bremen for three days but the cook had shore leave so I had to stay on board. Most of the pilots who assisted the larger ships into port were local men, so I spoke to one of them.

'*Darf ich fragen woher Sie Kommen?*' ('May I ask where you are from?')

'Farge.'

'*Kennen Sie Dr Heidbreder?*' ('Do you know Dr Heidbreder?')

'*Ja. Dr Heidbreder ist mein Arzt.*' ('Yes. Dr Heidbreder is my doctor.')

'*Wenn Sie ihn sehen Können Sie ihm bitte Grüße von Harry Callan bestellen.*' ('If you see him please give him greetings from Harry Callan.')

'*Werde ich. Harry Callan.*' ('I will. Harry Callan.')

The next day one of the crew told me that there was a man on the dock looking for me. I went on deck and there was Dr Heidbreder with Enno, who was now seven, and baby Hawke, who was now four. I hurried down to meet them and the doctor warmly shook my hand, while Enno stood shyly beside his father; he did not recognise me as his Onkel Harry. I suppose to a young child I was quite different; I was no longer skinny and I was not wearing a khaki uniform. I asked after Frau Doktor, Mareike and Uwe. I thanked him for all he had done for me and told him that I would always be grateful to him and his household. Dr Heidbreder did not tell me that in 1945 he had been arrested by the Allies and held captive for three years in Milag und Marlag Nord Westertimke. He did not tell me that he had been put on trial for his treatment of Allied nationals in the *AEL*-Farge camp; that Knott, Ryan and O'Dwyer had been called by the prosecution to testify against him, nor that he had been exonerated. We said our goodbyes; that was the last time I saw Dr Heidbreder.

When I went back on board the crew were curious to know how I was acquainted with a German and how I could speak the language. I told them that he was a friend of the family and left it at that. Two months later, Frau Heidbreder and two of the children came to Bremen to do some shopping. The children asked if they could see if Onkel Harry's ship was at the docks and as it happened the SS *Fanad Head* was in port. It was wonderful to see them. Mareike, now a young lady of fourteen, gave me a hug. Uwe, now twelve, seemed to have become a little quieter. He said 'hello', and I shook his hand. I was glad to be able to thank Frau Heidbreder personally for everything she had done for me. This time when I went back on board no one asked who my visitors were. I felt that I could move on with my life.

On 20 June 1950, Anne and I were married and, after our honeymoon, we lived with Jude, who was a great comfort and help to Anne while I was at sea. Catherine was born in April 1951 and Harry in October 1952. In 1954, the Headline Shipping Company began to sell some of its ships. It was the beginning of the end for the company. They were good employers and I had enjoyed working for them. On 20 March I signed on with Palgrave Murphy as ship's cook on the SS *City of Cork*. It was a short trip and I signed off on 15 April. As there was no other suitable position available at the time I took up relief work back on the SS *Fanad Head* and worked by on her in Belfast port as ship's cook until we sailed to Limerick where on 17 June I signed off. I took a train to Dublin and spent some time with Anne, Catherine, Harry and Jude.

Harry Callan and Anne McCabe on their wedding day,
20 June 1950.

While I was at home, Anne told me about a spiritual retreat being held in our church and she asked me to go with her. At this retreat I found a priest with whom I was able to speak openly. I told him about my experience with Fr Juno in Stalag XB and confessed that I had stolen bread from a dying man. He was very understanding. He told me that men do strange things during war; that I had not killed this man, that I had nothing to worry about and he gave me absolution. I left the church lighter and more content than I had been for years. The retreat was a regular fixture for me from then on.

Palgrave Murphy bought the *Dalkey Coast* in 1954 and I flew to Rotterdam and signed on as chief steward. They changed her name to MS *City of Ghent* and I worked on her until she sank in 1955. We were 3 nautical miles off the Lizard Lighthouse in Cornwall when the ship shuddered. There was a loud bang and she suddenly came to a stop. We had hit a rock and run aground. The bosun raced down below decks calling out as he ran, 'Harry! With me now!'

I followed him as quickly as I could. There was no damage under the hatches when we looked so we had to go lower. He reached a trapdoor. I was close behind him but we did not get a chance to lift it. At that minute the water burst through and forced the trapdoor up. The sea was gushing into the ship.

'Quick, Harry. Canvas and rope!'

I saw him trying to force the trapdoor back into position as I ran to get the items. Together we managed to get it shut by tying it down, but it would only hold for a short while. Already we could see the water seeping through other areas of the floor. We reported to the skipper and the chief officer. The lifeboats had been winched out and the crew were climbing on board. The skipper turned to me and said, 'Harry, go below and see if anyone is still down there.'

This was an order. I knew the water was pouring in but I had no choice.

'Aye, Skipper.'

I ran through the ship checking all the quarters shouting all the time, 'Abandon ship!'

I came across McCarthy, a greaser who was off duty, relaxing with a glass of beer.

'McCarthy, you'd better get up on deck quickly!'

'What?'

Harry and Anne with daughter Catherine and son Harry jnr at Butlin's holiday camp in County Meath, 1956.

Harry and Anne's sons, Michael and Brian on Ferguson Road, Drumcondra, Dublin, in 1967.

'The ship's sinking! Skipper has launched the lifeboats.'

He grabbed his bag and ran up top. The only other person I found was Joe Flynn. Electric razors had recently come on the market and Joe had just purchased this luxury item. He was proud of it and, after using it, always carefully cleaned the razor and returned it to the wrappings in its original box. Joe was trying desperately to get the box into his coat pocket. It was never going to fit. I could not believe it. He was risking both our lives for that bloody razor!

'Joe, will you come on? The ship's going down! Skipper says to the lifeboats.'

'Right, Harry, be with you now.'

Incredibly he continued to try to force the box into his pocket.

'What are you doing, Joe? Are you all right?'

'Yeah, fine. I'll be with you in a minute I just have to get this into my pocket.'

'The ship's sinking, Joe!'

I took the razor with its bag of attachments out of the box, shoved them into Joe's pocket, grabbed his arm and pushed him out the cabin door. Then he started to run. While he climbed into one of the lifeboats, I reported, 'All clear now, Skipper.'

'Lifeboats, lads!'

By now the MS *City of Ghent* was heavily listing and those of us still on board with the skipper walked down the side of her and into the lifeboats. We rowed away from our ship.

There was silence in the lifeboats as we watched her slip down. Watching our home disappear was dreadful and we were feeling the loss. I was remembering all the other ships I had seen sink. We also knew that jobs were harder to get now. The Cadgwith Lifeboat guided us back to shore.

From 1955 I worked on various Palgrave Murphy ships travelling to Europe, the United States and Canada. In July 1958 while in dry dock in Rotterdam, I felt really ill and thought I had a bad flu. We had been carrying live cattle and later I was diagnosed with brucellosis, which I caught from drinking unpasteurised milk. I had recurring bouts of brucellosis until January 1960, when the company doctor put me on sick leave until the end of June.

Our son Michael was born in April 1959, Jude died in February 1960 and another son, Brian, was born in April 1961. They were tough years for Anne but, happily for my family, the company paid me while I was sick.

I enjoyed working for Palgrave Murphy. Unfortunately, though, the company began to sell off their ships. My last sailing with them was on the MS *City of Cork* and I signed off her on 26 August 1966 in Dublin port. There were fewer shipping companies and those still in existence had their crews and weren't hiring anyone. I tried other jobs, such as taxi driving and door-to-door sales. I hated every minute of them. Then I got lucky. In May 1968 the British and Irish Steam Packet Company, fondly called the B&I, were looking for relief staff and I got a temporary job as assistant steward. By chance I met a supervisor from the Irish Shipping Office who asked me if I was looking for work.

'Yes, I am,' I replied.

'Are you ready to go now? There's a position for second steward if you want it? You need to fly out to Santander in Spain today.'

'I'll take it. I'll stop by my home on the way to the airport. Thanks, Sir.'

Because the air ticket was booked through the company my Discharge Book was sufficient identification for me.

When I arrived in Santander on 21 May 1968 I signed on the MV *Irish Rowan*. Once more we sailed up the River Weser but, thanks to Anne who had helped bring me back to my faith, I was able to pray for all those poor souls and for my dead comrades who had been left behind in Farge.

We docked in Bremen port for a couple of days so I decided to go back to Farge to try and find out about Katie. It was impossible to see the bunker because, thankfully, the Germans had planted a forest of trees around it. I knocked on the door and a woman answered. She looked like one of Katie's sisters but I could not be sure. She looked at me as though she was trying to remember who I was. I told her that I knew a girl called Katie Sause who had lived in the house a long time ago and that I was trying to find out what had happened to her. To my surprise, she replied that she knew Katie, that her married name was Kuhnert and that she lived in Blumenthal; she even gave me the address. I thanked her and walked the 4 km to Blumenthal. Now that I was here, I hoped that Katie was home. I recognised her immediately.

There was a moment's silence as she stood there looking at me. I was not sure whether it was a look of shock or surprise but then her face lit up with a smile.

'*Harry, kom herin, kom herin!*' ('Harry, come in, come in!')

I stepped in. I do not know what I was expecting. A handshake? A hug? But Katie turned, walked down the hallway and into the kitchen. I followed her. There was a man sitting at the kitchen table.

'Harry, *das ist mein Mann.*' ('Harry, this is my husband.')

'*Dies ist Harry Callan von Dr Heidbreders Haus.*' ('This is Harry Callan from Dr Heidbreder's House.')

Katie's husband stood up and we shook hands. Katie pulled out a chair for me and then busied herself making coffee for the three of us. I told her about meeting Anne, about my children and about my life at sea. Katie told me about meeting her husband and about her own children who were at school. They were due home shortly and she had to get dinner ready for them. It was time for me to go. Katie's husband just sat and listened to us, barely saying a word during the whole time I was there. He made me feel uncomfortable but I decided to ignore the feeling and enjoy the little time we had.

In German, I said, 'I want to thank you, Katie, for all you did for me. I will never forget that first cup of coffee and I will never forget your kindness to me. Thank you.'

I wanted to throw my arms around her to give her a big hug but I felt that her husband would not approve. So I said my goodbyes and left.

In December 1970 I signed on as crew cook with the B&I, working up to chief purser, which was my position when I retired in January 1987. When I think back on those years I realise how much I missed of my children's childhood. I was never home for their First Holy Communions or Confirmations, birthdays or other important events in their young lives. I can only recall being home once for Christmas Day. Working with the B&I meant that I was able to get home more often, and Anne, too, was happier with the shorter trips.

In December 1986, I became ill and spent that Christmas in hospital. I survived quintuple bypass heart surgery. Being a non-smoker and non-drinker certainly helped my recovery and I quickly changed my eating habits after that. I no longer snacked on raw mince but on grapefruit and

Harry and Anne Callan on their fiftieth wedding anniversary in 2000, with their children and their spouses. *Front row (l–r)*: Maeve, Marie, Anne, Harry, Michèle, Catherine Purcell; *back row (l–r)*: Brian and Harry Jnr, Michael Purcell, Michael Callan.

apples; I ate salads every day. I continued walking, which was the easiest part as I had been walking all my life. In January 1987, at the age of sixty-three, I retired. But instead of sitting around doing nothing, I helped my children with decorating and renovation jobs in their homes; they were all married by this time.

I missed the ships so on Sundays I went down to whichever of the B&I ferries was in Dublin port and went on board where I set up the altar and got things ready for the visiting priest. I served Mass, read and counted the collection afterwards.

Life was good. Our four children were happily married. We now had three grandchildren. Catherine and her husband, Michael Purcell, were the parents of Colette, aged fourteen, and her sister Eva who was five years younger. Brian and Maeve had a baby girl, whom they called Tara. All my family were well. Anne and I settled into our golden years together.

25

COMPENSATION AND GERMANY REVISITED

IN 2001, Anne's niece June heard an interview on RTÉ radio with Peter Mulvany, chairperson of The Irish Seaman's Relatives Association. She phoned Anne to tell her that this man had spoken about the German Forced Labour Compensation Programme. He wanted to contact survivors or their relatives. In July 2000, more than fifty years after the Second World War, the German government and German industry recognised that injustice had been done to millions of people, mainly from Eastern European countries, who had been forced to work for German companies or the Nazi regime.

'Wasn't Uncle Harry a prisoner of war, Auntie Anne?'

'Yes, June. He was.'

'Well then, he was a victim of the Nazi regime. He might be due some compensation. I wrote down the contact details for you.'

Anne and I had angry words about it and I told her that I did not want anything to do with it. 'But Harry, we're pensioners and we could do with the money.'

'Sorry, Anne, but no. I don't want anything to do with it.'

My nightmares, which Anne and I had accepted over the years as part of our life, became more frequent. I was exhausted during the day and had no interest in anything. It was Anne who decided to contact Peter Mulvany.

When he arrived at our home, I was furious; Anne had gone behind my back. I felt betrayed and slightly bewildered because Anne had never done anything like this before.

She asked me to hear him out and, to please her, I did. Peter explained that the association was a small group of relatives of seafarers who were lost on Irish-registered ships during the Second World War. The association helped families to get their entitlements, such as medals and death certificates, and, where necessary, to make representation on behalf of families. Following a query in Great Britain about the issue of Irishmen in the British Merchant Navy, the association was assisting the British authorities with the German Compensation Programme in Ireland. He offered to help me complete the forms to claim the payment before the deadline of 31 December 2001.

I knew I would have to tell Peter more than I had ever told anyone and I did not want Anne to hear what I had to say. I followed her into the kitchen where she was making coffee. I could not stay annoyed with Anne for long. She was right: as pensioners, extra money would be a help and it was not her fault that I had not told her my full story.

'I'm not happy about this but don't worry: I'll fill out the forms if that's what you want me to do.'

I was rewarded with one of Anne's wonderful smiles, a kiss and a hug. Peter and I filled out the application form. I told him that there had been thirty-one other Irishmen with me in Farge and he left to continue his quest to find other survivors. Most of them had been much older than me so the chances of them still being alive were slim.

Peter began to investigate the information I had given him and returned regularly to our house to discuss the war, my time at sea and my time in the camps. I still did not want to talk about my experiences and although I answered his questions, I did not tell him everything. I was able to confirm the names of the men who had died in Farge and Peter continued to try to trace the others.

At the age of eighty-one, my life had fallen into a routine. I was still able to do odd jobs for my children, I walked everywhere, I cooked and was generally in good health, except for my eyesight; I had been diagnosed with macular degeneration. Life was very quiet and I began to look forward to Peter's visits.

In 2003, Anne and I went on holiday to Crete. She had been thinking of my brother Edgar's death and had found out that there was a British and Commonwealth War Cemetery at Souda Bay in the northern part of the island. A lot of bodies had washed up on the shores of Crete and we hoped we would find Edgar's grave. At the War Cemetery the staff were very helpful but unfortunately, they could find no record of Edgar Callan on the HMS *Gloucester*. I lost all hope of tracing my brother.

When I told Peter about our visit to the cemetery on our return, he began his own investigation. He discovered a Matthew (which was Edgar's first name) Callan of 7 Derryview Terrace, Waterside, Derry, listed as an able seaman on the HMS *Gloucester*.

Edgar's body was never found. He is remembered with honour on the Plymouth Navy Memorial. He died on 22 May 1941, at the age of nineteen.

The person whom this scroll commemorates was numbered amongst those who, at the call of Monarch and Country left all that was dear to them, endured hardness, faced danger and finally passed out of the sight of men by the path of duty and self-sacrifice, giving up their own lives that others might live in freedom.

Let those who come after see to it that this person be not forgotten.

D/SSX 25344   Able Seaman

Matthew Edgar Callan

HMS Gloucester

Royal Navy

Date of Death: 22/05/1941

Commemorative Scroll for Matthew Edgar Callan, Royal Navy.

In March 2004 Peter told me that the International Organization for Migration had awarded me a payment of €7,700 as compensation for my years as a slave labourer in Germany. I did not want anything from Germany. Anne, however, was delighted. I hoped to hear no more about it so I was furious to read on the front page of the *Sunday Times,* 4 April 2004, for all to see, the headline 'Dublin man paid for Nazi slavery'.

> Harry Callan will receive up to €7,000 from the German government for his time as a prisoner of war. The first instalment of the payout, 75% of the total, was lodged to the pensioner's bank account last week. He will receive the remainder by August. Callan's was one of seven Irish claims submitted to the German Forced Labour Compensation Programme, a scheme established in 1999 by the International Organization for Migration (IOM) in Geneva to compensate victims of the Nazis.

'Where did they get this information? I never gave my permission. Did you talk to anyone about this, Anne?'

'No.'

Anne was as furious as I was. She was a very private person and would never have spoken about our finances to anyone. There were six other Irish claims, but we did not know who they were. Why were their names not printed in the newspaper? Now I could not get away from it. People from the neighbourhood stopped me to ask, 'Are you the Harry Callan that was mentioned in the *Sunday Times?*'

I was haunted by the thought that someone had betrayed me. I locked myself in the house and stopped going to church or the shops and for my daily walks. We went to Malta on holiday for six weeks, hoping that people would have forgotten about the article by the time we returned.

In July we received a gilt-edged invitation from the then Taoiseach, Bertie Ahern, to attend the National Day of Commemoration in the Royal Hospital Kilmainham, Dublin. This ceremony commemorates all those who fought and died in both world wars and all casualties of war. Anne and I were delighted to accept. On a lovely warm day, dressed in our Sunday best, we took a taxi into Dublin for the ceremony, which was attended by the President of Ireland Mary McAleese, the Taoiseach, members of the government, diplomats, church leaders and other dignitaries. There were prayers, speeches and music from the Army No.1 Band. Afterwards, as Anne and I did not see anyone we knew, we went home.

Peter and I never discussed the article but he spoke to me about returning to Germany, in particular to Farge and Bunker Valentin.

'I'm not going back there, Peter, no way.'

On the sixtieth anniversary of the liberation of the camps, there were commemoration ceremonies planned for April 2005 and he thought that I should go.

'I'm not going, Peter!'

But he was very persuasive. He had found Ginger O'Dwyer in Great Britain but he was not well enough to travel. Christy (Isaac) Ryan, who lived in Ireland, was the only other survivor to make the journey.

I never for one minute thought that Anne would agree to come with me but she did. On Wednesday 27 April 2005, we set off for Germany. We were a group of eight: Peter Mulvany, Christy Ryan, who was in a wheelchair, his daughter Deirdre, who as a nurse was there as her father's carer, Gerald O'Hara's son Edward and grandson Eamon, Deirdre Donnelly, who would document the proceedings for BBC Radio Ulster, Anne and I. Christy and I had not seen each other for over sixty years. There was not much conversation between us; too much time had passed.

It was a punishing schedule. After a two-hour flight to Hamburg Airport, Peter hired a minibus and drove us the three hours to Zeven where we stayed overnight. The following morning, we made the twenty-minute trip to Stalag XB Sandbostel. As we turned off the main road, there was the sign in large letters: Stalag XB. I got a sick feeling driving through those gates. There was no sand visible, just grass and molehills. But I could remember the sand blowing and the feeling of it in my eyes and nose and every other crevice in my body. Only the camp kitchen and a few of the barracks were left. Thousands of acres of farmland had been seized by the Nazis for camps during the war. Afterwards, the farmers who owned the land reclaimed as much as they could. Most of the camp had disappeared but earlier in 2005 the Sandbostel Camp Foundation had acquired a part of the former camp area, with nine historical buildings.

We were met and warmly welcomed by the project coordinator of the foundation, Dr Andreas Ehresmann, who spoke excellent English. Christy and I showed Andreas and Peter where our barracks had been. We described to them what it had been like to be there: what our guards were like and what the camp conditions had been. Andreas and his team were very courteous and interested in what we had to tell them. A simple ceremony was held in the camp grounds where a memorial stone had been raised for all who had been incarcerated there and for those who had perished. We laid our poppy wreath.

After lunch we left Sandbostel and drove to Milag und Marlag Nord Westertimke, about thirty minutes away. There was nothing left of the camp except one building, which had been renovated over the years and was now someone's home. The rest of the camp area had been turned

Harry laying a wreath at Milag und Marlag Nord, Westertimke, in April 2015.

over to nature and become a recreational park for the locals. Where the entrance gates had been, the eight of us joined other Navy and Merchant Navy veterans to commemorate the liberation of Milag Nord. A bagpiper played laments as a memorial plaque was unveiled in memory of all the prisoners of war who had been incarcerated there for up to five years and for those who had died. There were local reporters, as well as Deirdre Donnelly, covering the event and they asked Christy and me what we remembered of Milag und Marlag Nord. We told them it was a four-star hotel compared to where we ended up.

We left Westertimke and headed for Farge, about an hour's drive away. We had an early dinner, during which I noticed that Anne did not eat much.

'Are you all right, Anne?'

'Yes, Harry. Just tired.'

It had been a long, tiring day. All I wanted to do was to take Anne to our room and have a good night's sleep.

Peter had arranged a meeting with some local people in a private room in the hotel; the meeting would be recorded by Bremen TV/Radio and Deirdre Donnelly. This was the first I had heard about it and, although annoyed, I felt obliged to stay. Only Peter, Deirdre and I attended the meeting; the others had retired. I was introduced to Herr Heiko Kania, Herr Gerhard and Frau Rita Scharnhorst, and an interpreter, Constantin von der Schulenburg. While other people came in and took their seats, Peter explained to me that this voluntary group had managed to save the camp administration building from destruction and had arranged for it to be moved to its new position on a portion of the original Marine camp, which they had also acquired. The building was renamed 'Barrack 27'.

At Barrack 27, April 2015. *Front row: (l–r)* Dr Christel Trouvé, Gundela Kania, Harry Callan, Helen Dempsey, Rita Scharnhorst, Michèle Callan, Gerard Scharnhorst; *back row: (l–r)* Brian Callan, Dr Marcus Meyer, Rev. Evert Brink, Rolf-Dieter von Bargen, Petra Maurer, Vanessa Müller and Rainer Christochowitz.

The sixteen people in the room were second-generation Germans from Farge and the surrounding areas who were interested in their local history. They had been small children during the war and, like the Heidbreders and Günthers, their parents had also sheltered them from the horrors of it as much as possible. Some of them had lived on the boundaries of the camp and not known it was there. They never learned anything about this part of the war in school and their parents and grandparents did not talk about it either. They were now adults, some of them near

retirement age, and they wanted to know what had gone on
in their area during that time.

Through Constantin, they told me that over the years
they had gathered a lot of information and thoroughly
researched as best they could the *AEL* camp in Farge and
the Marine camp. Using Barrack 27 as their meeting room
and education centre, they had created a permanent display
from the information gathered and liaised with schools in
the region to include Barrack 27 in educational tours. In
all their research, there had been no mention of our group
of thirty-two Irish-born British Merchant seamen. They
needed to know the truth. The interview was conducted in
English. So many questions were fired at me that it began
to feel like an interrogation.

'There were 32 of us. We were Irish-born British
Merchant seamen, prisoners of war. We refused to work *frei*
for Hitler. We said "no" too often.'

I told them about the Marine camp and the move to the
AEL camp. They had difficulty believing what I was telling
them about our treatment and the treatment meted out to
the other prisoners. I did not realise that I had got to my
feet nor that I had raised my voice. I was telling them the
truth, but how could I convince them? I told them about
Herr Günther and working in his garden centre. I told them
about Dr Heidbreder and working for Frau Heidbreder in
her garden. Then a lady sitting in the room stood up and
said, 'I know you.'

I stopped talking and looked at her. I did not recognise
her at all.

'I know you! I lived in Blumenthal and Dr Heidbreder
was our family doctor. I heard my parents talking about
an *Irländer* working at the doctor's house. Once when I

was there I heard you talking to one of his children and on another visit I saw you working in the garden. When I asked my parents, I was told you were the *Irländer*.'

'That was me! I learned my German from the Heidbreder children.'

The relief. Someone remembered us! She might only have been a small child then but she was a mature lady now and she remembered us! Perhaps it was my imagination or my tiredness but I felt the atmosphere in the room change. 'Finally,' I thought, 'they believe me.'

Gerhard Scharnhorst brought me to a model of the *AEL* camp and asked me to confirm the layout of the camp.

'You've a few things wrong here. This was where the entrance was. The administration building was here and across from it was our barracks.'

I moved the little buildings around and indicated the rest of the layout to him: where our camp ended, where Camp Farge – the Neuengamme Satellite camp – began and where the covered-in oil tankers were.

The meeting ended. It was now 1 a.m. and I was sick with tiredness but my heart was singing; they knew we had been there.

Early next morning, we loaded our cases onto the minibus and at 8.30 a.m., after a ten-minute drive, we arrived at Bunker Valentin. The trees were gone and the bunker was clearly visible from the road. Word had got out that there were to be commemoration ceremonies held at the bunker and a lot of people were curious, especially when they saw the bagpiper and reporters. After the war the German Navy took over the building and used it as a storage and warehouse unit. There was a whole generation of German people who knew nothing else about it. The commemoration organisers had arranged with the Navy that we would be brought into the bunker to see it. Now, as the shadow of Bunker Valentin towered over us, and as we were led closer and closer to the building, the organisers were unaware that Christy and I were no longer part of their world. They had become kapos and we were being frogmarched onto the site. We were back there. We could hear the shouting of guards, the screaming of men as they fell to their deaths, dogs barking, the lash of whips, the pounding of the machinery, the groans of the building itself – it was unbearable. Christy was slumped in his wheelchair, crying. He had not been back to Bunker Valentin since liberation. I had passed by it many times on the River Weser and had thought I would be okay but I had not been this close to it. I completely broke down, and fell to my knees, distraught. I could not stop crying. Anne was very frightened for me. We were married fifty-five years and in all that time she had never seen me cry.

Later, at the monument which is named 'Annihilation Through Work' and depicts the workers being crushed under the building, Deirdre Donnelly bent forward with her microphone to ask Christy how he felt being there.

'It shows the truth,' Christy said, and I agreed.

Although it was very hard to be there, we were both glad we had made the journey. We were witnesses. It seemed that no one knew anything about the thirty-two Irish-born British Merchant seamen who had been there from the beginning and who had turned the first sod on this site.

'All right, Christy?'

'Okay now, Harry. And you?'

'Yes, okay now too. I'm glad we got into the bunker. It was terrible but I feel as if a dark cloud has been lifted off me.'

Harry Callan in April 2015 beside the memorial cross
erected for Patrick Breen at the site of the mass grave in the
Arbeitserziehungslager.

We climbed back into the minibus and drove the fifteen-minute journey to where the *AEL* camp and Camp Farge had been. The two camps had been demolished after the war and the land was now a forest and recreational area. Only the foundations of the barracks could be seen. We drove along the forest roads to the site of the mass grave where we planted a cross in memory of Patrick Breen. This wooden cross and brass plaque were commissioned by the Irish Seamen's Relatives Association with funds received from Dublin Bus personnel and carried from Ireland by Peter. At 10 a.m. we held a short ceremony there which was attended by our group, Heiko Kania, Gerhard Scharnhorst

Poppy crosses laid by Harry Callan at the graves of Thomas Murphy, Gerald O'Hara and Owen Corr at Rheinberg Cemetery in 2015.

and the military chaplain Rev. Martin Engelhardt. Deirdre Donnelly and the local newspaper recorded the event.

We had always thought that Patrick had died in Bremen Hospital and was buried in the mass grave outside the camp. Recently I found out that he had not been brought to Bremen Hospital, in fact, but to the hospital in Rotenburg-Unterstedt, 70 km southeast of Bremen-Farge, where his death is recorded. Unfortunately, there is no record of where he was buried but more than likely it was in the mass grave near Rotenburg-Unterstedt. Patrick Breen's body has never been found; he is remembered with honour as British Merchant Navy on Panel 11 of the Tower Hill Memorial in London.

It was a three-hour journey to the British Commonwealth Cemetery at Rheinberg, Düsseldorf, to visit the graves of Gerald O'Hara, Thomas Murphy, Owen Corr and William Knox. I was glad that Christy and I were with the O'Hara men at Gerald's grave. Together we read the poem 'For the Fallen' by Robert Laurence Binyon.

> They shall grow not old, as we that are left grow old:
> Age shall not weary them, nor the years condemn.
> At the going down of the sun and in the morning
> We will remember them.

I was physically and mentally exhausted by the time we reached our hotel. Anne, too, was overwhelmed. It was late when we eventually got to bed and fell into an exhausted sleep. On Saturday 30 April we drove the 240 km to Schiphol Amsterdam Airport to fly home. I was worried about Anne: she did not look well.

26

NEW FRIENDS AND OLD FRIENDS

WHEN PETER VISITED soon after the trip he told me that he had made arrangements with Dr Katharina Hoffmann, a professor of History in the University of Oldenburg, to come to Ireland to interview Edward O'Hara and myself; Christy was not well enough. She wanted a living-witness account for their academic records. I told him that I had done enough and that I did not want to be involved but, once again, Peter persuaded me to do it.

In June, Dr Hoffmann and her photographer, Wolfgang Wortmann, met Edward and me in Dublin. She made it easy to talk to her. At the meeting in Farge, I felt that I had to prove to the Germans that we had been slave labourers there and that I was telling the truth. Now, here was a university professor; by sending Dr Hoffmann it proved to me that they really wanted to know what had happened to us.

Peter took Dr Hoffmann to the German Military Cemetery at Glencree in Wicklow where there are 134 Luftwaffe and Kriegsmarine men interred. She also accompanied a group of us on a visit to the Seaman's Monument at City Quay in Dublin. This monument, which was unveiled by President Patrick Hillery in May 1990, is a large ship's anchor resting on a tall granite stone and is dedicated to all those Irish seafarers who lost their lives serving on Irish merchant ships during Second World War.

Dr Hoffmann and her photographer laid a wreath depicting the Irish and German flags with the following inscription on the accompanying card: 'In Remembrance of Irish Seamen who died and suffered in the Arbeitserziehungslager Bremen-Farge 1943–1945. From Memorial Site Bremen-Farge Schwanewede Germany.'

Peter encouraged me to attend the Remembrance Day ceremonies in London. I had never attended the annual ceremony in Derry partly because I was usually away at sea but also because it was not the done thing in the Catholic community; I had never worn a poppy. This time I went, with a poppy pinned to the lapel of my Merchant Navy blazer, and joined other seamen behind our flag standards. There was a wonderful atmosphere and I was glad I was part of it. In January 2006, on one of his visits, Peter suggested that we should travel to Germany again. I discussed it with Anne.

'Do you want to go back, Harry?'

'I'm not sure, Anne. Peter tells me I'm the only one fit to travel now and that the people at Bunker Valentin and Sandbostel have more questions to ask me. I think it's important to make sure that they record all about the thirty-two of us. They know very little about us.'

'If you want to go, Harry, that's fine. But I don't want you to be upset again.'

This year there was no fanfare or fuss at Bunker Valentin, just Dr Marcus Meyer and his team, who gave me a warm welcome. Whether it was this or the lack of crowds in the bunker I do not know, but I did not experience the overpowering shock of 2005, although I could still feel the ghosts and it was very emotional. On one of the days we made the seven-hour round trip to visit Rheinberg War Cemetery in Düsseldorf.

I also received a great welcome from Dr Andreas Ehresmann and the team of historians at Stalag XB. I was invited to lunch with the team at Barrack 27, the group that grilled me the previous year; they eagerly showed me the work they had been doing. I enjoyed my time with them and felt at home in their company. On one of his visits, Peter gave me a gift of a book containing excerpts from *War Crimes Trial 'Bremen Farge' Summing-up by Judge Advocate,* published by Curio House Hamburg in February 1948. He had marked various pages, highlighting references to the Irishmen. I put it to one side. When Peter and I returned to Germany in 2007 to pay our respects at all the memorial sites and visit the teams, we were invited by the Lord Mayor of Bremen, Jens Böhrnsen, to lunch in the Gold Room in Bremen Town Hall. It is a magnificent building, with gold everywhere: from the beautifully carved walls to the tableware and even the backs of the chairs. It was a great honour to be treated this way and we thanked Jens Böhrnsen for his hospitality.

In June 2007, Anne and I again attended the National Day of Commemoration in the Royal Hospital Kilmainham. I also received an invitation from Buckingham Palace to attend Her Royal Highness Princess Anne's Not Forgotten Association Tea Party. It was held in the palace gardens in July.

It was a great honour to be invited. Peter, too, had received an invitation so we travelled together and met up with other veterans from the British Merchant Navy. Princess Anne was very welcoming, and other members of the Royal Family also mingled with guests: it was great to be there.

Catherine, Harry, Michael and Brian hesitated when I asked them to come with me to Germany in 2008. They had grown up with my nightmares and I had no idea how they had been affected by them. They had also seen the effect the earlier trip had had on their mother. The little they knew made them angry with the Germans for what they had done to me and the other Irishmen. But I wanted them to meet some of the good German people. Reluctantly, they agreed to come with me.

Then, on 12 February 2008, our eldest son, Harry, suddenly died from an embolism. He was fifty-five. Anne was so shocked and heartbroken that she had a major stroke. I know now that I should have cancelled the trip to Germany but I was locked up in my grief and did not pay attention to what was happening around me. My children called a family meeting and eventually it was decided that Catherine's husband, Michael Purcell, would travel in her place and she would stay at home to mind Anne. Because there was funding in place, Michael, Brian and I felt obliged to go.

This year I was welcomed at Barrack 27 by Frau Marieluise Beck, the former Federal Commissioner for Migration, Refugees and Integration in Germany. Heiko Kania contacted the Heidbreder and Günther families and it was wonderful when Mareike and Uwe Heidbreder and Wilfried Günther walked through the door.

'Harry! Onkel Harry!'

There were hugs, tears, laughter and plenty of talk. Wilfried told my sons about the little boat I had given him and how, when he was older, his father Richard placed it behind glass in a cabinet in the house.

Once more, we were invited to lunch in the Gold Room by the Lord Mayor of Bremen, Jens Böhrnsen. To dine in the Gold Room once was a special honour; having my boys with me this time made it even more so. I was thankful that they had come with me but, like my father before me, I never talked to my sons about their feelings. At home, I grieved alone for Harry.

In April 2009, I returned to Germany with Peter once more. I was delighted to hear that numbers of visitors to the sites had increased, proving that there was a generation hungry for information about the war.

At the age of eighty-six, Anne had a major stroke and required full-time care. She moved to the Lusk Community Unit in the village where Michael and Brian lived, which was a short bus journey for me; I got used to living alone.

It was in March 2010, after an official trip Peter made to Argentina, that he told me he had met Frances Evans, the daughter of Frank and Joan Evans from the *Afric Star*. Joan had returned to Argentina after the war. Frances was writing a book about her mother called *Quiet Endurance* and would be launching it in La Cumbre, Argentina, the following January. Peter phoned her and when I heard the voice of a softly spoken woman with perfect English, I introduced myself and told her what I knew about her father. She told me that Sheila Jagoe had also survived the war and had remained great friends with her mother. I learned from her that Arthur Freeman and her father were buried in the Cimetière St Bris in Villenave-D'Ornon in

Bordeaux. In April 2010, Peter and I travelled by ferry from Rosslare to Cherbourg and drove the six-hour journey to the graveyard in Bordeaux. It comforted me to pray, to lay poppy crosses on their graves and to let them know that they had not been forgotten. We then drove to Bremen-Farge where my daughter Catherine joined us.

Our itinerary was the same as in previous years: we visited Rheinberg Cemetery; Milag und Marlag Nord in Westertimke; Bunker Valentin Stalag XB; and Barrack 27. Part of the Marine camp is currently an army base and we were all invited to lunch in the officers' mess.

In July 2010, Anne had another stroke and our children took turns to keep vigil at her bedside. On 31 July I whispered into her ear 'Anne, love, I'm going to Mass now. Catherine is here and I'll be back shortly. I love you.'

While I was at Mass she took her last breath; a huge chunk of my heart died with her that day.

I chose to spend Christmas 2010 on my own. In January 2011 Peter and I flew to Argentina for two weeks, for the launch of France Evans' book. Tim Lough, Vice-Chairman of the Buenos Aires branch of the Royal British Legion, showed us around before we flew to La Cumbre where Frances and her husband Walter live; it was wonderful to meet her in person.

The launch of *Quiet Endurance* took place at the former La Cumbre train station which is now the local hall. There were about 150 people there along with Francisco Capdevila, President of La Cumbre Historic Board, and Charlie Engel, the Lord Mayor of La Cumbre, who issued Municipal Decrees on 28 January 2011 naming Peter and me as 'Distinguished Guests of La Cumbre'. For the first time, I wore my service medals on my Merchant Navy blazer: the 1939–1945 War medal; the 1939–1945 Star medal and a Prisoner-of-War medal. Peter presented a framed document from the Lord Mayor of Dublin to the Lord Mayor of La Cumbre conveying greetings to the Irish, Argentine and British communities. He then asked me to make the following presentations to Frances: a badge from the Not Forgotten Association; honorary life membership of the National Ex-Prisoner of War Association; a commemorative Ex-Prisoner of War medal (Frances was the first British baby born in captivity); and a commemorative Ex-Prisoner of War medal in memory of her mother, Joan. We paid our respects at the British Cemetery in La Cumbre where we held a small memorial service for Frances' parents and deceased war veterans. It was a tearful goodbye; it was unlikely that Frances and I would see each other again but we promised to keep in touch.

In April 2011 Peter and I returned to Germany. I was recorded by Dr Marcus Meyer and his team at Bunker Valentin who were trying to piece together the information and history of the bunker site. They needed witness statements and I was one of the few who were willing to talk to them about our time there. I still had information about the camp that might be of help to them.

On our second last night, I got a phone call, via Heiko Kania, from a woman who introduced herself as Birgit Hyndes, the daughter of Katie Sause. I took the phone from Heiko and my heart was pounding.

'Hello, this is Harry.'

'Harry, my name is Birgit. There was an article and photograph of you in our local newspaper and my mother recognised you.'

Then, in a mixture of German and English, she said, 'Please, Harry, can you come to visit my mother? She is not well. She is dying and would really like to see you. Please, can you come?'

'Of course I'll come. I'll pass you back to Heiko. Give him the address and I'll see Katie tomorrow.'

I told Peter to cancel the arrangements he had made for the next day; I was going to visit Katie.

Birgit lived an hour's drive away. I was afraid I would be too late but when we arrived Birgit took me to her mother who was sitting in a big armchair with lots of cushions. She looked up smiled at me and held up her arms.

'Harry!'

'Ah, Katie.'

I quickly crossed the room, knelt down and put my arms around her, being very careful not to hurt her. We held each other for a few moments and the tears flowed down our cheeks. We talked about the first time we met and I reminded her of the day she threw the dictionary on the table; along with our tears we also laughed. I told her about Anne's death and she told me about her husband's. She had cancer and knew she was dying. She had wanted to see me once more and thought it was a miracle when Birgit brought her the newspaper article. Katie was exhausted; it was time to end our visit. We hugged each other and I told her that I would be in Farge on 8 May; I would call to see her then.

Birgit and Stephan, her husband, joined us for dinner that night and I told them about how Katie and I had met and her kindness to me; that I would love her all my life for what she had done for me. Then Stephan asked, 'Harry, was there ever more than a friendship? An affair?'

Birgit (Katie Sause's daughter) and her husband Stephan Hyndes
with Harry at their home in 2014.

I was shocked. I could not believe I was being asked
this. Birgit and Stephan explained that when I arrived back
in Bremen after the war asking people if they knew the
whereabouts of Katie Sause, the talk went around that an
Irländer was back looking for her. A rumour started that
we must have been lovers. Was that why Katie's husband
had been so unfriendly? I was angry, but I did not raise my
voice.

'There is absolutely no truth in that rumour. I won't have
anyone dirtying Katie's name like that. It was dangerous
enough for her talking to me and feeding me in the kitchen.

It was war! I was a prisoner of war. Katie was a good kind German girl. That's all.'

Stephan asked if he could interview me for Bremen Radio/TV. I agreed to do it with Katie, if she was well enough. It was arranged for 8 May in Barrack 27 because I was returning then for the official handing over by the Navy of the bunker to the custodial team of the 'Denkort Bunker Valentin' memorial.

It was 23 degrees Celsius on 8 May but only 7 degrees in the bunker. We sat in our coats and gloves but still the cold seeped into our bones. The ceremony was well attended by ministers of state, the army, academics, former prisoners, local people and descendants of some of the prisoners. After speeches from various ministers, an orchestra played beautiful, haunting music. The sound travelled around the walls of Bunker Valentin up into the roof and when it stopped its echo could be heard further on in the bowels of the building. As the last notes faded and silence returned, the building filled with applause, which lifted the mood. After a few hours we came outside into blinding sunlight.

Birgit brought Katie in her wheelchair to Barrack 27 and I was there to meet her. I took her inside where Rolf-Dieter von Bargen, Barrack 27's new chairman, greeted us. We held hands. At times we were crying and other times we were smiling. The interview lasted a little over one hour and was in German. I got stuck on some words but Katie helped me and I reminded her again of the time she threw the dictionary down on the table.

'*Dar war ich wohl eine gute Lehrerin.*' ('I must have been a good teacher so.')

We both laughed. On Sunday 5 June I received a phone call from Stephan to tell me that Katie had died. I phoned

Peter and asked him if he would be able to travel with me to her funeral. I had a little money put by which I used to cover our expenses and Peter made the necessary arrangements.

During the year I attended the Irish memorial ceremonies with my daughter-in-law Michèle, Michael's wife. In January 2012, I received an invitation to the Holocaust Memorial Day in Dublin's Mansion House. I did not know what to expect but it was a very dignified and inclusive ceremony and was very moving. In April, Peter and I flew to Germany where, at Stalag XB, I joined four other survivors – a Belgian, a Pole, an Italian and a Russian – to give our witness statements to Andreas and his team. When I heard their stories I was thankful that I had been there for only a short time in 1941.

Shortly after we arrived home from Germany, Peter stopped visiting. He told me that he was involved in another project and that he needed to devote more time to it. He also passed Michèle's contact details to the Bunker Valentin team. Michèle and Michael discussed the situation, as they both knew how important these visits had become to me, and soon after Michèle called to say she would look after future trips to Germany and she would also bring me to the commemoration ceremonies in Dublin.

27

WAR CRIMES TRIAL FINDINGS

A TRIAL TOOK PLACE in a military court convened in Hamburg between 19 December 1947 and 24 February 1948, presided over by Judge Advocate Guy Sixsmith. Thirteen men were accused of allegedly ill-treating Allied nationals interned in an *AEL* camp in Bremen: Hans Hasse, Walter Heidbreder, Wilhelm Plothe, Frank Sauer, Karl Walhorn, Friedrich Gaertner, Ludwig Zehnter, Walther Grauer-Carstensen, Johannes Meyer, Guenther Velke, Erich Voss, Heinrich Breckner and Daniel Van Der Veen.

In addition, five of them were accused of the second charge of being concerned in the killing of Allied nationals interned in the same camp: Heidbreder, Meyer, Plothe, Velke and Walhorn.

I knew nothing about this at the time. It was not until Michèle read excerpts from the book Peter had given me that I learned details about the men who haunted my nightmares. I was shocked and horrified at some of the things that Michèle read to me. Knott, Ryan and O'Dwyer had been called by the prosecution and she was now reading their accounts of life in the camp. I was very angry by their comments about Dr Heidbreder. Why had they been called but not the rest of us? Two of them called him 'a goat skinner' (an Irish expression used by poor Irish farmers for the veterinarian who came to look after their livestock but who himself was too poor to have modern medicine and equipment). To someone who had never heard it before, it must have sounded derogatory – it made him sound like a butcher. Someone should have explained what it meant. I would have spoken up for the doctor. He had done everything he could for us. There was no medicine, not even for his own patients in the village.

I suddenly realised that I had never asked the lads who had remained in the camp while the rest of us went to the village and farms what it had been like for them all day on their own with some of the guards. What had it been like for them during the typhus shutdown while I was safely hidden in Dr Heidbreder's? We had never talked about these things. We knew the dangers of casual talk. I had seen Corr, O'Hara and Murphy sick and bedridden but they died in hospital. I could not imagine the horrors of the sickbay where up to 200 men died from the disease. What had Ginger Ryan and Knott seen? They must have thought the doctor was useless.

From Dr Heidbreder and Karl Walhorn's depositions, Michèle read:

Walter Heidbreder, born in 1902 in Düsseldorf, was a doctor of medicine and from 1930 practised in Bremen-Farge. He joined the SA (*Sturm Abteilungin*) in 1933, a group of mainly unemployed and some former soldiers, whose function was to break up meetings of Nazi opponents. He joined the NAD (*Reichsarbeitsdienst* or State Labour Service – formerly the NSDAP (*Nationalsozialist-Arbeitdienst* or National Socialist Labour Service) in 1937. In 1942 he was called up by the army and was ordered by the medical board at Bremen to look after the welfare of three camps in the Bremen-Farge area. He made regular reports to the Authorities about conditions in the camp and protested against the punishment, which consisted in giving the prisoners no food, and also against the condition of the cells.

In spring 1945, when the Russian prisoners' doctor, Dr Nowitzki, asked for his help concerning the increase of cases of death by force in the camp, he made an urgent telephone call to Herr Hesse, a senior official in Berlin who was in charge of the *AEL* camps, and the following morning the Gestapo arrested Schauwacker and two or three guards. Regarding his practice of medicine, he stressed that he always did his best considering the conditions. He was exonerated of all charges.

Karl Walhorn was born in 1914 in Osnabrück and was a window dresser by profession. He said that he was employed with the Gestapo at Bremen from 1937 until 1940, when he was appointed Camp Commandant of the Labour Education Camp Bremen-Farge. During his time in the camp, he claimed that not more than four or five prisoners were shot dead while trying to escape and that he did not allow prisoners to be beaten. He said that the British sailors told him that when they had refused to work freely for Germany, they were sent to the labour education camp.

He stated that the head of the Bremen Gestapo, Dr Zimmermann, ordered that the British sailors be sent to a concentration camp as they refused to work. He ensured that this was not carried out; they stayed in the camp nearly until the end of the war. He also said that the British sailors had privileges and that he had helped them in every respect. He admitted occasionally hitting internees himself and firing at prisoners who were trying to steal potatoes. He accepted responsibility for everything that went on in the camp while he was there. He was convicted under the first charge but not under the second. He was sentenced to four years' imprisonment.

Erich Voss was born in 1908 in Saxony and was a dairy assistant. He served as a policeman in the police prison in Oldenburg and was commandant in the *AEL*-Farge camp for fourteen days between the arrest of Schauwacker and the appointment of Schrader. He was exonerated of all charges.

The one man who deserved to be punished was missing from the list: Heinrich Schauwacker. He has never been brought to trial for war crimes. I knew nothing about Schauwacker except that he was vicious; everyone was terrified of him. The warrant for his arrest was among the documents shown in the book. My blood turned cold when Michèle read what Schauwacker had done before he came to Farge. There was a letter from him to Dr Goebbels boasting of his success in killing Russians. He wrote in the letter that he was 'ordered to take part in the executions of JEWS, GYPSIES and RUSSIANS'. He also stated: '… at the castle of the SIPO and the SD in KLEIN TROSTINAZ I had to shoot 3,600 Men WOMEN and Children in a barn in two days. This number of people came from all the surrounding

Prisons and Camps near MINSK and they were all shot by Sturmscharführer WALTER OTTE and myself.'

That was the sort of monster he was. Michèle read on:

> While Schauwacker was arrested in February 1945 in Bremen Farge by the Gestapo he mysteriously disappeared and a warrant for his re-arrest was issued. He was tracked, found and twice escaped while using false identification papers and identities, known aliases Heinz Joachim Adamovsky and Jonny Bindhammer and his last sighting was at a hotel Hotel Zum Dampfboot owned by one of his relatives in Berlin …
>
> He was arrested towards the end of the War (Feb. 1945) for ill-treatment of prisoners … but is believed to have been released on special conditions i.e. He had to become a member of the <u>AKTION BUNDSCHUH</u> (SIPO stay-behind organisation) and is believed to have led a 'Grupp'.

Then Michèle read Dr Alfred Paul Schweder's deposition: 'After my return to Bremen I arranged for Schauwacker to be detained in the Gestapo building and the two others in a Wehrmacht-prison. Furthermore I wrote a comprehensive report on the case. Warnke had continued with the investigations and it is possible that he had arrested two further persons …'

I found out from Grauer-Carstensen's deposition that he named those arrested: 'They were: Schauwacker, Plothe, Velke, Witt and Luchinski.' Schweder's deposition continued:

On two occasions I personally gave Schauwacker
short leave from the prison, once for the funeral of his
child and the second time for assistance in connection
with air-raid damage to our premises. Schauwacker
was a trained member of the fire service. Both his
leaves extended over several hours at a time. I know
that later on, after the 1st April, 1945, Schauwacker
and the others whom I had arrested in the Farge affair
were released by Dr Kiessel, the commander of the
Security police at Bremen. I met Dr Kiessel later in
the camp of Nirenberg. We were there together for
several months. I have heard that he [Schauwacker]
was sent to Yugoslavia as a witness. I could not say
whether he has come back.

Michèle read that Captain R. W. Rose of the War Crimes
Investigation Unit reported:

If this man is found; he is of Automatic arrest category.
Will the Officer who makes the arrest please ascertain
whether or not he <u>has</u> been at Bremen Farge. <u>If so
He is responsible for the deaths of hundreds of Allied
Nationals including a few British.</u>

I could not believe it. They actually had him and let him
go! Where was he now? How could they have released that
monster? It was from the depositions that Michèle learned
that, thanks to Dr Heidbreder, this brutal man had been
reported and removed.

From all the statements and depositions, nobody correctly
recorded our nationality or number. Even Brigadier R.C.

Halse DJAG (Deputy Judge Advocate General) recorded us as: '30 or 40 British and natives of Eire …'

Reading the book, Michèle realised just how close we came to being sent to Neuengamme Concentration Camp where we would surely have died. After they completed their prison terms, Kommandant Walhorn returned to his wife and children in Neunkirchen and Dr Heidbreder returned to his home in Farge and his practice.

These two men had done the best they could for us. They got us off the work detail and treated us as prisoners of war, letting us work for the villagers and farmers. I wished that I had been called to give evidence. I kept thinking about the Heidbreder children and Kommandant Walhorn's little girls. I felt really sorry for these innocent children. It is always the children who suffer during war.

28

KEEPING THE MEMORIES ALIVE

IN 2013 Michèle organised the trip to Germany. My children Catherine, Michael and Brian, my niece Martina and Anne's niece June joined us. On our first day in Farge, I met Birgit and Stephan and went with them to place flowers on Katie's grave.

The next day we went to Bunker Valentin to meet the Denkort team. We were joined by Wilfried and Helga Günther and Enno Heidbreder. The senior students from Oberschule an der Egge in Blumenthal had assembled at the memorial outside Bunker Valentin to run a 5 km race, ending at the site of the administration building in Camp Farge. The tradition had begun in 2005 but it was the first time that I had seen it. I was asked to speak to the students before their run about my war experiences.

There were about fifty teenagers in the room but as soon as Dr Marcus stood up to introduce me there was silence. I spoke in English and told them about daily life in the *AEL*-Farge camp. There was a short question-and-answer session after my talk.

One of the students asked me in English, 'Mr Callan, how did you feel when you received the payment from Germany of €7,700 for your labour at Bunker Valentin? Were you insulted by this amount?'

'The amount of money meant very little to me but by writing that cheque the German government finally recognised the fact that we had been here and that acknowledgment of me and my thirty-one fellow Irishmen as slave labourers was more important than the amount.'

Another student asked, 'Mr Callan, did you think of your family while you were in the *Arbeitserziehungslager*?'

'No, never. You didn't let yourself think about your family. That would lead to despair and melancholy and you could not let yourself go there. So no, we didn't talk about our families and we tried not to think about them either.'

And another question: 'Mr Callan, how did you keep going?'

'We kept going with a four letter word. It's a little four-letter word but it is a huge word. H – O – P – E. We lived on hope. Without it, we were dead men.'

Afterward, Marcus and his team showed us their plans for the new interpretive centre, which would open to the public in 2015. Architect and design students from Alwin Lonke-Road School, using information from prisoners like Raymond Portefaix and me, were designing a model of the cement mixer for display at the site. It was good to see young people getting involved with historians.

At Westertimke, we were greeted by the Bürgermeister (or mayor), Hans-Joachim Nikolaus, before attending the sixty-eighth anniversary of the liberation of Stalag XB, Sandbostel on 29 April 2013, when the new permanent Interpretive Exhibition Centre was opened. Among the attendees were over a hundred relatives of former prisoners and there were three former prisoners of war at the ceremony: Sergei Litvin, aged ninety-one from Russia who had spent three years there; Roger Cottyn, aged ninety-two from Belgium who had spent five years there and who was one of the first survivors to come back and to give witness at the commemoration ceremonies; and I was the third. This year, Sergei Litvin was going to speak for us. The guest of honour was Dr Hans Engel, a Jew and a member of the Medical Corps of the Royal British troops. In April 1945 Dr Engel had participated in the liberation of the camp and its satellite concentration camp of Neuengamme. It was Dr Engel who ensured that German nurses were brought in after liberation to provide aid to these concentration camp prisoners. He also developed a special nutrition programme for the starving inmates and organised recovery measures for the typhoid patients in the region. It was also his birthday: he was ninety-seven on 29 April 2013 and he gave a speech about his time at Sandbostel. He died just months later, on 23 October 2013.

Enno arranged a tour of what had been Dr Heidbreder's house. The present owner, Frau Schultz, graciously welcomed us all. The parquet floor in the dining room was the same one from which I had removed the original varnish with wire wool. I told Frau Schultz about this. She laughed and was delighted to hear stories about the house.

Michèle accompanied me to all the Irish commemoration ceremonies that year and in November I celebrated my ninetieth birthday with family and friends in Skerries. It was a very emotional birthday for me because I had all my family around me; I was a very lucky man. I was finding it hard to breathe again and was struggling to walk to Mass

On the dyke in 2013 *(l–r):* Enno Heidbreder, Harry Callan, Babs Daehr and Uwe Heidbreder.

but I said nothing to my family. Before I went to Germany, Michèle insisted that I have a medical check-up and fortunately all I needed was a change in my medication.

In the autumn of 2013 Joe Kearney, a freelance journalist, asked if he could make a documentary about the thirty-two of us for RTÉ Radio. In April 2014, Ronan Kelly (the series producer and acting sound engineer of *Documentary on One*) and his son Dara joined Michèle, Brian and me on our annual pilgrimage to Germany. The radio documentary *Clouds in Harry's Coffee* was aired on 13 September on RTÉ Radio 1. It was broadcast in Ireland, Great Britain, Germany, Poland and other European countries and, through the power of the Internet, as far away as the US,

Canada and Australia. We received emails from relatives of the Irishmen thanking us for the documentary and telling us that they had never known anything about that period of their relative's life, other than they had been a prisoner of war. Like me, none of the Irishmen had spoken about it. They were surprised to hear their relative's name read out on the radio and to know that they were remembered in this way each year at the commemoration ceremonies in Germany.

That year I was recorded in Denkort Bunker Valentin for their archives. After the annual race, one of the students, who was studying English and had been designated spokesperson for the group, came up to me and said, 'Mr Callan, we would like to change the name of our run in 2015. With your permission instead of "Memorial Run" we want to name it the Harry Callan *Lauf* [Run].'

I certainly was not expecting this. 'But you need to discuss that with your teachers and Dr Marcus,' I said.

'They said it was all right if you agree. We would like to do this.'

I heard the sincerity in his voice and was moved to tears. 'I thank you for this honour. I accept on behalf of my fellow Irishmen, my comrades.'

'Mr Callan, we are the honoured ones that you come back to speak to us,' said his teacher, Herr Schiller, as they both bowed to me.

We visited Neuengamme Concentration Camp, a ninety-minute drive from our hotel, because I wanted my family to see the boxcar, used for the transportation of POWs, displayed there. Among other things, we saw the ruins of the crematorium where we stood for a while and prayed for all those lost souls. Then we went to Westertimke. Herr

Students from Oberschule an der Egge, Blumenthal, laying wreaths with Harry at the commemoration ceremony at Bunker Valentin in April 2015.

and Frau Heitmann maintain the monument and the little garden surrounding it on a voluntary basis. Herr Heitmann installed a garden bench so that people can sit and spend some time in contemplation at the monument. In their own quiet way, the Heitmanns have honoured the memory of all those who passed through the camp.

We made a special trip to Bremervörde to meet Karola, the cousin of our Irish-German friend, Heinz Glier. Heinz had told them of my experience in 1943, when the villagers had stoned us. Over *kaffee und kuchen* Karola told me her story. She spoke slowly and emotionally, and Heinz translated.

I was very young at the time. I remember being kept inside the house with the door locked and the curtains drawn. I remember Grandfather, Father and other villagers taking bread and water from the house and trying to give it to the prisoners while they were lined up outside the station. The Gestapo shoved them back and told them that if they were 'good Germans' they would not feed the enemy. They were told to throw stones at the prisoners while they were being marched out of the village. They were to show these prisoners that they were our enemy; anyone who didn't like it could join them. So the men threw stones and turnips, but not all of them aimed to hit. Father and Grandfather were very upset that they had done what they were told. It was the first time I saw my father and my grandfather cry. It was the first time I felt fear in my home and in my village. A couple of weeks later, the Gestapo came back to our village and the men were conscripted into the army. Only the very old men and very small boys were left and I lived with fear every day after that.

We were both crying as we held each other's hands.

'I am sorry, Harry, that this happened to you. How can you forgive us?'

'You have nothing to be sorry for. You were only a small child. I'm sorry that your father and grandfather and the village were punished in this way because of us.'

Afterwards there was a feeling of release and calmness.

In April 2014, at the sixty-ninth commemoration ceremonies in Stalag XB, the Polish people who had been detained there were especially remembered. Wiktor

Sitting on the bench at the monument at Milag und Marlag Nord, Westertimke, in 2014: *(l–r)* Frau Heitmann, Harry Callan, Harry Heitmann and his son Uwe.

Listopadzki, one of the resistance fighters from the Warsaw Uprising who was interned in 1944 as a prisoner of war in Stalag XB, was with us to give witness. Also there were Roger Cottyn, Michele Montagano, a former Italian Military internee who had not been there the previous year, and myself. Our Russian internee survivor, Sergei Litvin, was unable to be with us and we missed him. There was a one-minute silence to honour Dr Engels, who had died the previous year.

In June 2014, Michèle accompanied me to the Not Forgotten Association Garden Party at Buckingham Palace; this year Her Majesty Queen Elizabeth II attended. We met Charlie Mayhead, who had been a prisoner of war in another camp, Stalag XIB/357, Fallingbostel in Lower Saxony and had written a book about his wartime experiences. At

In the *Arbeitserziehungslager* in 2014: *(l–r)* Markus Günther,
Harry Callan, Frau Günther, Michèle Callan, Brian Callan and
Wilfried Günther.

ninety-six, he was still a sharp man but needed a stick when
walking. He was the last survivor of his comrades from
Fallingbostel and I was the last survivor of my comrades
from Bunker Valentin. We had a lot of stories in common
and we understood each other.

In July, at the Irish commemoration ceremonies in
Kilmainham, I met two of my old British Merchant Navy
friends, Captain Bernard (Benny) Forde and Barney
Crossan, and Benny introduced me to the Flag Officer
Commanding Naval Service Commodore of the Irish Navy,

Hugh Tully. Commodore Tully invited me to give a talk to the general body of the Naval Service about my wartime experiences. Imagine, the Irish Navy wanted me, a British Merchant Navy seaman, to talk to them!

On 21 October 2014, one month before my ninety-first birthday, I sat with Michèle in front of over 100 Navy personnel, from new recruits to senior staff, including Commodore Hugh Tully, at the Naval Base, Haulbowline, in Cobh, County Cork, and made a presentation to them about my life at sea. My son Michael prepared a slideshow for the backdrop and acted as sound engineer while Michèle conducted an interview with me. After a question-and-answer session, and lunch in the officers' dining room, Commodore Tully presented me with a wooden plaque in memory of my visit.

I celebrated my ninety-first birthday on 19 November 2014. Seven days later, I fell and broke my hip and was in hospital until late January 2015. It became obvious to my children that I could no longer live alone and so Michael and Michèle asked me to move in with them.

At the end of March, we received an email from Denkort Bunker Valentin. Kommandant Walhorn's grand-daughter Petra Ebel had contacted them to say that, while cleaning out her grandmother's attic, she had found letters written by the *kommandant* to his wife while he was in charge of the *AEL* camp in Farge. In one of the letters he mentioned the Irishmen who were imprisoned there. She made an appointment with Dr Marcus Meyer to visit Denkort Bunker Valentin; her mother, Heidi, Kommandant Walhorn's daughter, accompanied her. When Petra learned that I returned each year to Farge she asked to meet with me.

Michèle asked me, 'Would you like to meet her, Dad?'

'Yes, I would. She will only hear bad things about Walhorn and, while he was strict, he was never cruel to us Irishmen. If it was not for him and the doctor we would have ended up in Neuengamme. Will you tell her that I'll meet her?'

So Michèle made the arrangements to meet in Düsseldorf on our last day in Germany.

In April 2015, Michael, Brian, Michèle and her friend Helen flew with me to Düsseldorf. For the first time, I needed wheelchair assistance at both airports. At Arrivals, I heard a voice call out, 'Onkel Harry!'

Uwe Heidbreder was waving and walking towards us. I was delighted to see him again. We followed the same itinerary as before, this time visiting Rheinberg Cemetery en route to Farge. There was a serious accident on the motorway so the three-and-a-half-hour journey took seven hours. I was in dreadful pain with my hip and, though I said nothing, Michèle knew and insisted that I take a painkiller and lie down for an hour.

We woke to rain the following morning. Enno Heidbreder was waiting for us at Denkort Bunker Valentin. We were introduced to Herr Peter Nowack, the *Ortsamtsleiter* (chief officer) of Bremen-Blumenthal, who joined us on our tour of the bunker. When we stepped through the door into the huge empty space, I stopped for a moment.

'Do you still hear them, Dad?' Michèle asked me.

'Oh yes. I still hear the noises, but they no longer swamp me like they did the first time I came back.'

Linking my arm in hers she led me over to the family. We saw the progress that had been made on the new reception area for visitors and the new café area and its facilities, which were in their final construction stage. Another part of the bunker had been boxed off for exhibits and this area was being fitted with air conditioning. In the administration building, I addressed an attentive audience of over forty students from Oberschule an der Egge. I told to them about my daily regime in the camp and about the good people that I met, too: the people who kept the twenty-seven of us alive. Then the students were encouraged to ask me their questions.

'Mr Callan, what did you tell about your time here when you got home?'

'Nothing. I never spoke about it.'

'Mr Callan, what did your family say when you got home?'

'My father met me at the railway station. He put his arms around me and he hugged me. Then we went home. I said nothing to him or to my family. I never talked about it.'

And the questions kept coming. Finally one student asked me, 'Mr Callan, you come back here to Farge every year. How do you not hate us?'

I took a deep breath before I answered. 'I don't hate you. I don't hate the people of Farge. I met very good people here. How many of you have small brothers and sisters? If you saw something dreadful happening in the street, would you hide them from it? You must remember that, when I was here, the Gestapo were judge, jury and executioner. Everyone lived in fear. Most of your parents and some of your grandparents were young children then. When the prisoners arrived and were marched through the village, parents pulled their children into the houses, drew the curtains and warned the children not to look out. When the children went to school, they were brainwashed. Children reported their parents for things like not giving the correct Hitler salute to their child and the Gestapo would visit the house and threaten to send the parents to the *AEL* camp. Fear set in. Families and neighbours no longer trusted each other. But even with all this fear and mistrust, some of the people of Farge, Neuenkirchen and the surrounding villages helped prisoners by secretly hiding food along the route the prisoners took and, in our case, by allowing us to work on their farms and in their gardens. We cut wood to store for the winter, we dug ditches, laid hedges, planted gardens and did house repairs. These people shared their rations with us. But there was always the fear that someone would find out and report them to the Gestapo.'

I told them about Dr Heidbreder's family and Herr Günther's family too.

'So no, I don't hate the German people and you should not hate your grandparents or your parents. You shouldn't blame them for not speaking out during that terrible time. I hope that you will go home today and hug them and tell them that you love them.'

After a few more questions we all left together to participate in our commemoration ceremony at the monument.

This year, Oberschule an der Egge had arranged a certificate which I signed for every participant of the race. Jakob Günther, one of the class of 2005, was also a participant. Although now a grown man working in Berlin, Jakob makes a point of returning each year to take part in the memorial run. He is the first past pupil to do this. In his own way, he, too, is honouring the memory of what happened there. I was deeply moved by his commitment.

From there, we drove through the Farge camp to the mass grave where we laid a poppy cross in memory of Patrick Breen and then on to Barrack 27.

We visited Baracke Wilhelmine, which was located in the *Marinegemeinschaftslager* in Schwanewede-Neuenkirchen, only a few hundred metres from Barrack 27. Baracke Wilhelmine is now a museum documenting the history of the camps in Bremen-Farge and later the *Lebensborn* home in Schwanewede-Löhnhorst. (This was an SS-run home for unmarried mothers.) Now Baracke Wilhelmine is a meeting place for these lost children and they come from all over the world to try and find more information about their birth mothers and their roots.

We spent Sunday as a family day with the Heidbreders in Enno and Elisabeth's home and attended the usual commemoration ceremonies over the next few days, including a visit to Katie's grave. Unfortunately, I had to leave Stalag XB early because my hip was giving me a lot of pain and I was exhausted. I was unable to return to the former camp for the conclusion of the ceremonies and instead returned to the hotel.

29

THE IRISHMEN REMEMBERED

THE NEXT MORNING, 30 April 2015, we left Farge and returned to Düsseldorf. Michèle and I were to meet Kommandant Walhorn's daughter and granddaughter, Heidi and Petra Ebel, at 4 p.m. in our hotel. I still wanted to meet them but now I had misgivings. I told Michèle how nervous I was feeling and why. But she assured me that everything would be okay.

'You're telling Heidi about your memories of her father and Petra about her grandfather. If they have questions for you, just answer them truthfully and don't worry: I'll be with you. Remember too, Dad, they only know about you through Dr Marcus and Dr Christel and then through emails with me. For all they know, this could be a ploy to get them here so that you can harangue them about the *kommandant* in Farge and not to tell them anything good about him so I would think that they are feeling pretty nervous too.'

'But I wouldn't!'

'I know that but they don't know it do they?'

I said a quiet prayer to Anne asking her to help me.

'There are two ladies coming in the door now, Dad. I think it's them. You wait here and I'll bring them over to you.'

I heard the footsteps coming closer and then I saw the shadowy figures: one very tall woman wearing white and one shorter woman wearing grey. I stood up and shook hands with them. Introductions were made. While we waited for coffee and cake there was general conversation. Then in one of the pauses in the conversation I spoke up.

'Well, Heidi, I hope I can help you. Have you any questions you want to ask me? You can ask me anything and I will answer you truthfully.'

There was silence. I repeated, 'Anything at all?'

Heidi said, in a very quiet voice, 'No, Harry, I have no questions.'

'Well, so. I'll tell you about the Kommandant Walhorn I knew. I know you'll have heard things about him but I can tell you that personally I never saw him ill-treat anyone. He was strict, yes, but I never saw him treat anyone cruelly. There were others there during the times Walhorn was absent who were vicious.'

I told her about our daily regime. I told her that when I got sick Walhorn gave Dr Heidbreder permission to let me work in the doctor's garden and that he then pulled the other Irishmen off the site and arranged for them to work on the local farms and in the village. I told her about Billy English and me going to work for the merchant farmer who did not give us any food or water and about my knocking on Walhorn's office door to ask for food. I laughed as I told her about the following day and all the little sandwiches and cups of coffee that the gardener and his wife gave us.

Then Heidi spoke.

'I remember the Irishmen.'

This surprised me. Petra turned to her mother and said, 'You remember them?'

'Yes. Since you told me about this meeting I have been trying to remember. I was only about four when we moved to Farge but I remember the Irishmen.'

Heidi continued, 'My sister died of typhus before we moved to Farge. My mother, my younger sister and I came to live in the bungalow outside the camp with my father. I have a memory of hearing marching feet. My mother closed the curtains and told my sister and me to stay inside and not to peek out. But, being curious, I lifted the corner of the curtain to see and I was shocked. Who were all these people marching along? To my child's eyes, they looked all wrong. They were being made to march fast by guards and there were so many of them. They kept marching past the bungalow and I grew scared. I remember letting the corner of the curtain fall again and being really scared.'

Heidi's voice broke; Michèle and Petra comforted her and when she was more composed she went on.

'I remember the Irishmen. I have been thinking hard, trying to remember their names. There were three Irishmen who came each day to our bungalow.'

'If you can't remember their names, Heidi, perhaps you might remember what they looked like. With a description I might be able to say who they were.'

'Well, I think I have their names right. There was Cooney – Thomas Cooney – a big jolly man.'

'Ah, God! Yes and he was half his size then, you know!'

'He was still a big man to me as a small child. He was looking after the pigs and one day he called me out to the garden and told me to close my eyes and hold out my arms.

I did and I felt something warm and heavy and wriggly being put into my arms. I opened my eyes and squealed with delight. A baby piglet! And he told me to make sure that I took good care of it. He laughed at my delight and I remember his laugh. There was O'Dwyer. I can't remember his name; he had another name.'

'What did he look like?'

'He had red hair.'

'Ah, Ginger!'

'Yes, that was it! He was called Ginger. But that was not his real name.'

'No, it was Michael. But we always called him Ginger because of his hair.'

'Yes. Ginger cooked for us. He made orange jam which he put on my bread each morning and he made me eat it. I hated the taste of it but he said it was important that I eat it as it would keep me healthy and I wouldn't get sick. And then there was Patrick Kavanagh. He minded us and played with us. We had a long runner rug in the hall of the bungalow and I would sit on one end and Patrick would roll up the runner and then pull it and it would flick into the air and I would roll off and laugh, and Patrick would laugh with me and then start the game again.'

We were all delighted at how much she remembered for different reasons: Petra because they were happy memories for her mother and Michèle and I because these three Irishmen would be remembered by this family for their kindness to a little child. I told her then that her father had always walked like he had an injury and, using my hands, indicated the way he walked. She laughed and said, 'Imagine you remembering that about him! Yes, my father had a car accident and was always in dreadful pain with his back. He found it very difficult to walk. Later in life he had osteoporosis and suffered dreadfully with broken bones. He never spoke to us about his time during the war. It was forbidden to talk about it.'

Then Heidi continued. 'I remember another day playing in the garden. There were Polish children there. I never knew where they came from or where they lived but my father told me to be kind to them and to play with them. We had great fun that day. Later on, the planes flew overhead. I know now they were the Allies. They started dropping bombs. My mother called out to us to come into the cellar and my sister and I ran as we had been taught to do. My father came and saw the Polish children huddled together in the garden. He called to them to come and told them to hurry down into the cellar with us. He followed us in and closed the door and we all huddled together. I felt really safe there with my father. Afterwards, I assumed they went home. I never asked. They came to play again but then one day they were gone.'

Heidi told us that the *kommandant* and his family left the bungalow and moved to Neuenkirchen; that explained why I had not seen them again.

'I remember one day the soldiers, the Allied soldiers, coming to our door and ordering my father out of the house. I was terrified. Why were they shouting at my father? They took him away from us. My father was arrested and I didn't see him again for four years. I remember being confused and scared and angry. Why had they taken my father? What had he done? I was a child and didn't understand. My mother refused to answer my questions and it was forbidden to talk about it. Now, of course, as an adult I understand. I know why my father was arrested but it is still hard to know that my father did some terrible things. I am sorry for what happened to you, Harry, and to the others. I am sorry that my father was involved in all that pain and suffering.'

There were tears running down her cheeks. This was what I did not want to see: another child suffering for something that was not of their doing. I assured her that she had nothing to apologise for.

'Nothing is purely black and white, Heidi. I believe there is good and evil in everyone and sometimes you have to look hard to find the good. Your father was good: when he did his best for his family and had my fellow Irishmen watch over you; for keeping you safe; for pulling the Polish children into the cellar to safety; for trying to put the Geneva Convention into practice; for never allowing anyone else into our barracks; for taking us off the work on Bunker Valentin; and for not sending us to Neuengamme Concentration Camp – all that was goodness. Yes, he was strict. He was the *kommandant* so he had to be.

'Petra, Michèle tells me you're researching your family history. You're going to find out a lot of bad things about your grandfather and others, and you'll be shocked. It will be difficult for you to reconcile the two men – your grandfather and the *kommandant*. I hope, Heidi, that you and Petra will be able to remember today's conversation and the happy memories that we have shared. You need to keep those happy times close to your hearts.'

With that, Heidi stood and put her arms around me. The tears were running down our cheeks but we were also smiling as we were crying. Petra and Michèle joined in laughing and crying and embracing. Then Michael joined us to take photographs; we promised to send them copies.

The meeting had gone well but it had been an emotional and exhausting day. Uwe Heidbreder and his partner Babs joined us for dinner and I listened to the banter and conversation in two languages. My children and the Heidbreder children had become good friends. It would be up to them and the students at the Oberschule an der Egge to remember for me. I toasted everyone's good health and silently hoped that I would be able to return again next year. I also hoped that more people would visit Bunker Valentin where they would learn about the thirty-two Irish-born British Merchant seamen who, when asked to work *frei* for Hitler's Germany, had answered 'no.'

ACKNOWLEDGEMENTS

WHEN I FIRST ASKED Harry to share his life story with me, I had no idea what to expect or where it would take me. We have shared a long road together and with support and encouragement from so many, I finally completed my task.

A very special thanks to my father-in-law, Harry, for sharing and entrusting his story to me and to my husband, Michael, who supported and encouraged me on this journey.

I would also like to thank my family for their encouragement: my mother Brenda, my brothers and sisters – Patrick, Ian, Audrey, Elaine and Lynne – and my brothers- and sisters-in-law, Catherine, Michael, Brian, Maeve, Marian, Roseanna, Gerry, Danny and Paul; my nephews and nieces, Laura, Eimear, Ciara Lee, Collette, Conor, Niamh, Hayley, Eva, Eoin, Alan, Fiona, Aidan, Ciaran, Áine and Ronan.

To Harry's family, Eileen, Drew and Helen, Robin and Betty, Yvonne, June, Coleman and Ruby, Cyril and Judy, Martin and Mary, and to his many nieces and nephews, particularly Martina, Michelle, Irene, Teresa, John, Tony, Matthew, Drew and Emma, thank you all for your help and encouragement.

To June Harte, Doris and John McCormack, thanks for your continued support. You have been there from the beginning. To Heinz Glier, our German/Irish friend, thanks for your introduction to your cousin Karola.

My sincere thanks to Paul Barker and Deirdre Piquard, who stuck with me, reading the many drafts along the way, and to Antje and Constantin von der Schulenburg for correcting my German dialogue. Your help was invaluable.

My deepest gratitude to Helen Dempsey for editing my work and to her husband Joseph for the endless cups of tea and coffee that helped us keep working.

Thanks also to the following:

- Deirdre Donnelly of BBC Northern Ireland for your help with research and for your documentary *A Journey Through Time*, which was aired on BBC Radio Ulster on 26 December 2006.
- Joe Kearney, for your empathy and honesty in creating the documentary *Clouds in Harry's Coffee* and Ronan Kelly, producer of *Documentary on One* on RTÉ radio for the wonderful production of the documentary which was aired on RTÉ Radio 1 on 13 September 2014 and reached many thousands of listeners.
- Martin Dwan, director and producer of Zampano Productions, for being a good friend to Harry and a great support to me.
- Peter Mulvany, chairman of The Irish Seaman's Relatives Association, for encouraging Harry to return to Farge on the 'Heroes Return' trip in 2005 and organising and accompanying him on eight of his return trips.
- Commanding Naval Service Commodore of the Irish Navy, Hugh Tully (FOCNS), for inviting Harry to give a presentation about his life at sea during war, to the Irish Navy Recruits.

- Captain Benny Forde of the Commissioners of Irish Lights for his introduction to the Commodore of the Irish Navy.
- Billy McGee from the British Merchant Navy, for all your help and encouragement.
- The staff at The Poppy Appeal in Aylesford, Kent, for looking after the poppy wreaths and crosses each year for Harry.

In Germany, thank you to the following:

- Thomas Weis, Navy Archives, Wurttemberg State Library, for photographs of the ships.
- Dr Katharina Hoffmann, Oldenburg University and Wolfgang Wortmann for taking the time to travel to Dublin to interview Harry for Oldenburg University History Department.
- Heiko and Gundela Kania who have been there since the start of Harry's journey, thank you for finding his old friends and reuniting them.
- **Barrack 27**: Rolf Dieter, Rita and Gerard Scharnhorst, Otto Guido, Evert Brink, Vanessa and Rickard for your friendship and for keeping the history of the *Arbeitserziehungslager* alive for future generations.
- **Baracke Wilhelme**: Harald Grote and Wilfried Blumentritt for the visits to your museum and for keeping the history of Bunker Valentin, the Camps and the Lebensborn for future generations.
- **Denkort Bunker Valentin**: Dr Marcus Meyer, for providing Bunker Valentin photos and to Dr Marcus Meyer, Dr Christel Trouvé and their team for all the hard work over the years, which has cumulated in the preservation of Bunker Valentin's history and the present Interpretive Centre.

- **Schulzentrum Eggestedterstrasse**: Principal Frau Julia Hofer (now retired) for allowing younger pupils to participate in the memorial run and to act as tour guides, for family and friends, in Bunker Valentin.
- **Oberschule an der Egge, Blumenthal**: School director Herr Ingo Schiller and Principal Herr Andreas Kraatz Röper for encouraging the students to participate in the memorial run, 'Harry Callan Lauf'.
- Jakob Günther (past pupil): thank you for returning each year to take part in the 'Harry Callan Lauf'.
- Monika Eichmann, for translation during presentations with the pupils, you are always there when we need you.
- Uwe Heitmann, Herr Harry and Frau Heitmann in Westertimke. Thank you for the care you take of the memorial and its garden at the entrance to Milag Nord.
- **Stalag XB**: Dr Andreas Ehresmann and his team for all the years of hard work. The Interpretive Centre and site are a credit to you and your team.
- Sarah Mayr, photographer, for your Survivor photographic exhibition which is now on permanent display in Stalag XB. And to Corinna, our Interpreter in Sandbostel, for your help every year.
- To Sonja Stöver, management and staff of Ringhotel *Fährhaus* Farge and to Frau Schultz in Dr Heidbreder's old house, for their hospitality.

Thank you to the following officials for their continued support of the projects:

- Minister of Bremen State, Herr Bernd Neumann
- Herr Peter Nowack, the *Ortsamtsleiter* [chief officer] of Bremen-Blumenthal
- *Bürgermeister* of Bremen, Herr Jens Böhrnsen
- Frau Marieluise Beck, Bremen Government

- Bürgermeister of Westertimke, Hans-Joachim Nikolaus
- For their hospitality and friendship, Frances Evans and Walter Bengtsson in Córdoba and Tim Lough in Buenos Aires, Argentina.

Special thanks to:

- Karola and Jürgen Bosch, Bremervörde for their hospitality and especially to Karola for sharing her memories of the prisoners.
- Heidi and Petra Ebel who remembered the Irishmen, especially Ginger O'Dwyer, Thomas Cooney and Patrick Kavanagh, in Farge, 1944.
- Birgit and Stephan Hyndes for renewing Harry and Katie's friendship and for their support and to Wilfred, Helga and Marcus Günther for sharing their memories of Harry and Billy English with us.
- Rita and Gerhard Scharnhorst, Bastian Spille and Franziska Scholl for their friendship, assistance and their support.
- Last but not least a very special thanks to our German family, Uwe, Babs, Enno, Elizabeth and Mareike Heidbreder, for their love, friendship and encouragement to write Harry's story.

Thanks to the following organisations for their funding and sponsorship:

- Bremen Government
- British Legion
- Bunker Valentin
- Irish Seamen's Relatives Association
- Stalag XB
- UK Lottery Funds

FURTHER READING

Frances Evans, *Quiet Endurance* (Argentina: Gráficamente Ediciones, Córdoba 2010)

Chas Mayhead, *Rumours a Memoir of a British POW in WWII* (New York: Pleasure Boat Studio: A Literary Press, 2002)

Raymond Portefaix, *L'Enfer que Dante n'avait pas prévu*, (Imprimerie modern: Aurillac, France, 1988)

Raymond Portefaix, Andre Migdal, Klaas Touber, *Hortensien in Farge Überleben im Bunker "Valentin"*, ed. Barbara Johr and Bärbel Gemmeke-Stenzel (Donat Verlag: Bremen, Germany, 1996)

War Crimes Trial, 'Bremen Farge' Summing-up by Judge Advocate (Curio House, Hamburg, February, 1948)

Websites

www.baracke-wilhelmine.de

www.denkort-bunker-valentin.de/startseite.html

www.geschichtslehrpfad.de

www.rte.ie/radio1/doconone/2014/0904/647700-clouds-in-harrys-coffee

www.stiftung-lager-sandbostel.de

PHOTOGRAPH CREDITS

Dr Marcus Meyer, Denkort Bunker Valentin: pp. viii, 87, 99, 101 (both), 108, 114 (both), 115 (both), 124 and 127 (both).

Harry Callan: pp. 2, 4, 77 (both), 221 (both), 238, 241, 247, 251, 253 (both) and 258.

Eileen Callan: p. 7.

The T.S. Vindicatrix Association: p. 14.

www.wrecksite.eu/wreck.aspx?16294: p. 29.

Private collection: p. 37.

Thomas Weis, Bibliothek fuer Zeitgeschichte in der Wuerttembergischen Landesbibliothek: pp. 49, 57, 58 (both) and 59 (both).

Michael Callan: pp. 69, 267, 269, 273, 274, 284, 297, 299, 301 and 302.

Birgit Hyndes: pp. 153 (both), 164 and 173.

Wilfried Günther: p. 159.

Michèle Callan: p. 263.